CREWELWORK EMBROIDERY

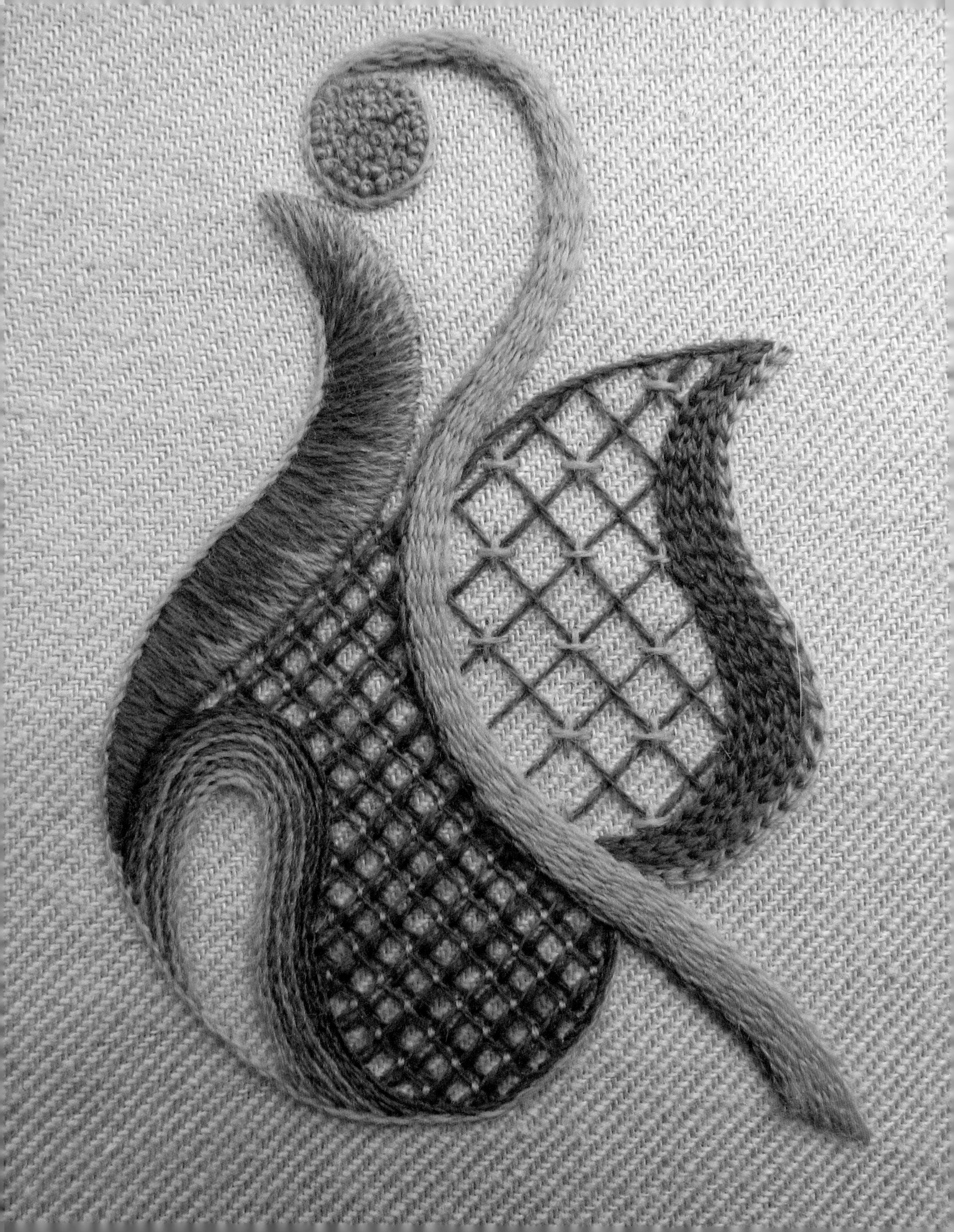

Crewelwork Embroidery

Becky Quine

CROWOOD

First published in 2020 by
The Crowood Press Ltd
Ramsbury, Marlborough
Wiltshire SN8 2HR

www.crowood.com
enquiries@crowood.com

British Library Cataloguing-in-Publication Data
A catalogue record for this book is available from the British Library.

ISBN 978 1 78500 543 5

Acknowledgements

I would like to start by thanking my family for their support, my father Paul for the loan of equipment, my sister Natalie for her proofreading and photographic skills and my mother Lyn for her words of encouragement. Thanks also go to Helen Richman for suggesting the idea for this book, to Lizzy Pye for her support and to Shelley Cox for the loan of her studio, which was essential to the process of writing this book. The wise words and encouragement from Jacqui Macdonald and Rachel Doyle were also invaluable. I am grateful to Shelley Cox, Flo Collingwood, Lizzy Pye, Helen Richman, Jess Aldred, Rachel Doyle, Jenny Adin-Christie, Helen Stevens, Marg Dier and Chrissie Juno Mann for the privilege of allowing me to share their work in this book. Thanks also go to the Royal School of Needlework for allowing me the privilege of viewing and photographing pieces from the collection, and for permission to reproduce those images in this book. Great thanks go to Noleen Wyatt-Jones for her proofreading skills and to everyone for their patience during the writing of this book.

Graphic design and typesetting by Peggy & Co. Design
Printed and bound in India by Parksons Graphics

Contents

The History of Crewelwork

The term 'crewel' is defined as a loosely twisted thin woollen thread used for surface embroidery. So quite simply, crewelwork refers to any surface embroidery worked in wool. In the UK crewelwork has been practised for centuries and has grown to include a large number of surface stitches, some of which we will cover in this book.

Crewelwork and embroidery in general has a long history. Sheep were one of the earliest animals to be domesticated for use in agriculture, so it is easy to speculate how old the technique actually is. There is evidence to suggest that crewelwork was practised in both Ancient Egypt and Ancient Greece; there are even biblical references to it. Over the centuries crewelwork has evolved under the influences that also affected more visible disciplines such as architecture and art, and as a result has faded in and out of fashion.

From the Royal School of Needlework Collection (RSN Grove Book), this small fragment is from a much larger monochromatic piece. Often depicting a collection of motifs drawn from the natural world, these pieces lack perspective.

From the RSN collection (RSN 214), this picture shows a detail from a larger piece that was most likely intended to be a household item. The depiction of flora and fauna is one of the most common themes throughout history.

From the RSN Collection (RSN402/582/1222/2234a), this sample was worked as a training piece by a Diploma student of the RSN in the first half of the twentieth century. The traditional shapes and motifs are reminiscent of the Elizabethan/Jacobean interest in the natural world.

The Bayeux Tapestry is one of the oldest existing and most well-known examples of crewelwork. The piece is 70m/230ft long, 51cm/20in wide, and contains seventy-two scenes depicting the Norman conquest of England in 1066. Surprisingly for such a big piece, it is worked in only ten colours and uses very few stitches, including Stem Stitch, laidwork, couching, Chain Stitch and Split Stitch. The date of this piece is unknown; however, it is believed to have been worked just a few years after the conquest. It is unclear who worked it, although many believe it to be connected to individuals closely related to William the Conqueror.

From the tenth century onwards wool threads became less expensive, which led to a rise in interest in the technique. Crewelwork had its heyday in the sixteenth and early seventeenth centuries. During the reign of Elizabeth I (1558–1603), the Elizabethans were looking beyond their shores, exploring the high seas and colonizing new lands. With this activity came new opportunities and money. As a result, families and individuals found greater wealth and greater status within society. Women in particular benefited from this change by turning more and more to needlework. Crewelwork as a technique was used to create all manner of household items such as bed hangings, curtains, covers for chairs, clothing, book covers and many other things. These items all worked to brighten and insulate rooms, particularly in large, draughty houses, and were often worked by the lady of the house. Their value was clearly recognized at the time, as they were itemized in inventories and even referred to in wills. There was also a thriving commercial embroidery industry that provided employment for both men and women, which was regulated by a Guild that still exists today, known as the Worshipful Company of Broderers.

Although silk was available at the time, it was expensive as it was imported; wool, however, was home-grown, readily available and often spun into a suitable thread by the stitchers themselves. At this time the motifs used reflected the fascination of society with herbs, plants and the natural world. The influence of Elizabethan costume can also be seen, as designs that had been previously rendered in blackwork for clothing were scaled up and used on larger embroideries such as wall hangings and curtains. The oriental influence is also noticeable in pieces from this time, although it later went on to develop a greater presence alongside motifs of exotic flowers, oversized leaves and mounds. This was the grounding for the Jacobean style that was to follow.

The reason for the introduction of the oriental flavour present in many embroideries is open to debate. Many believe this was a result of the formation in 1600 of the East India Company to open up trade routes between England and the Far East, and the huge influence on embroidery of the items they imported, which included pearls, spices, furniture, silks, and painted cottons adorned with a variety of plant and animal motifs called pintadoes, palampores and chints (chintz). Just three years later, in 1603, James I ascended the throne and the Jacobean period began. However, a study of the East India Company records conducted during the 1950s and 1960s by John Irwin, a historian of Indian art at the Victoria and Albert Museum in London, would suggest that, primarily, English embroideries were sent out to India. Although some textiles were imported from India, this trade did not reach its peak until after 1660 and the end of the Jacobean period. The East India Company paid close attention to those items that were popular in the English market; they were even known to request alterations to products from their suppliers in India to tailor them to the taste of their customers.

It is also possible that the oriental style was introduced into England with the silk trade routes through India and Persia, via the sea lanes established by the Portuguese in the early 1500s. By the 1600s most of Europe was trading with Asia. The oriental aesthetic was much appreciated by the English, and through their efforts to translate it into their own decorative arts, the 'chinoiserie' style started to develop. It is likely that this style of embroidery travelled with the early settlers to America in the early 1600s, and there in turn developed into a different style that took influence from the locality in both materials used and design inspiration.

In 1624 a book of motifs and patterns, *A Schole-House for the Needle*, was written by Richard Shoreleykers and proved to be immensely popular. It was a favourite of professional travelling craftsmen, who used it to design pieces for large country estates that were to be stitched by the ladies of the household.

From the RSN Collection (RSN232), this leopard motif is commonly seen in historical pieces. Used from the sixteenth century through to the present day, it is often seen on contemporary pieces where the Jacobean style has been imitated.

For the domestic stitcher, materials used in embroidery would have been home-made, with spinning, dying and weaving all being tasks that could be performed in the home. The fashion for crewelwork became immensely popular and was a staple in the life of women of the time. Crewelwork fell out of favour somewhat during the Civil War and the formation of the Commonwealth in 1649. The Puritan influence meant that the extravagances of the previous fifty years were frowned upon. Little in the way of crewelwork was executed in the following years; however, stumpwork, a type of raised or embossed embroidery, become more prominent.

After the dissolution of the Commonwealth and the installation of Charles II as king (1660–1685), social and religious changes caused a resurgence of interest in embroidery, and particularly crewelwork. With the introduction of upholstered furniture to England, there was less demand for chair, stool and bench coverings; instead, attention was turned to larger scale projects. Diarist Samuel Pepys (1633–1703) noted that every woman was involved in producing new 'furniture' for beds, such as hangings and pelmets. These items were time-consuming to produce, despite the background being left bare so that the motifs could be worked with relative speed, particularly in comparison to other types of embroidery. The technique had evolved, and although fewer stitches were used, they were worked more effectively. Long and Short Stitch was used prolifically with subtler shading than before. Other popular stitches of the time include herringbone, stem and Coral Knot Stitches. As the work of this time was on a much larger scale than before, it is likely that this was the reason why the stitches and colours used were limited. Monochromatic colour schemes were popular, with greens and reds appearing frequently.

From the RSN Collection (RSN1443), this piece, started in the late twentieth century, references a seventeenth-century wall or bed hanging and was intended to be a *portière* (door cover).

Throughout this time the East India Company continued to trade with and export to India, and by 1670 Indian artists were producing textiles from patterns provided by English businessmen. This proved so popular that the Indian artisans requested that the Company send a regular supply of patterns to stitch, as the Dutch and French were already doing. Often these designs were translated into textiles reflecting local culture, so that motifs leaving England depicting shepherds returned to England with figures wearing robes and cloth headwear. To the English eye, this gave an exotic appearance to the embroidery that was very desirable.

By the early 1700s there had been a huge outpouring of embroidery, although silk was overtaking wool as the preferred fibre. Counted work on canvas with a mixture of wool and silk came into vogue, and whilst crewelwork showed something of a decline in Britain, its traditions continued to evolve in America.

Although crewelwork survived in the eighteenth century – and historical examples demonstrate this – the fashion for it

From the RSN Collection (RSN 231), this piece demonstrates the diverse ongoing cultural influences in British embroidery as seen in the Jacobean period.

was very much on the wane. In the early nineteenth century a new form of embroidery came to the fore, evolving from the trend of canvas work, with the first Berlin wool work pattern introduced to the market around 1805. By the 1830s mass production of these patterns was in full swing thanks to the Industrial Revolution and the resulting rise in mechanization. This technique took advantage of the production of new aniline (synthetic) dyes producing vibrant colours, and soon most household surfaces were adorned with some form of Berlin wool work.

However, towards the end of the nineteenth century crewelwork again saw a resurgence, along with a number of other traditional hand crafts. Born in 1834, William Morris grew up through the latter part of the Industrial Revolution and the resulting impact it was to have on Victorian society. Morris, Marshall, Faulkner & Co was founded in 1861 as a decorative arts company by Morris and a number of partners with the intention of using and promoting craftsmanship within the jobs they undertook and the items

From the RSN Collection (RSN214), this unfinished piece was most likely intended to be a household item.

they produced. Considered by many to be a response to dubious Victorian work practices, the company became very fashionable and had a heavy influence on decorative arts throughout this time period. After some internal strife, including the loss and replacement of various founders, Morris took control of the company in 1875, renaming it Morris & Co, which continued trading until 1940. It was after this change that Morris developed his interest in textiles. He rejected the new and fashionable aniline dyes and returned to organic dyes. The ranges of colours available to him had expanded significantly over the years due to the established trade routes between Britain and the USA. In 1885 his daughter May Morris became the director of the Embroidery Department at Morris & Co, and she continued to work with the company while also becoming involved with a number of other organizations.

Morris's philosophy of returning to craftsmanship was highly influential, particularly throughout the 1870s when a number of organizations were formed to preserve and promote what was known as Art Needlework. These included the Leek Embroidery Society and the School of Art Needlework (later to become the Royal School of Needlework).

The School of Art Needlework was formed in 1872. Its original focus was to preserve the art of needlework, and through this to provide a suitable form of employment for women who found themselves without financial support, in many instances due to the loss of their father or husband. The School of Art Needlework worked closely with notable artists of the day including William Morris, Edward Burne-Jones and later May Morris.

In 1885, the same year in which May Morris became a director at Morris & Co, Elizabeth Wardle of the Leek Embroidery Society decided that Britain should have its own copy of the Bayeux Tapestry. She set about researching the piece and recruiting skilled embroiderers to stitch the replica. By 1886 the piece had been completed and was exhibited in the same year at the Nicholson Institute in Leek. Purchased by Alderman Arthur Hill in 1895, it is now on permanent exhibition at the Reading Museum and Art Gallery.

All these influences ensured that different forms of needlework, including crewelwork, became more accessible to hobbyists and homeworkers. The production of house linens and decorative pieces has a long history of embroidery and continues to influence not only design, but materials as well. Whilst crewelwork can only be called crewelwork if it is worked in wool, there is also scope to mix in different fibres and embellishments such as goldwork threads, beads and sequins.

In this book the focus will be on surface stitches in wool and their application. However, these stitches are not exclusive to crewelwork; they can be worked in any fibre and in conjunction with many techniques.

From the RSN Collection (RSN 2226), this large four-panel screen was advertised as a kit in the March 1934 edition of *The Needlewoman*. This large-scale piece was worked by one individual.

Modern Folk 1 designed and worked by Chrissie Juno Mann. This contemporary piece draws inspiration from the natural world and utilizes traditional stitches to create a fresh take on crewelwork.

Chapter 1

Materials

Using the right materials and equipment is the first step to producing a successful piece of embroidery. There is a huge variety of materials and threads to choose from and it can be tricky to narrow the list down to items suitable for this technique. Similarly, the array of equipment, such as hoops and scissors of different sizes and prices, can be daunting.

Many of the choices to be made, such as background fabric or brand of wool, are personal. Everyone has their own preferences as to the materials and equipment that work best for them. However, it can be expensive experimenting and finding the right items for you. Therefore, when starting out in any technique, it is best to begin on a smaller scale to test the waters. With experience comes confidence that allows the stitcher to gradually move on to bigger and more complex projects. Working on a larger scale will have different requirements in terms of equipment and quantity of materials. Remember that equipment and materials used in this technique can be used for other forms of embroidery too, so it is always good to buy the best quality materials and equipment that you can afford.

The following information is designed to act as a guide for putting together a basic sewing kit and for selecting equipment and materials for the first few projects.

Choosing the right equipment for a project will greatly influence the end result.

Art Deco rocket designed by the author worked by Rachel Doyle. This piece draws on traditional stitches in an unusual Art Deco style to create a striking contemporary embroidery.

Fabric

There are many fabrics that can be used for crewelwork. Here is a selection:

- **Linen twill** – possibly the most traditional of fabrics to use with this technique. It is a closely woven thick fabric that is neutral in colour, strong and slightly textured. This fabric can be used for large hangings, upholstery and other soft furnishings.
- **Normandy linen** – a closely woven fabric that is slightly lighter and smoother than linen twill.
- **Calico** – a plain woven fabric made of cotton which is most commonly unbleached, giving it a neutral cream colour. White calico is also available. Using a medium or heavyweight calico produces the best results, although two layers of lighter weight calico can be used at the same time. It is a low-cost fabric, so ideal for use when practising or 'sampling' stitches, and is also used in mounting.
- **Silk** – this fabric can make a lovely contrast to the wools used in crewelwork. However, silk can be quite delicate and will not take the weight of surface embroidery on its own. So it is important that it is applied to a backing fabric such as calico or a close-weave linen before the embroidery is worked.
- **Denim** – a closely woven cotton fabric, woven in the same way as a linen twill. Just like twill it can be heavy-duty and will support the weight of the surface stitching.
- **Miscellaneous fabrics** – there are a number of other fabrics that could be used for crewelwork; however, consideration should be given to the density of the fabric before commencing work. Generally speaking, thicker fabrics such as banner silk or duchesse satin can be worked on directly. Finer fabrics should be backed with a stronger fabric such as calico or a close-weave linen before starting to stitch.

There are a number of fabrics to choose from. A good starting point is a closely woven fabric that is neutral in colour.

Threads

In order for the embroidery to be crewelwork, it needs to be worked in wool. The best wool to use is a two-ply or worsted wool. Most wools are sold in either a skein or a hank; a skein is approximately 25 metres/27 yards in length, and the length of a hank can vary, but is usually over 150 metres/164 yards. The colour of the wool can vary slightly from dye batch to dye batch, so it is best to order a little more wool than is necessary to complete the piece to avoid a colour mismatch if you run out in the middle of stitching. Most projects will only require skeins; however, if working a very large project, it may be worth considering buying a hank. The thickness of the crewel wool depends on the manufacturer and their process, and this will influence the size of the needle used.

Hints and tips

Keep your threads and fabric clean by wrapping them in tissue paper and storing them in a dry place. Fabric is better rolled than folded.

Two-ply or worsted wool is best for crewelwork; however, the thickness of the thread can vary.

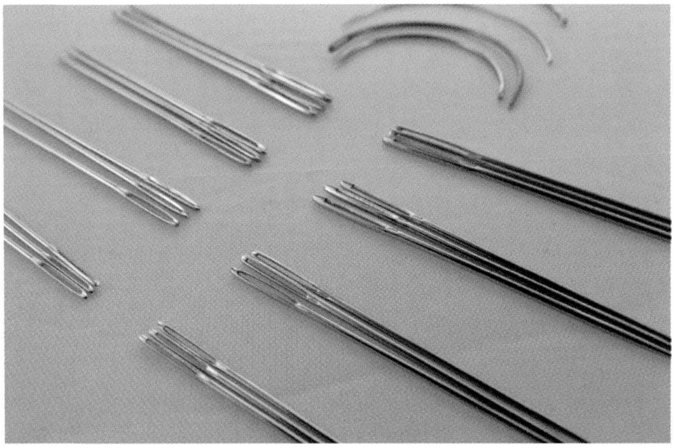

A variety of needles can be used for crewelwork. It is important to always have spares.

Needles

There are a variety of needles suitable for crewelwork. The most commonly used are crewel or chenille needles, although tapestry needles can be used for certain stitches. Needles come in a variety of sizes and it is important to select the correct one. The needle should be big enough to create a hole in the fabric that is fractionally larger than the stitching thread. Using a needle that is too small can damage the thread. A needle that is too large could leave marks or holes in the fabric.

Needles are sized by number; generally, the larger the number, the smaller the needle. The needle size most often used in crewelwork is a size 24 chenille needle (for use with one strand of wool). If working with multiple threads, it is important to switch to a larger (lower number) needle. When working with finer wools, it is important to use a finer (higher number) needle.

- **Chenille needle** – this is a sharp needle with a large eye that is easy to thread and can be used for the majority of stitches.
- **Tapestry needle** – this is a blunt needle with a large eye that is easy to thread and is useful when working stitches on the surface of the fabric such as woven or whipped wheels.
- **Crewel needle** – this is a sharp needle with a small eye and can be used for the majority of the surface embroidery stitches in crewelwork.
- **Curved needle** – this is a sharp needle that has been deliberately shaped into a C or half circle. It is used for mounting a piece of work, so it is important to have a curved needle that is sturdy but flexible. One of the most commonly used curved needles is a mattress needle. Avoid using curved beading needles for mounting as they will be too fine.

Hints and tips

Tapestry and chenille needles share the same sizing system.

Sewing Equipment

There are a number of items that make up a good general embroidery sewing kit that will be used throughout the process of working a piece of embroidery. The following will make a good basic kit:

- **Fabric scissors** – a good-quality pair of scissors are useful for cutting out fabric.
- **Embroidery scissors** – these should have a sharp point with a fine blade in order to cut threads close to the fabric.
- **Scissor sharpener (optional)** – it is important to keep scissors sharp.
- **Thimbles (optional)** – using a thimble can feel awkward at first; however, they are essential for working a large project.
- **Tweezers** – tweezers can be useful for removing stray fibres and fluff.

Hints and tips

Keeping scissors in good condition, clean and sharp is essential and will help prevent stray fibres and fluff appearing on the work.

- **Screwdriver** – a short screwdriver is useful when working with a ring frame; the tighter the screw of the frame, the more the tension will be retained in the fabric.
- **Pliers** – pliers are handy to use if the needle gets stuck when working over a particularly dense area of stitching.
- **Pins** – glass-headed pins are the best because they are sturdy, which is important when working with thick fabric. Pins are used throughout a piece of embroidery: from framing up, to applying fabrics and during the mounting process.
- **Tape measure** – this is an essential for any embroidery project, and is used mostly for measuring fabric when framing up. Take care when using a fabric tape measure as it can stretch over time.

> **Hints and tips**
>
> Screwdrivers and pliers should be purchased new and for the sole purpose of embroidery. Adopting 'pre-loved' tools could result in dirt and grease being transferred on to the embroidery.

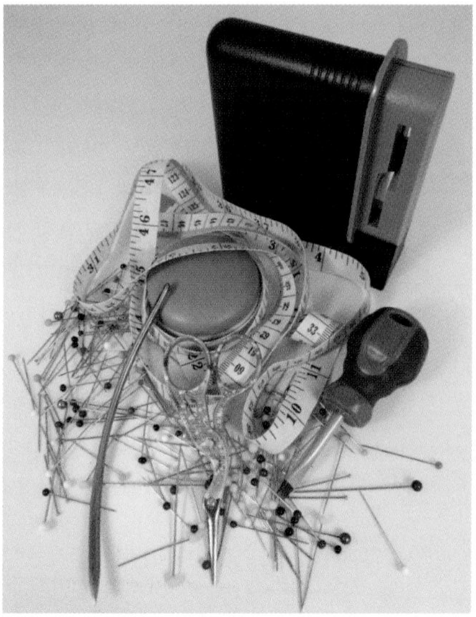

Equipment such as scissors, pins and screwdrivers are essential to any sewing kit.

Embroidery Frames and Hoops

To ensure a good finish on a piece of embroidery, it is important to keep the fabric tight while it is being worked. This will help to prevent ripples and bubbles appearing when the embroidery is completed. The best way to do this is to work the piece on a frame, and there are a number of styles to choose from:

- **Ring frames** – these come in a multitude of sizes and are normally sized in inches. Hoops that are thinner in depth are useful for finer fabrics; however, when working with thicker fabrics, a deeper frame is preferable. There are a couple of different styles: hand-held frames (which are probably the most readily available), seat frames and barrel clamp frames to name a few. The latter two have a dowel attached to the frame that fits into either the seat or barrel clamp, allowing the embroiderer to stitch with both hands. The most common sizes are 6, 8 and 10 inches. The size of frame used should be appropriate to the motif. As ring frames can leave marks in the fabric, it is best to use a frame that is not only larger than the motif but also leaves a rebate of fabric around the stitched area; this extra unmarked fabric will give flexibility when finishing the piece.
- **Roller frame** – roller frames are the next step on from ring frames. They are lightweight and readily available. The preparation of this frame takes a little longer than a ring frame; however, it will hold the fabric tighter with a more consistent tension across the piece. When working with this type of frame, it is preferable to have minimal excess fabric. Extra fabric can be rolled around the bars; however, this will reduce the amount of tension that can be achieved and cause the fabric to slacken more quickly. When working with a roller frame it is important to have some way of supporting it; despite it being lightweight, it will still be heavier than a ring frame. A floor stand or set of trestles are recommended.
- **Slate frame** – slate frames come in larger sizes and are more robust than roller frames. As a result they are larger and heavier, so some form of support, usually trestles, is recommended. When properly constructed, a slate frame gives the best overall tension on fabric compared to other types of frames.

> **Hints and tips**
>
> If a piece will not be worked on for an extended period of time, it is best to reduce the tension on the fabric. This can be done by moving the bars and slackening the strings on a slate or roller frame, or removing the fabric from a ring frame.

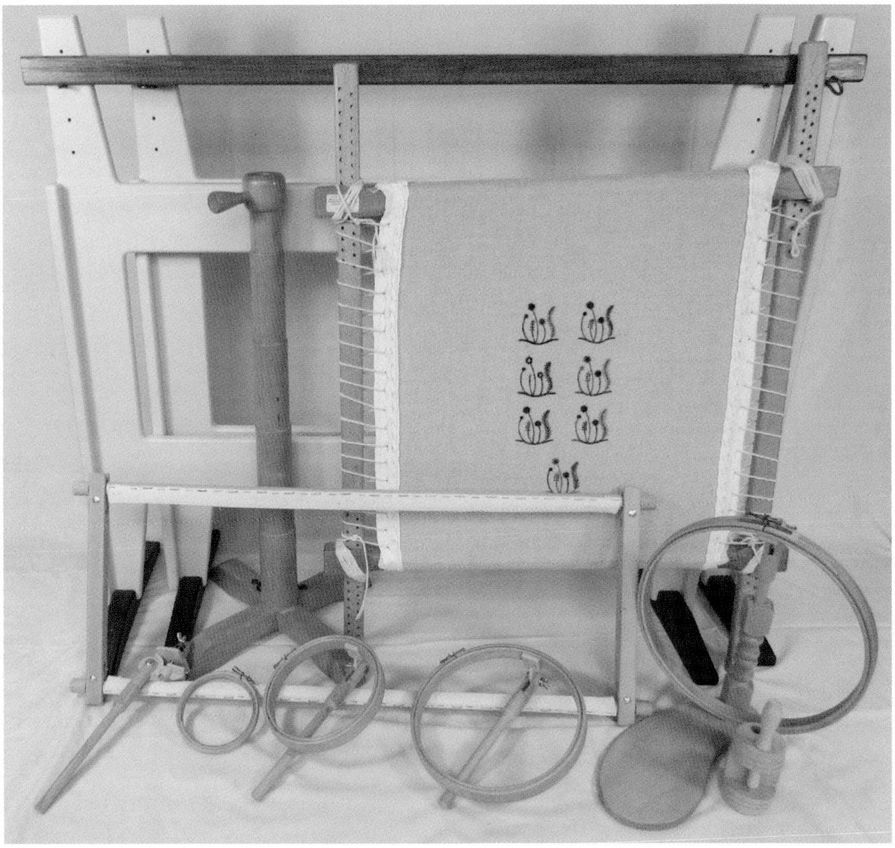

A set of trestles is essential when working with a slate frame; a floor stand, seat or clamp allow the stitcher to work hands-free when using a hoop.

Equipment for Framing Up

The following equipment will help you achieve a professional finish:

- **Crewel/chenille needles** – a sharp needle is necessary when framing up due to the thickness of fabric to be stitched through.
- **Button or upholstery thread** – when the frame is made up, there will be a huge amount of tension on both the fabric and the holding stitches, which is why it is important to use a strong thread. Threads that are thick with a high twist are preferable, in particular a button or upholstery thread.
- **Herringbone tape and parcel string** – a closely woven cotton tape that is at least 2.5cm/1in wide is necessary for framing up. This will take the parcel string, which is then wrapped around the arms of the frame to achieve an even tension on all sides of the fabric.
- **Bracing needle and cork** – a large bracing needle is used to apply the parcel string to the herringbone tape. This is a large and very sharp needle which, when not in use, should have the point covered with a cork or similar so as to avoid injury.
- **Tissue paper** – this is used cover the work to keep it dirt and dust free. Acid-free tissue paper is preferable, but white paper is a must; coloured tissue paper, if wet, can leak dye into a piece of work. Alternatively, a clean pillowcase or cloth can be used.

Equipment for Designing and Transferring On

You will need the following equipment to draw your design and then transfer it to the fabric:

- **Drawing pad or paper** – these are used for sketching out shapes and planning designs.
- **Tracing paper** – a good-quality thick tracing paper is necessary to create a pricking, but can also be used for tracing elements of the design.
- **Drawing pencils** – pencils with a variety of leads, such as H, F and HB, can be useful for transferring on and designing. Keeping the lead of a pencil sharp will create finer, more accurate lines, which makes a pencil sharpener another essential piece of kit.
- **Shade cards (optional)** – made by thread manufacturers, they help with the comparison and selection of colours for a project, but are not essential. On occasion, manufacturers may change the range by introducing new colours and removing old ones, which means shade cards can go out of date.

Pounce and watercolour paint can be used to transfer on a design.

- **Colour wheel** – this is a useful reference point when selecting colours, as it makes it easy to see warm and cool colours, along with complementary and contrasting colours, and how they work together.
- **Colouring pencils and pens** – when designing, it is important to plan both the colour scheme and the stitches to be used. Good-quality pencils or pens in a variety of colours will help with this.
- **Circle template (optional)** – drawing a perfect circle freehand can be very challenging, particularly when working on a textured fabric. Using a circle template will make this easier.
- **Sticky tape** – a low-tack sticky tape, often known as Magic™ Tape, can be used to create a collage when designing.
- **Watercolour paint and paintbrushes** – these can be used to transfer the design on to the fabric and at the planning stages to determine the placement of colour. It is preferable to use watercolour paint from a tube due to its consistency. When painting on a design, a small, fine paintbrush will produce finer lines.
- **Water dish and artist's palette** – when painting on, colours may need to be mixed together on the palette and the brush should be kept clean using the water dish.
- **Pricker** – this is a tool that is used to hold a sharp needle, which is then used to create a pricking to transfer a design onto fabric.
- **Pounce** – this is a mixture of ground cuttlefish and charcoal. It is a fine grey powder that is applied to a pricking to create a temporary outline on the fabric.
- **Soft bristle brush** – this is used to remove pounce from the fabric once the design has been transferred; a baby brush is perfect for this.

Equipment for Mounting

You will need to mount your work before it can be framed and the following equipment will be required:

- **Mountboard** – this comes in many thickness and colours. Plain white is the best to use because, as with tissue paper, the addition of colour adds extra chemicals to the board, which can leak colour into the work in certain circumstances. Conservation board is the best, as this has been manufactured to be used with delicate vintage and antique textiles; sadly, this can be expensive and difficult to source. The most readily available is a 2mm mountboard. When using thinner mountboard, two identical pieces should be cut and glued together to make the board sturdier. A single piece will be too thin, causing it to buckle under the weight of fabric and the tension it is put under.
- **Ruler** – this is used to mark out the correct dimensions on the mountboard. A heavy metal ruler that can be used to cut against is preferable.
- **Set square** – a set square is used to create and check the square corners on a piece of mountboard and is essential for producing a well-mounted piece of embroidery.
- **Craft knife and spare blades** – a sharp, sturdy craft knife is used for cutting mountboard. It is important that the blade is sharp in order to achieve a clean cut.
- **Cutting mat** – this is used to protect work surfaces from damage when cutting a piece of fabric, paper or card. Cutting mats come in a variety of sizes and are usually made of vinyl or rubber.

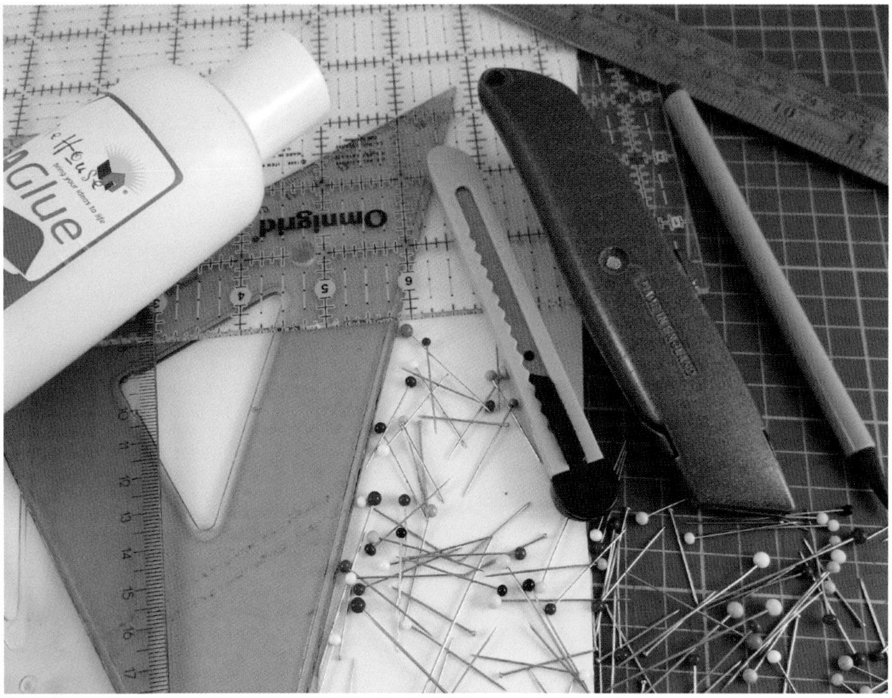

When cutting board for mounting a good-quality knife, cutting mat, set square and ruler are necessary.

- **Glue** – this is used in moderation in the mounting process. A conservation glue is preferable; however, as with the mountboard, it can be difficult and expensive to source. A good-quality PVA glue will work in the same way.
- **Sateen or cotton fabric** – a good-quality sateen or cotton fabric in a neutral colour can be used to back a piece once it has been applied to the mountboard.

Optional Equipment

The following equipment is useful but not essential:

- **Trestles** – these are an adjustable pair of wooden stands on which to lay a large frame and are a good way of supporting heavier slate frames.
- **Magnifier** – this can be particularly useful when working with finer threads on a smaller scale. It can also greatly improve the accuracy of stitches.
- **Light box** – this can be used in place of the prick and pounce method to transfer designs onto thinner fabrics. However, there are some fabrics that are too thick to be used with a light box.
- **Anglepoise lamp** – whilst natural light is the best for stitching, the addition of a lamp can help to extend the number of stitching hours in the day. It is important to have a good-quality bulb that produces a white light that replicates daylight, as this is better to stitch by.

SPLIT COMPLEMENTARY
COMPLEMENTARY

CHAPTER 2

DESIGN

Designing can be a challenging process when starting out; however, there are a number of things to bear in mind. Staring at a blank piece of white paper can cause any design ideas to instantly flee; to combat this, coloured paper can be a less-intimidating alternative. It is best to avoid symmetrical or repeating motifs as most designs will alter subtly throughout the transferring on and stitching processes. Any variations between the elements at the start of the process will become enhanced as it is worked, which can throw out the symmetry. This is particularly true for an inexperienced embroiderer.

First, gather together interesting images, pictures and fabrics to provide inspiration for the basic shapes and layout of the final piece. A design doesn't have to be drawn freehand in its entirety; tracing shapes from photographs or books (such as the motif templates section in this book) is an easy way to compile a design, particularly when starting out. These motifs can be enlarged/reduced on a photocopier or manipulated in a computer to aid the design process.

Taking inspiration from the natural world can make a great starting point and is a very traditional approach. However, modern crewelwork designs can be of any subject and stylized to suit the embroiderer's personal taste.

A good piece of embroidery starts with a strong design.

Designed and worked by Lizzy Pye, this crewelwork monogram uses a variety of stitches. Monograms make an excellent motif, particularly for a beginner.

Generally speaking, design elements work best when combined in odd numbers; for instance, when drawing a tree, a main trunk with either two or four branches would create a pleasing basic structure. This would leave three or five points on which to include additional elements such as animals, leaves or flowers.

The following examples show the evolution of a tree of life design, which is a very traditional motif in British embroidery, particularly crewelwork. This type of design gives a lot of scope to work a variety of stitches and, depending on the size, colour as well.

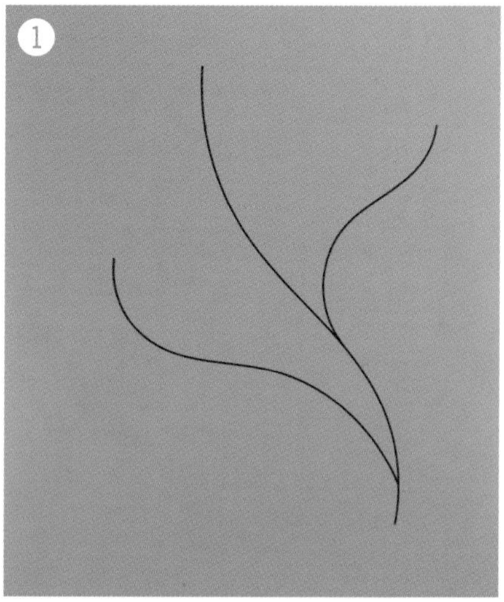

An easy way to start a design is by drawing a single curving line across the piece of paper. Draw an additional line on each side. These should also curve out but be shorter than the central line. This creates the basic framework for the tree.

Fill in the shape of the trunk by sketching lines around the marks already on the paper. Try to keep the base broader and curve the lines up to a sharp point at the very top. Repeat this process with the branches. Note how the new outlines aren't always equidistant from the mid line.

When the tree is complete, the shape needs to be 'grounded'. This means elements need to be added at the base in order to prevent the tree from appearing to float in mid-air. Use a sweeping motion to run a pencil line across the bottom of the paper; this should create a curved line to represent a hill on which the tree will sit. It is worth considering adding additional hills in odd numbers, but take care not to overcrowd the design by adding too many.

Once the basic structure is in place, trace off various elements such as animals, leaves and flowers to embellish the image. These can be resized to suit. Tracing the elements is preferable as substructure will be visible that can inform the placement of the element. Remember: when tracing shapes they don't have to be copied exactly; they can be altered or stylized to the taste of the designer.

Lay the elements on the paper over the existing lines. Take time over this process; have more elements than necessary as this will give plenty of options to swap them in and out to create a pleasing design.

Tape the traced elements to the paper to secure them in place. Then trace the design on a fresh piece of tracing paper. Alternatively, the design can be photocopied before tracing. As the design is traced, the joins between elements should be refined, reshaping these where necessary and leaving out any lines that fall behind another element. Take care to ensure the lines are smooth as this tracing will become a pricking, which is used to transfer the design onto the fabric. Make at least four copies to be used for the next few stages with one spare.

Once the layout is complete, take a moment to look over the design. Are there any particular elements or areas that the eye is drawn to? If there are, this could suggest an imbalance. Consider adding additional elements into an empty space or resizing a shape if it is either overly dominant or lacking in impact. Throughout this process extra hand-drawn elements can be added at any time.

When tracing off the final design, it is important to ensure the areas where elements join are smoothed together. This example shows the uneven join where the flower shape has been placed over the trunk.

In this example the flower shape was ineffective and the eye was drawn to the right-hand side of the design. To correct this, the top middle motif was enlarged and a tendril added to fill the right-hand gap. The three leaves across the main stem were moved down and an additional wandering tendril was added to the left-hand branch. Whilst the overall layout of the design is pleasing, it still has potential for additional small details such as flowers or insects. As these will be very small details, they have not been included in the final drawn image. This gives flexibility during the stitching process, as if a mark is made on the fabric, it *must* be covered.

By removing the point at the base of the flower and broadening the trunk, the shapes flow together. This seamless transition through the shapes helps to draw the eye through the design.

Designed and worked by the author, this piece is worked in three stitches; the simplicity of the approach creates an elegant but dimensional embroidery.

Designed and worked by Lizzy Pye, this simple leaf design is worked in four outlining stitches to create a repeating motif.

Designed and worked by Lizzy Pye, this contemporary piece is worked using the principle of odd numbers. Five flowers are depicted, three of which are larger and therefore more dominant.

Hits and Tips

Additional elements such as smooth curves can be created by using the pivot points in your arm. Keep your elbow stationary on the table and make a sweeping motion across the piece of paper. The same can be done using the wrist as a fixed point.

Designed and worked by the author, this tropical design utilises densely worked and careful shading to create a stylised piece of embroidery.

Designed and worked by Helen Richman, this piece focuses primarily on outlining and accent stitches to create a contemporary motif.

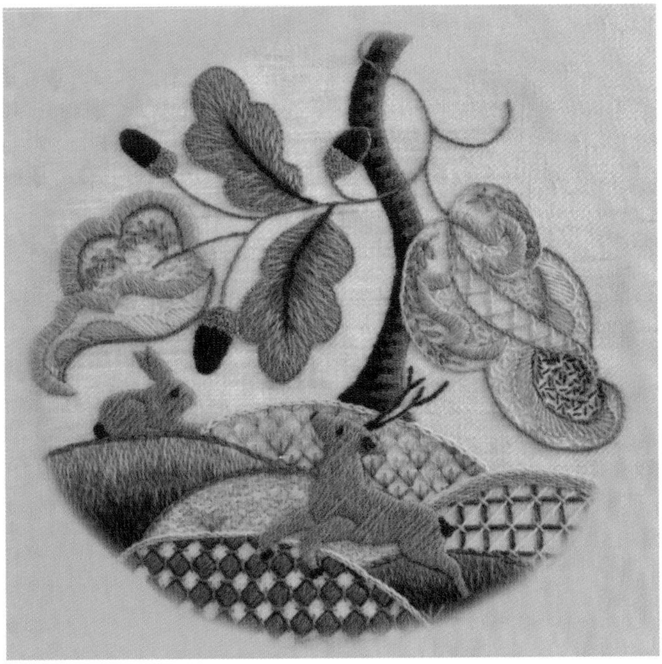

Designed and worked Helen Richman, this more complex motif references the Jacobean period in both design and execution.

Designed and worked by Lizzy Pye, this piece is uses Long and Short Stitch and careful shading to create a realistic embroidery.

SPLIT COMPLEMENTARY
COMPLEMENTARY
TRIAD
TETRAD
Sew Easy
Sew Easy

CHAPTER 3

CHOOSING COLOUR

Choosing a colour palette can be an intimidating and challenging process as there are multiple ways of selecting colours and a huge variety to choose from. In order to simplify this process, it is best to focus on a starting point; for instance, honing in on the selection of one colour and building a palette around it is much easier than trying to choose all the colours at once. This can be as simple as picking a favourite colour to use in combination with a colour wheel and the principles that are outlined in the next few pages. If narrowing it down to one colour is tricky, try taking inspiration from a photograph, fabric or drawing, which can provide excellent resources to determine which colours work well together. When studying resources like these, it is important to identify the main colours and their variations, the number of colours present and how they work together – for instance, do they create a sense of harmony or is there a vibrant clash of colours?

Choosing a colour palette can be intimidating. However, taking inspiration from fabrics or other colourful items can help to guide choices.

Nature has had a huge influence over embroidery throughout history by showing us which colours work well together. For instance, the vibrant blue-purple of a pansy is often complemented with a touch of yellow-orange at the centre of the flower, and the subtle colours of an autumn leaf can appear to be monochromatic but often reveal an interesting blend of analogous colours. Paying attention to these details will help you build and expand your colour knowledge, making the process of selecting colours easier for future projects. Similarly, taking inspiration from the home environment is a good way to start; a lot of people lean towards colours that are present in the main areas of their home, meaning the new piece will sit well within their existing decor.

Those confident in selecting and assembling colour palettes can consider colours that do not first spring to mind or are in fact are actively disliked. Don't be afraid to take risks; grey and black are rarely seen in crewelwork, so working in the grey scale or sepia tones would be a departure from the traditions of this technique. Think, too, about the feel of the embroidery. Is the intention to create a piece that is dramatic and striking? If so, bold primary colours work well. Or is the intention to create a piece that gently draws the eye into a calm and subtle piece? If so, softer, paler colours would be preferable. Ideas such as these can add an additional challenge and push personal boundaries – a necessity for keeping the technique fresh and interesting.

The number of colours used in a piece is often dictated by the size of the design. As a general rule of thumb, the smaller the design, the fewer the colours used in it. Use too many colours and the design could look cluttered; use too few colours and the piece will lack dimension and punch. When designing and choosing colours, odd numbers work well and is a basic principle to use when starting out.

Primary colours – these are the basic colours that make up the heart of the colour wheel. All of the other colours stem from these three.

Secondary colours – these are the colours that are created when two adjacent primary colours are mixed together.

Tertiary colours – these are the colours that are created when a primary colour is mixed with an adjacent secondary colour.

The Colour Wheel

The first step in this process is to understand how the colour wheel is constructed and how to use it to create colour palettes.

There are multiple versions of the colour wheel that each have different attributes. However, there are commonalities across each variation. The most useful one for artists is comprised of multiple tiers of colour. When starting out, working with Primary, Secondary and Tertiary colours will provide a range of colours to use and an understanding of how the process works.

At the centre of the colour wheels are the Primary colours – Red, Yellow and Blue (RYB colour model; other versions may start with subtly different colours). When mixed with their neighbour, each of these colours produce the tier of Secondary colours, which are:

Yellow + Red = Orange
Red + Blue = Purple
Blue + Yellow = Green

Tertiary colours are created when a Primary colour is combined with its neighbouring Secondary colour:

Yellow + Green = Chartreuse or yellow-green
Green + Blue = Teal or blue-green
Blue + Purple = Violet or blue-purple
Purple + Red = Magenta or red-purple
Red + Orange = Vermilion or red-orange
Orange + Yellow = Amber or yellow-orange

This method of mixing two adjacent colours together can continue to create additional tiers of colour.

The colour wheel can then be split into two halves – cool or passive colours (those that lean towards the blue scale) and warm or active colours (those that lean towards red/yellow colours). Generally speaking, cool colours create a calming and serene effect whilst warm colours can create an energizing and fiery feeling. Considering this in conjunction with the shapes and motifs included in the design can greatly influence the overall tone of the finished piece.

Choosing Colour Schemes

The following colour palettes have been selected to show how adding and changing colours can alter the appearance of a palette. For the purpose of the following examples blue has been chosen as a starting point; note that this colour is not the only one that can be used. Selecting one colour will help to reduce the number of options available, which makes the process of colour selection easier.

After reading through this chapter, it will be worth assembling the colours in a colour wheel and stitching your own version. This will not only create a reference point for future projects but will also solidify your understanding of how the colours flow together.

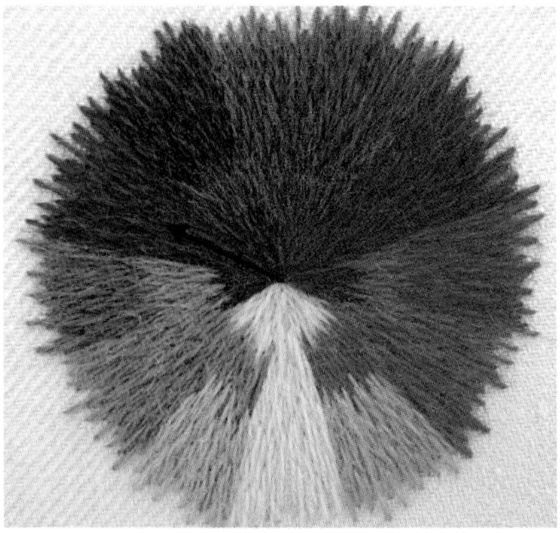

Monochromatic – this palette is made up of tones of the same colour.

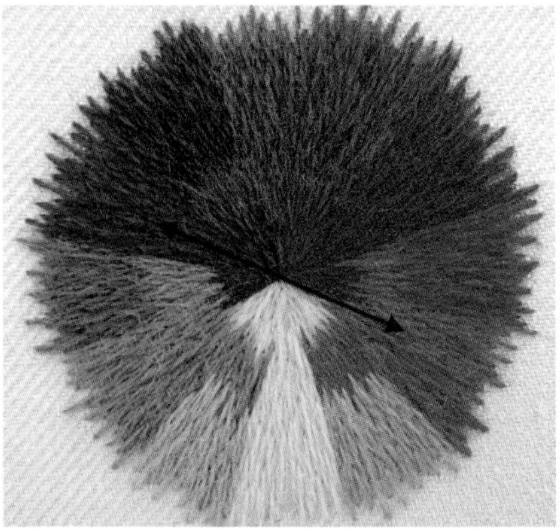

Complementary – this palette is made up of two colours that sit opposite each other in the colour wheel. Variations of the complementary palette are known as side/near complementary, split complementary, double complements and mutual complements.

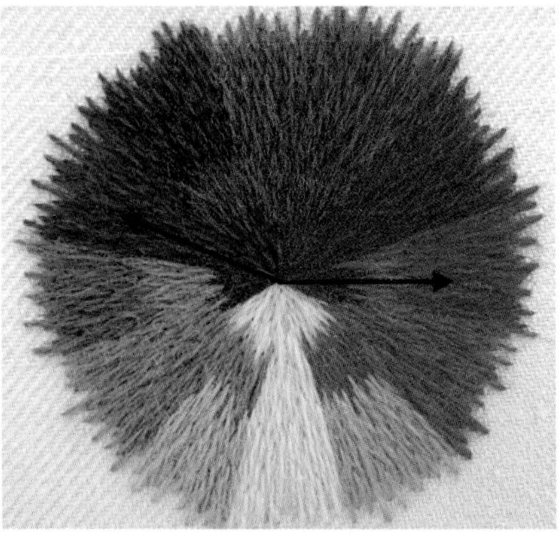

Side/near complementary – this is a variation of the complementary palette: a main colour and the colour that sits either to the left or right of its complementary colour.

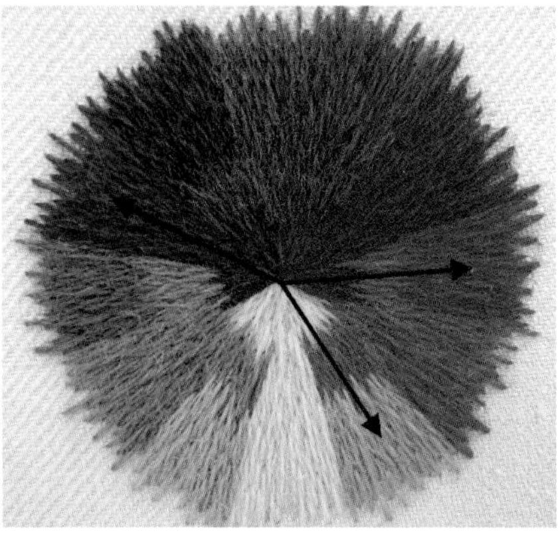

Split complementary – this variation of the complementary palette is made up of three colours: a main colour and the two colours that sit either side of its complementary colour.

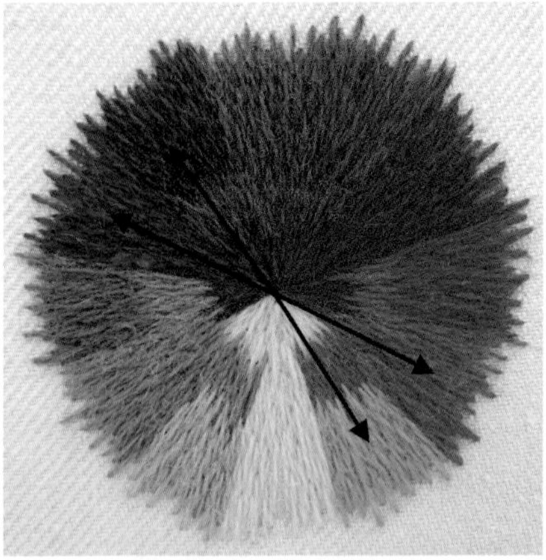

Double complements – this variation of the complementary palette is made up of two sets of complementary colours: two colours that sit side by side and their complements.

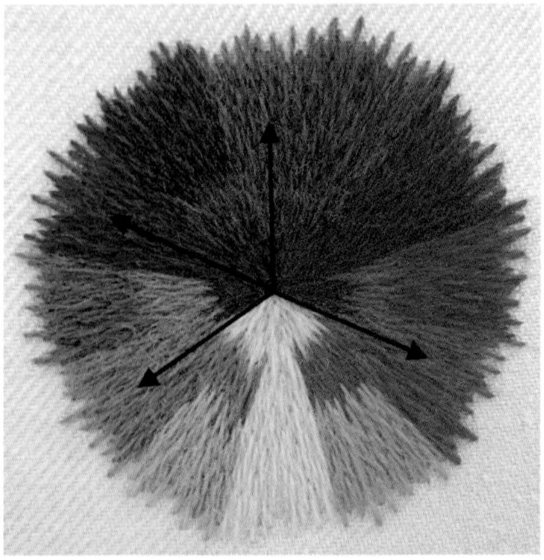

Mutual complements – this variation of the complementary palette is made up of four colours: three that are equally spaced across one half of the colour wheel and the complement of the middle colour.

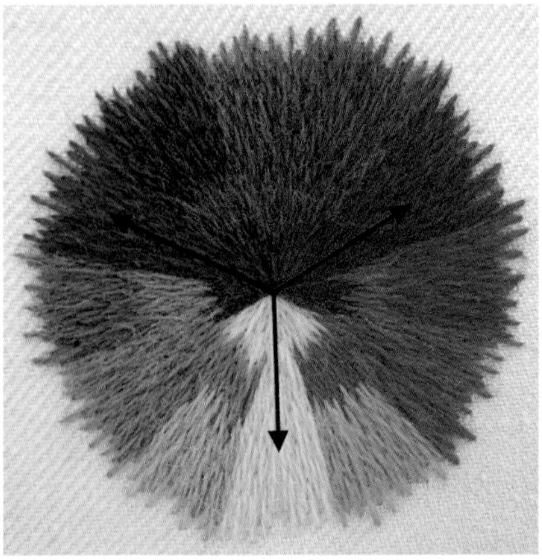

Triadic – this palette is made up of three colours that are evenly spaced across the colour wheel. When looking at a colour wheel, they will make a triangle.

Hints and tips

When selecting colours, always try to work in natural light. Artificial light can change the way colours appear.

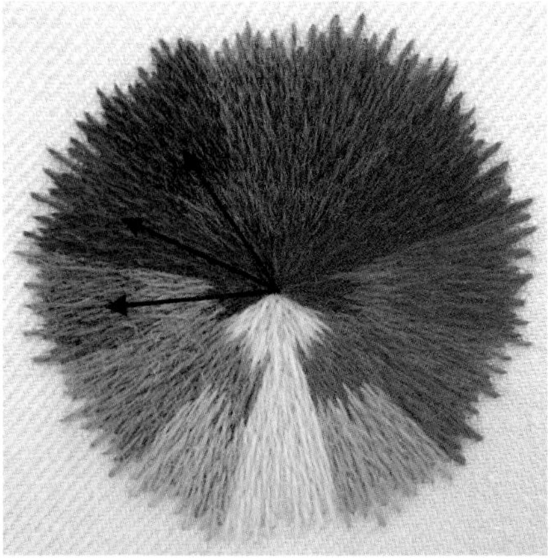

Analogous – this palette is made up of three colours: a main colour and the two colours that sit either side of it.

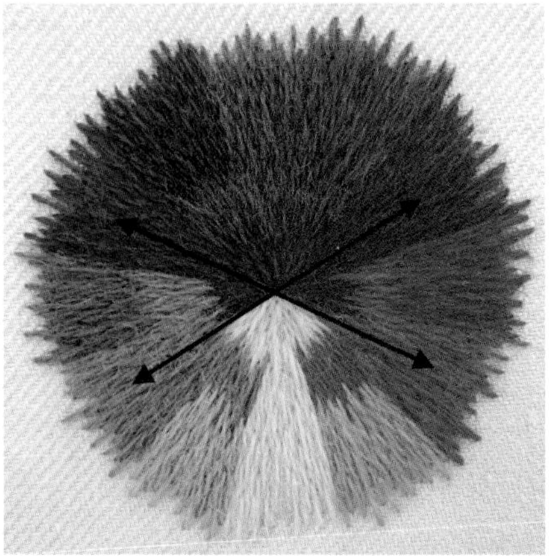

Rectangular – this palette is made up of two sets of complementary colours. When looking at the colour wheel, they will make a rectangle.

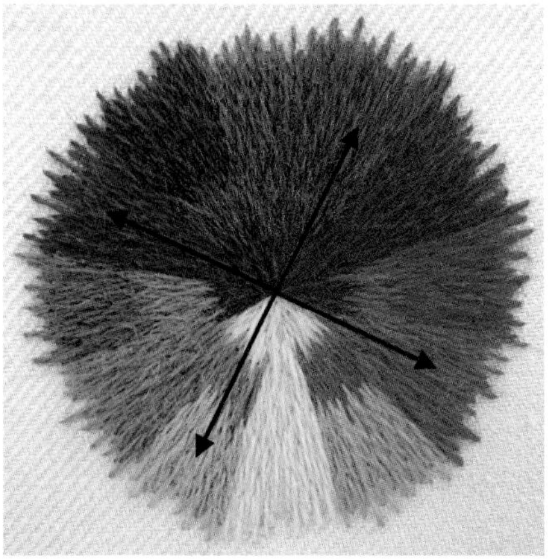

Square – this palette is made up of two sets of complementary colours that are spaced evenly across the colour wheel (unlike the rectangular palette). When looking at the colour wheel, they will make a square.

Hints and tips

When working through this process for any piece, regardless of its size, it is useful to have a shade card nearby to check what colours are available in your chosen brand of wool.

HEAD, SHADE, TINT AND TONE

Once the base colours have been chosen, take time to consider that there are variations of those colours that can be substituted. Using the pure bold colours of the colour wheel can create a striking and impactful piece; however, this is not necessarily to everyone's taste. Using the variations of a colour can create something that is just as impactful but a little more subtle. These variations can be defined as follows.

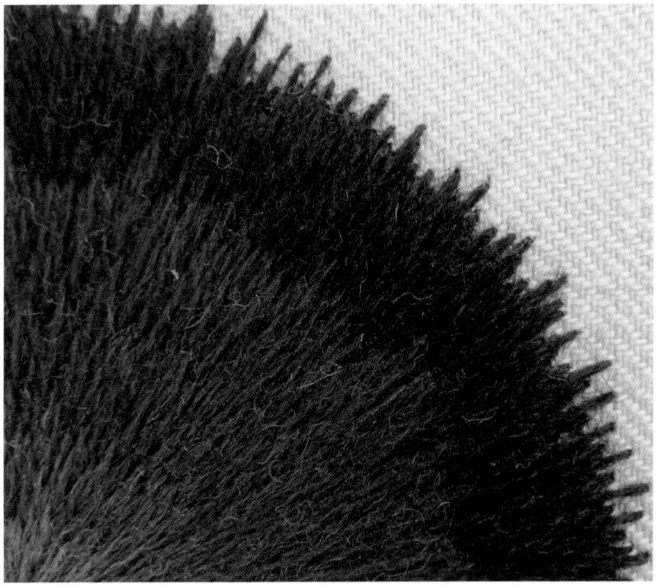

Hue – this term is used most frequently when naming a colour (red, green, yellow etc.). In this instance, the hue used is blue.

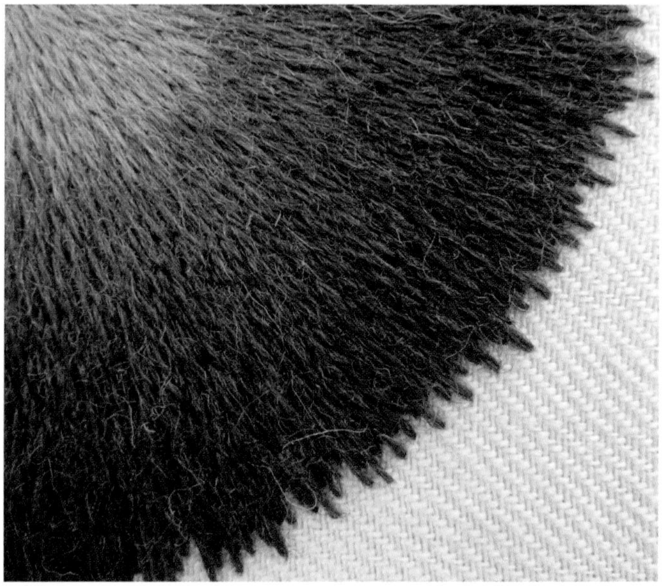

Shade – this term is used to describe the result of mixing a hue with black.

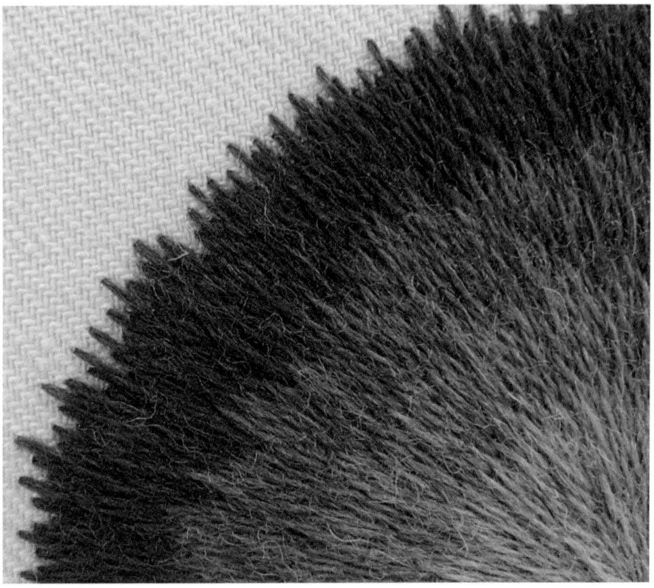

Tint – this term is used to describe the result of mixing a hue with white.

Tone – this term is used to describe the result of tinting and shading a hue and then mixing it with grey.

When considering any colour palette, regardless of the number of colours used, it is important to ensure that all of the colours work together. Often the best way of doing this is to hold thread in the chosen colours in a bunch and consider how they react to one another. Do they enhance each other or do they detract from each other? This effect can be seen in the image below.

The bright blue hue in the top right-hand corner seems much brighter and more vivid when sat next to the tint and shade variations. Similarly, these two hues appear quite different when compared to images isolating the same sections – the tint appearing to be much paler and conversely the shade much darker. The tone, in the bottom left-hand corner, has taken on an almost greenish tinge, which again is not present in the image of this same isolated section. This is often referred to as one colour 'draining' another. In this instance the hue is responsible for compromising the other colours.

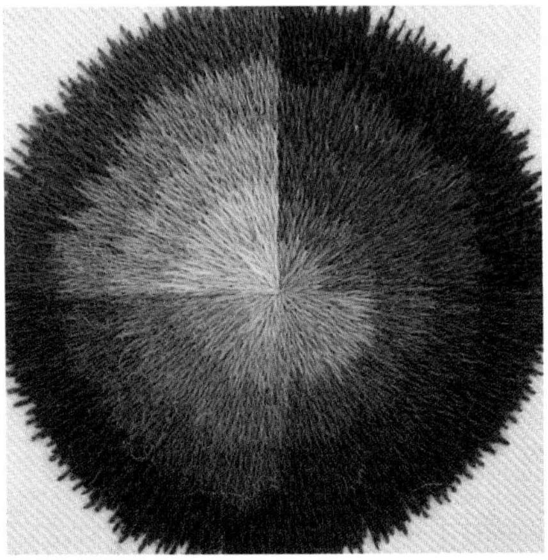

This image compares the hue to its variations of tint, shade and tone.

Neutral Colours

Pure neutral colours are black and white, which create grey when mixed. All of these are used to shade, tint or tone a colour. Other neutral colours, such as brown, are not present on the colour wheel but can be created by mixing complementary colours. Neutral colours work well in most colour palettes, but take care that you select the right one. For instance, a brown made by mixing blue and orange can become warm orange/brown or a cool blue/brown, which can influence the other colours. When considering using a neutral colour, don't be tempted simply to add it to an existing colour palette; if the colour palette is too large, it will be a struggle to place all of the colours, which could leave the piece looking muddled. Take care when selecting a neutral if the piece is being worked on a natural coloured fabric; often very light shades can be indistinguishable from the background fabric.

When working with black and white in embroidery, it is often best not to use pure black or pure white; these colours can appear very harsh and unnatural when in situ. It is worth considering a charcoal grey, very dark brown or very dark navy blue instead of black and a soft cream colour instead of white.

Designed and worked by Helen Richman, the colour choice for this piece is augmented by the addition of a neutral colour, which in this instance is brown. This addition enhances the vibrancy of the red and blue palettes.

Developing the Range of Colours

Ensuring that the intensity of colour is consistent across the different ranges will greatly enhance the final piece.

When the main colours have been selected, you can add to them to develop a range of colours that blend through from light to dark. Most thread brands dye in colour 'families', which are numbered consecutively within the colour range. This can make building your range quite easy. However, it is important to look at how the colours blend through each other. If the colours are too close, they will not have enough contrast and will appear flat. Alternatively, if there is too much contrast, they will not blend properly, causing the shading to jar and draw the eye. It is therefore important to edit out colours appropriately. Generally, colour palettes work best with odd numbers of colours.

If in doubt, select three colours from each of the main colour families; this provides a light, medium and dark colour to work with. For new stitchers, this approach will be more manageable as larger palettes can be overwhelming; revisiting this approach is also beneficial for the experienced stitcher, as it requires them to draw on their knowledge and creativity to work a dimensional and interesting piece with a limited colour palette.

Once the number of colours in a range has been decided, it is important to check that the intensity of each colour matches that of its counterparts across all colour ranges used. To do this, lay the all of the skeins out in order from dark to light and compare the colours. It will be obvious when there is a large difference.

The final stage of this process is to lay the chosen colours out on the fabric to be used and check that they work together against the fabric; as previously stated, the colour of the base fabric can enhance or detract from the colour palette. It is also important that the colours stand out against the fabric. If there is little or no contrast between the thread and the fabric, the stitches could disappear, leaving the piece looking disjointed.

This can be an intimidating process, and one that is easily overthought. However, the more you deal with colour, the easier it gets. Instinct can play a valuable role in this process, so don't be afraid to go with initial impulses. Whilst taking inspiration from traditional pieces can be a great starting point, using green for leaves or brown for a trunk is not always necessary. Don't be afraid to experiment with colour. A realistic colour palette can create a beautiful piece, but it is not a requirement to always be faithful to the colours found in nature.

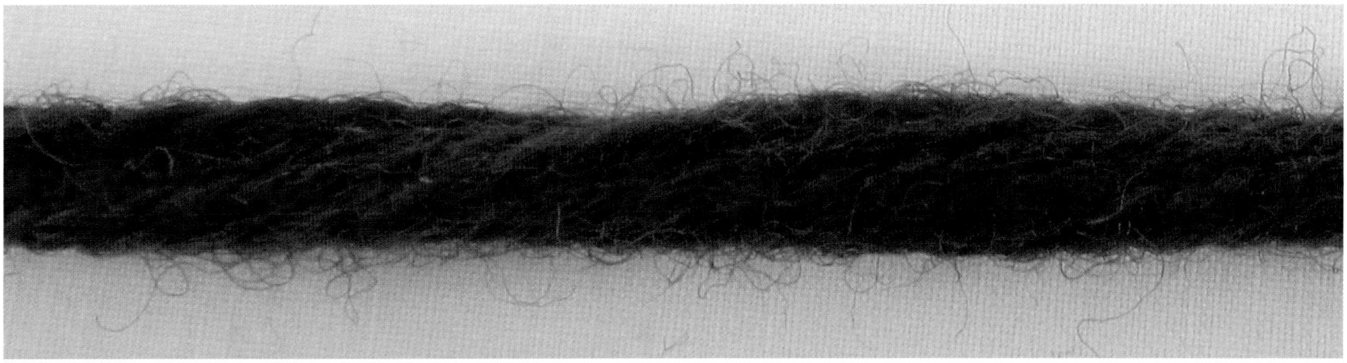

In this image, the two colours are barely distinguishable from each other. As there is a lack of contrast, these two colours will blend together too well, which will cause the worked area to appear flat and will therefore lack depth.

In this image, the two colours contrast strongly with each other. This strong contrast means that they won't blend or flow through each other when worked together. This could cause the worked area to become stripy.

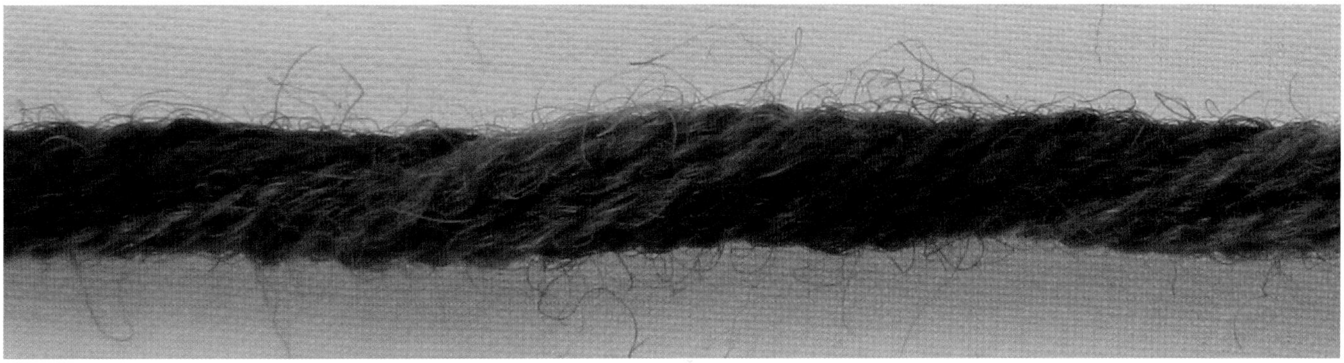

In this image, the two colours are close but distinguishable from each other. This slight contrast means that they will blend well together and you will achieve a smooth transition through the colours.

CHAPTER 4

PLANNING

Once the colours have been selected, it is important to plan where they should be placed in the design. This can be done by colouring in a copy of the final outline drawing. The purpose of this exercise is to create a sense of harmony with the colours; this won't necessarily happen with the first attempt. Working multiple versions of the colour plan is not only often the best way to troubleshoot balancing colours, but also helps you to explore the possible outcomes that can be achieved. It is worth playing with the ratios of colour in each version and being open to revising which colours are used as accents and which will make up the main colour families. When working with many colours there is the risk that one will become too dominant, and, as a piece is often worked in small sections, this dominance is not always obvious until the piece is almost finished. Similarly, if one of the motifs is overly saturated with one colour, this can draw the eye and disrupt the flow of the piece.

A similar process is required for planning the stitches. Just as with colour, it is important to have an idea of where the stitches will be placed. A good piece of embroidery will have a balance of open and closed areas that are appropriately placed. Keep in mind what the stitching is supposed to represent; for instance, grassy areas or hills are solid and dense, and therefore stitches chosen to replicate them should be dense or closely worked. This is particularly true if there are other motifs such as trees or animals resting on them. Densely worked areas are often described as adding weight to an area. Similarly, the wings of a bird or insect can be worked in an open manner that reveals more of the fabric to bring a lightness to the motif.

It is a good idea to consider the different characteristics of stitches and the way they meet or overlap in advance of stitching. Planning the order in which stitches are worked is another important step to ensure a sense of perspective is achieved within the piece. Whilst the crewelwork technique is often more stylised than realistic, it still provides an opportunity to achieve dimension and depth. This can be done by ensuring that areas that appear to be in the background are worked first and then those in the foreground are worked over them.

These planning stages will provide a starting point when the stitching begins. They also help to ensure the different factors of colour, density and perspective are combined harmoniously so as to lead the eye gently through the piece.

To start, gather together pens, pencils or paints that most closely resemble the chosen colour palette and copies of the original line drawing. In this example, the colours used are blue, green, purple and orange. They were selected by looking at the mutual complements on the colour wheel. The orange range is used as an accent colour, which will be used sparingly to create impact.

Designed and worked by Helen Richman, this piece demonstrates how open and densely worked areas along with textured stitches can be combined to create a striking effect.

Colour Plan

The completed colour plan is used as a starting point and a guide; the colours can be changed as the piece is stitched. For instance, in this colour plan there are two areas where the purple range stands out – in the middle leaves and the turtle. While there is purple present in the left-hand leaf, it doesn't stand out as it should do. Adding a touch of purple to the bottom of the trunk may help with this.

In this instance, the tree trunk is one of the most dominant features; it is present through most of the height of the piece and is the main connection between the motifs. Choosing the colours for this area first can set the tone for the rest of the piece.

In this example the top of the stem fades from green into a combination of both blue and green, with blue being the dominant colour at the bottom.

The flower head is worked in green with a touch of blue, which will echo the stem. The orange accent colour will be worked in the centre of the flower head.

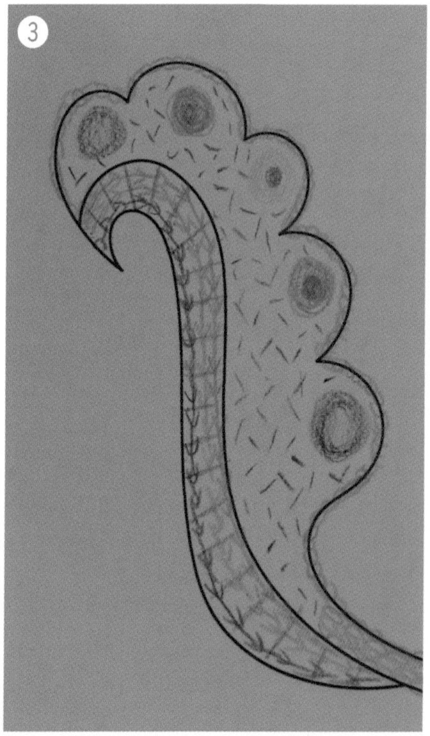

The left-hand leaf will have all the colours in it. The two dominant colours will be green and purple, with small touches of the orange accent colour and a little blue.

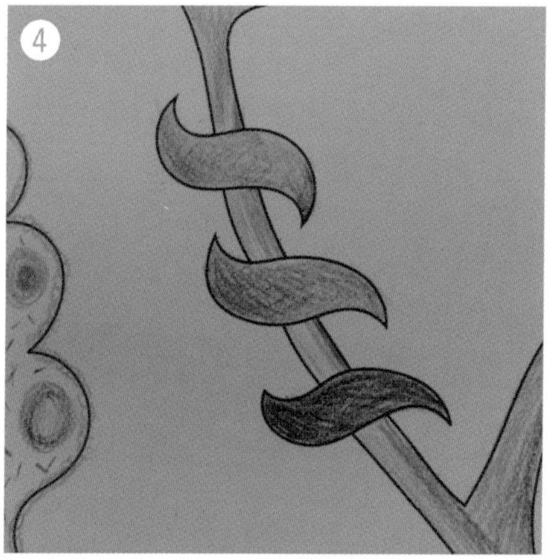

The three middle leaves will be worked in purple, which will be the first block of this colour in the piece.

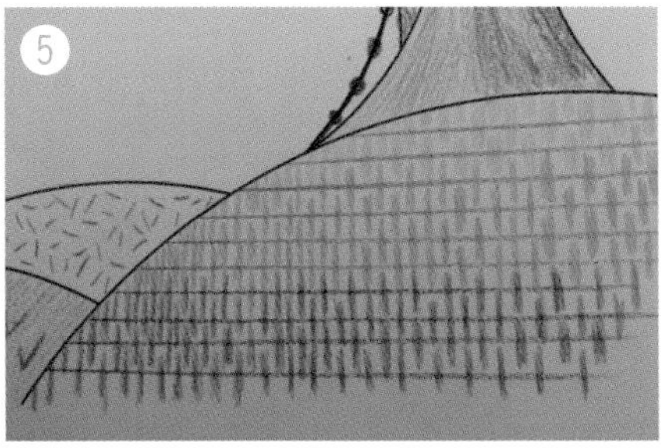

The next most dominant feature are the hills at the bottom. The stitches have been drawn in as this will give a more accurate impression of how the colours will appear in the final piece. The biggest and most dominant hillock will be worked in the green range with a hint of orange, the remaining two in blue with small touches of purple.

The turtle will be worked mostly in purple with a small touch of the orange accent colour. The head and limbs will be worked in the pale end of the blue range.

Drawing Stitches

The process of planning colour and stitches is intended to provide guidance to the stitcher, giving them a place to start and a path along which to travel. Therefore, taking time over these stages will greatly improve the effect of the finished piece. To get the best representation of how the finished piece will look, consider drawing in the stitches.

This is a straightforward process that comprises looking at the stitch that is to be used and trying to replicate it with pencil and paper. For instance, using a ruler to

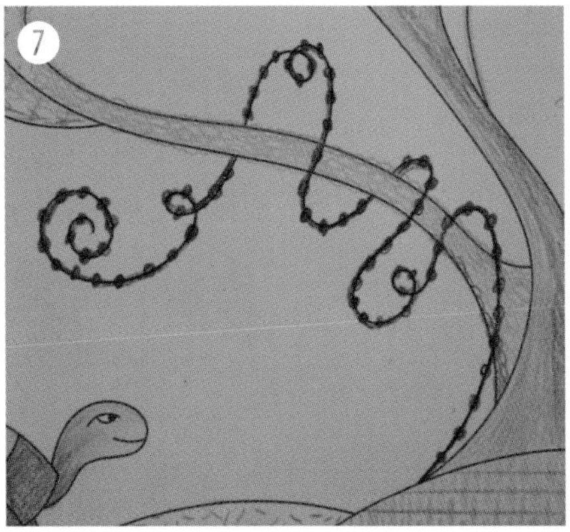

The right-hand branch is worked in green, which could leave a distinct dividing line between the right side (blue) and the left side (green). However, the wandering tendril helps to draw the blue through to the left-hand side.

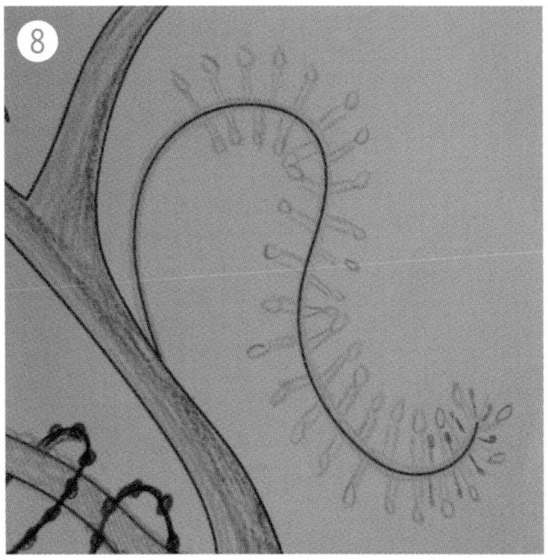

Just like the left-hand tendril, the green trellis in the top right-hand leaf draws the green into the right-hand side, in conjunction with the right-hand tendril.

Drawing in the stitches shows the embroiderer how much colour is present in each area.

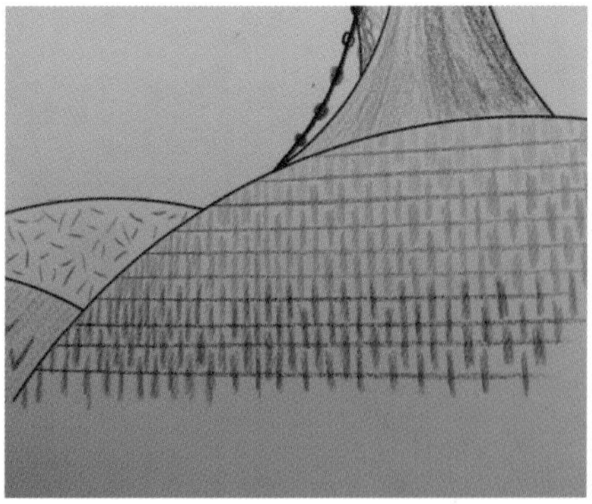

Comparing areas of dense and open stitching will help to balance the piece.

draw a series of straight lines can create a trellis, dots can represent French Knots and a teardrop shape can represent Chain Stitch/lazy daisies. When it comes to areas of dense stitching such as Long and Short Stitch, raised stem band or block shading, it is best to simply colour in these areas in order to replicate the density of the stitching. Following this simple process will give a greater sense of not only the balance of open and closed areas but also the density of colour. For instance, drawing short dashes to represent seeding will give the embroiderer a greater sense of how much colour will be present in an area than can be achieved by simply colouring in the shape.

Gaining a better sense of the balance created by open/closed areas and colour distribution will make the stitching process much easier and less stressful. Decisions made now can be subject to change throughout the stitching process.

The colour plan is not intended to be a great work of art, and once the embroidery is complete, will probably never be looked at again. This means it doesn't have to be perfect and is a process that should not be feared.

Creating Depth with Colour

Using the height and texture of a stitch to create depth is not the only tool available to the embroiderer. Using a range of colours or a colour family will help to add depth to the piece, but this needs to be worked carefully and with consideration.

Whilst working out the colour plan, it is worth deciding where the light is coming from. If this is in doubt, the top left-hand corner is a good choice. Then think about where shadows would fall: for instance in the bottom right-hand corner a darker green has been used, then a lighter colour has been introduced through the middle and the lightest colour at the very top, which is where the most light would fall.

When working with colour in this way, it is important to be consistent across the piece. For instance, the treatment of the turtle shell could be modified slightly so that the darker areas extend across to the middle of the shape in the lowest purple row to create a more rounded effect. This effect would have been enhanced by leaving the dark colour out of the very top row. The colour placement in the blue hill was designed to create the effect of the turtle casting a shadow. If the darkest colour extended into the centre of the hillock and a little more of the next colour in the range was placed on the left outer edge of the shape, this effect would have worked a lot better.

For the most part the flower head works well with the colours matching on each side. However, the area could have been greatly enhanced by working slightly darker shades on the right to give a subtle impression that the right-hand side was slightly in shadow.

Similarly, the right-hand side of the tree trunk is worked in darker blues, which fade through into the lightest blue and green. When working elements that sit in the background, it is better to choose a mid to dark colour.

This can sometimes mean that multiple colours are used in one area, or even within a line of stitching. Careful management of the transition of colours (as described in the instructions for laidwork in Chapter 6) can create great depth. However, take care not to overcrowd small motifs with colour. Just as with design, odd numbers work well, so consider if there is enough space to work three or five colours. If working multiple colours in a line of stitching, it is important to 'park' the needle (see Chapter 6).

Planning Stitches

When planning the stitches to be used in a piece, there are a number of things to remember: first of all, what kind of texture is being created? For instance, Chain Stitch or Split Stitch would work well to create the rough texture of a tree trunk; Stem Stitch or raised stem band make a good alternative, although the texture will be finer. Stitches such as Fly or Cretan can be used to replicate the veining on leaves or the feathers of a bird.

The shape and size of an element should also be considered when placing stitches; for instance, if the shape is too big, the chosen stitch will potentially be too long and therefore unstable. This type of instability can cause an eye-catching disruption that will ruin the overall effect. If the shape is too small for the chosen stitch, it could create a crowded effect or simply not show the stitch to its best advantage.

Stitches have different scales and heights. For instance, Stem Stitch is quite thin and hugs the fabric. Chain stitch is slightly broader and shorter; the nature of this stitch means that it sits a little higher than Stem Stitch. Both of these stitches work well as outlines, but can also be worked in rows packed together to cover an area. Raised stem band is a form of Stem Stitch that is worked over a series of bars, resulting in a dense area that becomes slightly domed and can sit higher than surrounding stitches. Other stitches such as Satin Stitch can be padded to create height within the piece. This difference in the height of stitches can be used to the embroiderer's advantage; a sense of depth can be created by using stitches that lie flatter behind those that sit higher.

An embroidery of this style works best when there is a balance between open and dense areas of stitches. For instance, Long and Short Stitch, when worked properly, should cover the fabric completely, and will create a dense and colourful area. Seeding is a series of short stitches that are distributed over an area to introduce colour whilst leaving the area open, which creates a sense of 'lightness' within the piece. Considering the qualities of the object depicted is also an important aspect to consider. For instance, a tree trunk is a solid and heavy object, which means it is best worked densely to create the idea of it being a sturdy element; the lightness of seeding would sit at odds with this and spoil the illusion.

Using the design in Chapter 2 in the following example, you can start to see how the stitching order can be used to enhance the design.

Taking into consideration the different heights of stitches will add depth and a sense of perspective to the piece.

There are certain core stitches that will always be useful and will make up the heart of a range of skills, such as stem and Chain Stitches or long and short and Satin Stitch. However, there are many other stitches and variations that can also be used.

When starting out it is best to keep to simpler stitches, often reusing them in similar areas on future projects. But with experience comes the opportunity to experiment with new and interesting stitches. It can be all too easy to stick to the same stitches over and over again. However, pushing boundaries by researching and trying new stitches can be very rewarding and will add extra dimension to a piece.

Approaching the planning stages of a project with the idea that the piece could be a 'stitch sampler' can encourage the stitcher to experiment more. A stitch sampler is the name given to a piece which is worked with the intention of exploring and using as many stitches as possible.

Trunk and branches – these are worked in raised stem band, stem and Chain Stitch. These stitches will fill the areas. However, the Chain Stitches will be lower than the raised stem band, which makes the branches appear to sit slightly behind the main trunk. As the trunk rises up through the piece, the raised stem band will migrate into Stem Stitch, giving the effect of it falling behind the leaves, the padding in which will emphasize the fact that the leaves sit above the trunk. At the top Long and Short Stitch is used to continue the effect of the trunk sitting behind the leaves. However, the top edge will be outlined in Split Stitch prior to working the Long and Short Stitches; this will raise the Long and Short Stitches above the areas next to it .

Flower head – the centre of the flower head is worked in battlement couching, which is a variation of trellis. This stitch creates an interesting texture to the flower head, but also helps to stylize the shape. As this stitch doesn't fully cover the fabric, it is a step towards lightening the area and is combined with the increasingly open stitching surrounding it. The overall effect is to open up the motifs so that the piece doesn't become top-heavy. The stitches chosen are Fly, Cretan, Long Arm Feather and Van Dyke. These stitches are all similar in texture and create the illusion of leaves.

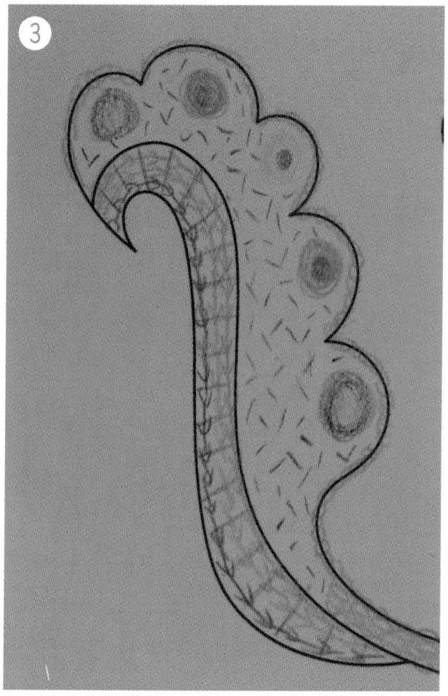

Left-hand leaf – the two sections will be worked to create a strong contrast, the narrow section with raised chain band, which will be worked quite densely, and the wider section in seeding. The addition of whipped and woven wheels will break up the seeding and add a little height in this area.

Middle leaves – as these shapes are quite small, working Long and Short Stitch on a curve would be challenging. Open stitches such as Fly or Cretan would work well in this area. However, they would sit level with or slightly lower than the trunk. Padded Satin Stitch is a better choice as the stitches would not be too long and the padding will help to raise the area and add dimension.

Right-hand leaf – the left-hand side of this leaf works well in Long and Short Stitch, and the resulting curve will help to draw the eye through the area. The contrast of trellis next to it will prevent the area from appearing too heavy. There is also the possibility of adding additional stitches to embellish the trellis.

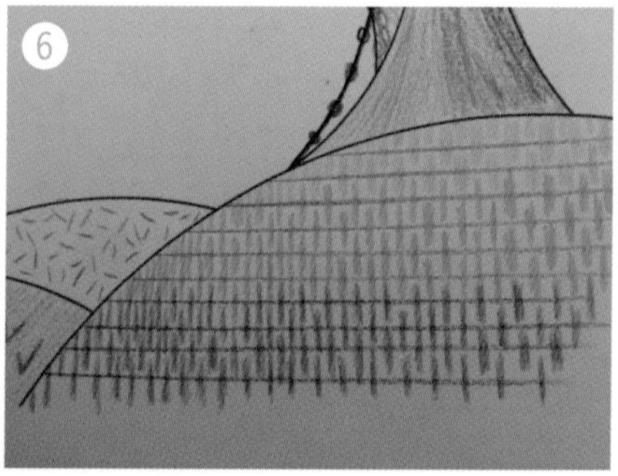

Hills – these are all worked in flat stitches: Burden Stitch, laidwork and detached Fly Stitch. The back hill (which has nothing resting on it) is worked in seeding. These areas will all require an outline; however, the colour for this can be determined when you are closer to finishing the piece.

Turtle – to give this motif weight, it will be worked in solid stitches: block shading and Long and Short Stitch.

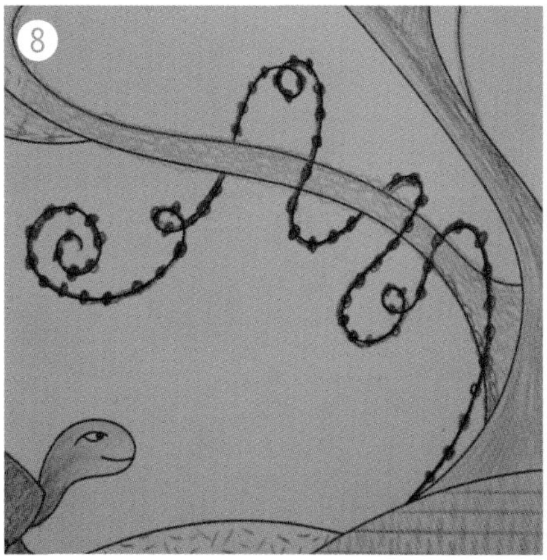

Left-hand tendril – this will be worked in Coral Knot Stitch. The dark colour depicted in the colour plan is a little eye-catching, so it would be preferable to use a lighter colour.

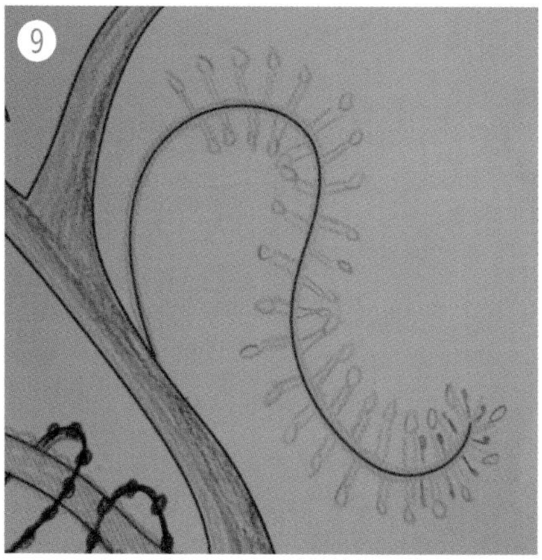

Right-hand tendril – using Up and Down Buttonhole Stitch will create a spiky texture, which will sit in contrast to the left-hand tendril. This stitch will then be further embellished with lazy daisies (detached chain) and possibly French Knots.

As with colour, odd numbers work well in design, as can be seen in this example in the three open areas (leaves and hills) and the three areas of trellis (flower, leaf and hill), and so on.

There are a wealth of stitches to choose from that would work equally well in this design. The description above is designed to offer guidance on how to choose stitches by considering texture, size, height and density. Although a good plan makes a solid foundation for working a piece, at this stage it is not yet set in stone. There will be times when it is a struggle to put a stitch in place. When this happens, don't be afraid to change the stitch. Selecting a stitch that is similar in style or from the same family is a good place to start.

Order of Work

When working a large and complex piece like this, it is important to consider the order in which the stitches are worked. There is no point in taking the time to carefully consider stitches and the texture they create only to work them in the wrong order, which could potentially spoil the effect. It is best to start in an area that is furthest in the background and work forward. This means that areas will overlap appropriately, leaving the areas in the foreground sitting in front of or, in some instances, on top of those in the background.

Here the petals in the flower are worked first, starting with the topmost petals and working down. Next, the right-hand tendril, the narrower section of the left-hand leaf and middle hillock should be worked.

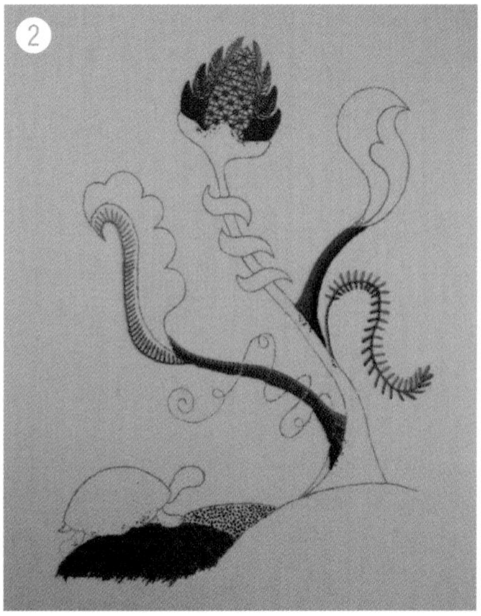

The next step is to work the bigger areas, such as the two branches that sit behind the main trunk. The left-hand hillock needs to be completed before the turtle and right-hand hillock. The centre of the flower head can also be completed at this point.

Before the main stem can be worked, the right-hand hillock should be completed.

With the branches and hillocks complete, the main stem can be worked, including the two areas between the middle leaves. Outline Stitches around the flower head need to be added, again starting with the top petals and working down, then working the outlining stitch around the central area. This is in preparation for the hard outline around the lower section of the flower.

The area of Long and Short Stitch at the bottom of the flower head should be outlined with Split Stitch, which has the effect of raising the area above the rest of the shape. The outlines around the middle and left-hand hillock are worked in preparation for working the turtle's feet, head and tail. Trellis in the right-hand leaf is added now, as it will sit slightly lower than the Long and Short Stitch.

The two feet of the turtle are now worked, along with the Satin Stitch in the middle leaves and the Long and Short Stitch on the right-hand leaf.

The turtle is now worked, and at this stage the wandering tendril on the left-hand side could be worked. However, if left to the end of the piece, it can be used to balance the colour if required. For this reason, it is now necessary to complete the left-hand leaf in order to be able to make this decision.

All of the major elements are now complete. Additional stitches are used to enhance the design and balance areas of colour and density.

On the left-hand leaf the addition of weaving through the Chain Stitch outline has given a subtle frill to the edge of the shape. To balance this, a whipped detached chain and French Knots have been added to the right-hand leaf. The right-hand tendril has been embellished with Pistol Stitch and Long Armed Chain Stitch has been added to the turtle shell.

Overall this piece has worked well. The eye is drawn through the piece following the long elegant curve of the tree trunk. Although the trunk is a little dominated with the blue colour range, it is broken up with the other colours and balanced with the green and orange hill that it rests on. There are no large gaps in the motif that draw the eye, similarly the piece isn't over-crowded. Whilst the accent orange colour is a little dominant in the bottom left corner, it does add a pop to the piece. The left-hand leaf has worked particularly well in terms of the textures created.

The Plan vs the Piece

Changes to the stitch and colour plan have been made as the piece has been worked. Some of these changes are due to challenges of fitting a stitch into a particular area, and others are made to improve the colour plan. Throughout this process it is important to pay close attention to the colour balance and areas of dense and open stitching. If necessary, a second colour plan can be worked to troubleshoot any changes.

The original intention was to work the centre with battlement couching. Creating the colour and stitch plan demonstrated this would use too much of the accent colour and leave the area a little too dense. A double woven trellis was worked instead with the woven element worked in the accent colour. This leaves the area more open and uses less of the accent colour.

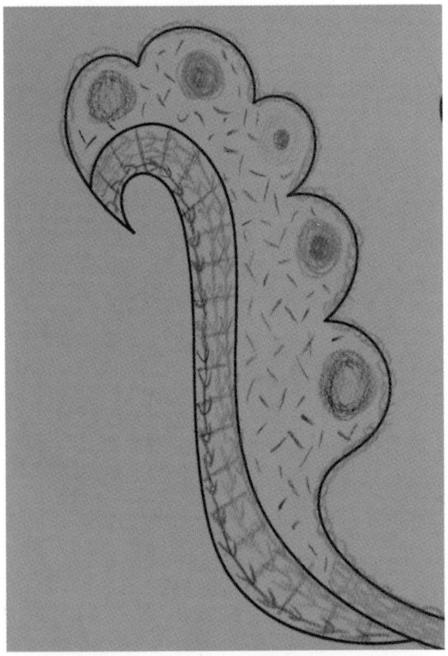

It proved too challenging to work raised chain band around the tight curve and top of the left leaf shape. This was replaced with open Buttonhole Stitch, which left space for straight stitches in a different colour. The purple seeding proved to be a little pale, so a darker shade of blue was used instead. In addition, weaving was added to the Chain Stitch outline. The colour plan called for the accent colour to be used within the whipped and woven wheels; however, this proved to be too strong.

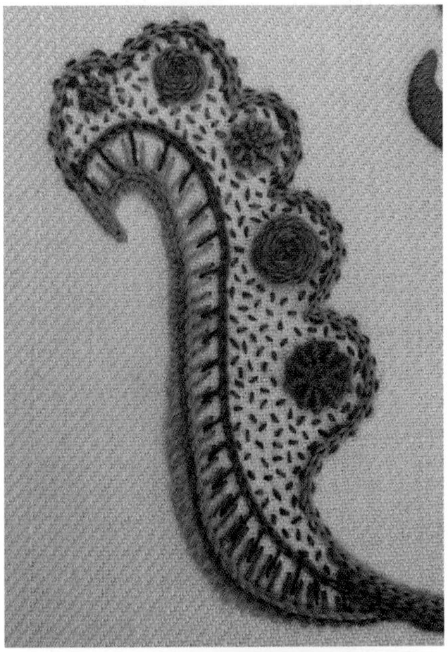

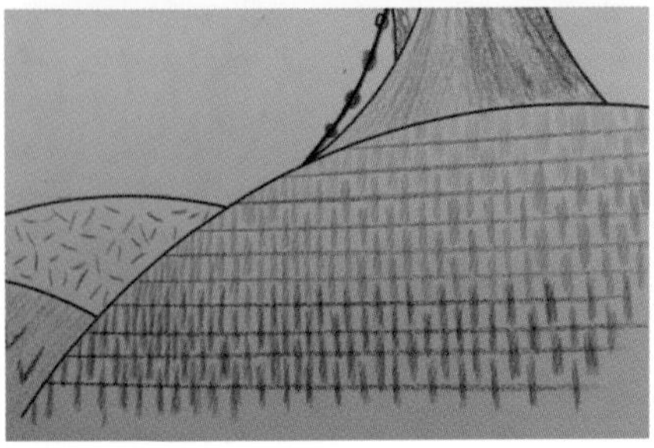

Burden Stitch was worked In the right-hand hillock. However, the stitches were worked closer together and in groups of three, exposing a little more of the underlying bars to reveal some of the accent colour. A touch of purple was added to the trunk to balance out the other purple elements.

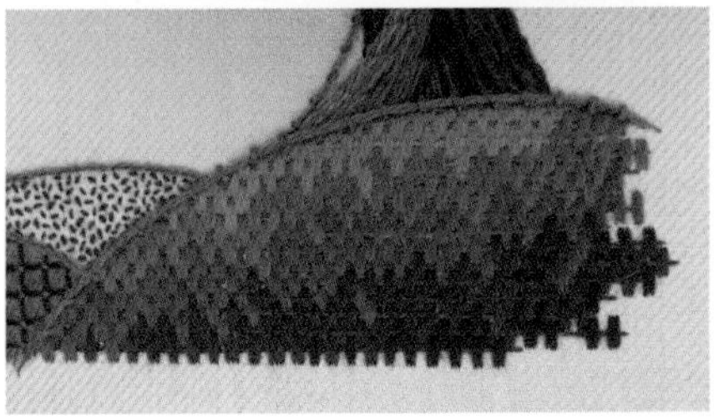

The left-hand leaf was kept relatively consistent with the original plan. The addition of whipped detached chain and French Knots breaks up the area and adds a little more colour.

When working the lower part of the shell in the darker purple, the definition between shell and hill were lost. Therefore, the colours were flipped with the accent colour placed at the bottom and the darker colours worked on the right-hand side of the shell. Trellis was used in place of detached Fly Stitch to hold the laidwork in place on the hillock.

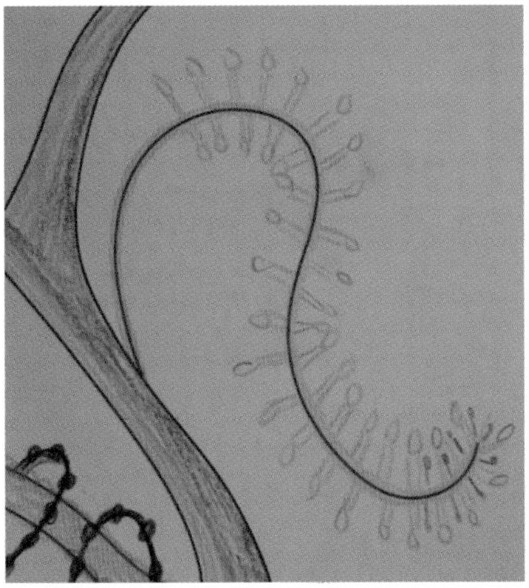

The inclusion of detached chain and French Knots had the effect of overcrowding the right tendril. Therefore, a simple Pistol Stitch was used instead.

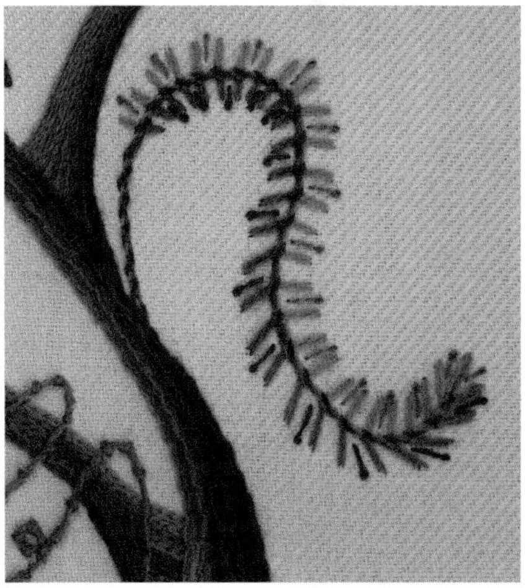

BLACK
POUNCE
8ml
0.27 U.S. floz.
Bracknell, England
150

CHAPTER 5

GETTING STARTED

FRAMING UP

Once the design has been finalised and the colours selected, it is important to frame up the fabric correctly. Working a motif under tension is preferable as it helps prevent wrinkles and puckers appearing in the fabric. When working on any frame, it is important to ensure that the fabric stays taut by checking the tension periodically. The type of frame should be selected based on the size of the motif, and there should be a suitable rebate of unworked fabric surrounding the motif. For instance, working a large piece in a small ring frame may require the piece to be moved multiple times. This could potentially abrade the fabric and will most definitely leave ring marks from the frame. It is important that a ring frame never be placed over stitched areas as this will crush the stitching, disrupting the overall effect and potentially damaging and even breaking the wool.

Framing up a design in the correct way will make all the difference to the end product.

When considering what method of framing up to use, it is worth thinking about how the piece will be presented when finished. For instance, if working the piece for a cushion cover, excess fabric will be needed for seam allowances as well as a rebate around the worked area; the same is true if the piece were to be placed in a picture frame. However, more fabric will be required if the piece is to have additional picture mounts over the top of it than if it were to not. Smaller items, such as needle books or small pouches, can be worked with less fabric as they are less likely to require a large rebate of unworked fabric. If you are unsure how the piece will be presented, it is best to work it on a larger frame with a good amount of unworked fabric, as it is easier to cut excess fabric away than add it later.

Framing up and transferring on a design are important stages that should not be rushed.

Ring Frame

For this process you will need the following:

- Ring frame
- Fabric
- Screwdriver

Did you know?

Tissue paper can be added to the frame by placing it onto the outer hoop before laying the fabric over the top. After the inner ring has been added and the hoop tightened, some of the tissue can be removed from the middle to reveal the fabric.

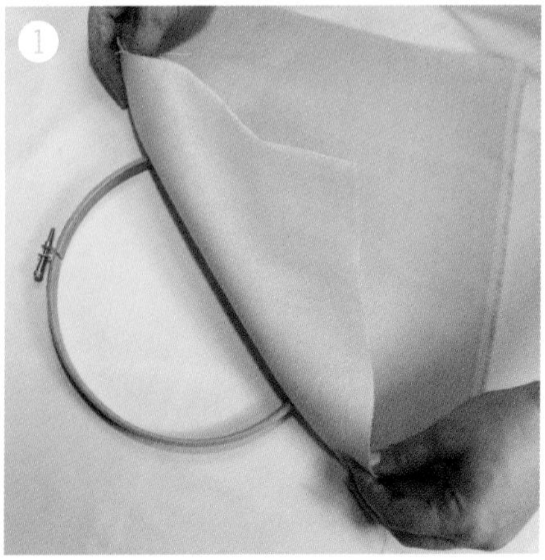

Remove the outer hoop from the frame and lay on a clean flat surface. Place the fabric over the ring; ensure that the ring is centrally placed in the middle of the fabric.

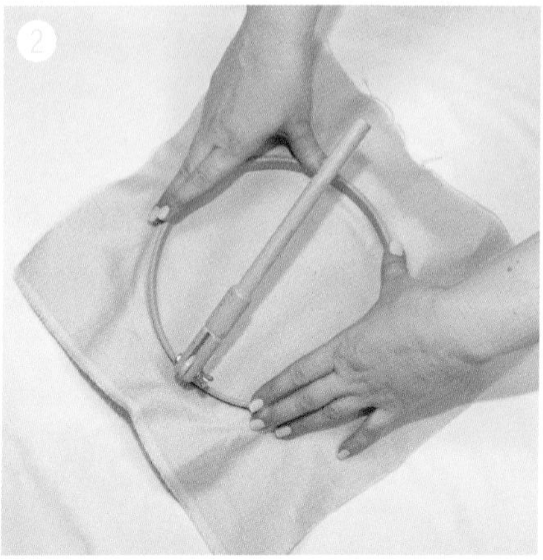

Place the inner hoop over the fabric and align it with the outer hoop. Push down firmly so that the inner hoop sits within the outer hoop.

Turn the frame over and if the screw is very loose, tighten it slightly so that the two hoops stay together. Pull the edges of the fabric to remove wrinkles and tighten it within the hoop. Finish by using a screw-driver to fully tighten the screw.

Slate Frame

When working on a slate frame, it is important to keep the fabric taut and square. This will greatly enhance the finished embroidery. The fabric should be large enough to accommodate the design with an additional rebate to allow for mounting.

For this process you will need the following:

- Slate frame
- Fabric
- Size 24 chenille needle or similar
- Button thread
- Glass-headed pins
- Tape measure
- Pencil
- Scissors
- Herringbone tape
- Parcel string
- Bracing needle

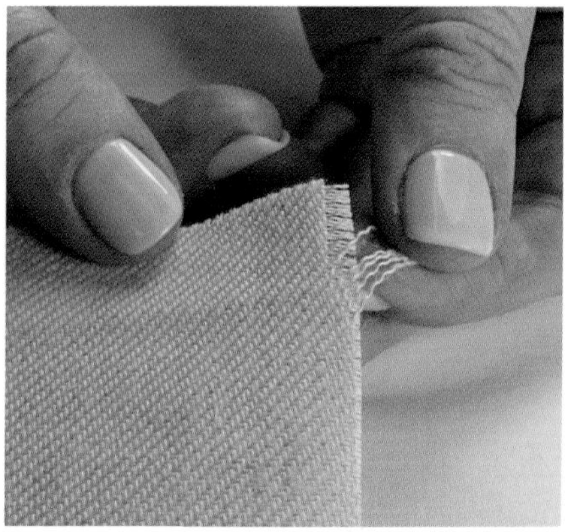

Take time to make the fabric into a square: once it has been cut, fray out each edge until a single continuous strand is extracted. Carefully trim away any long threads.

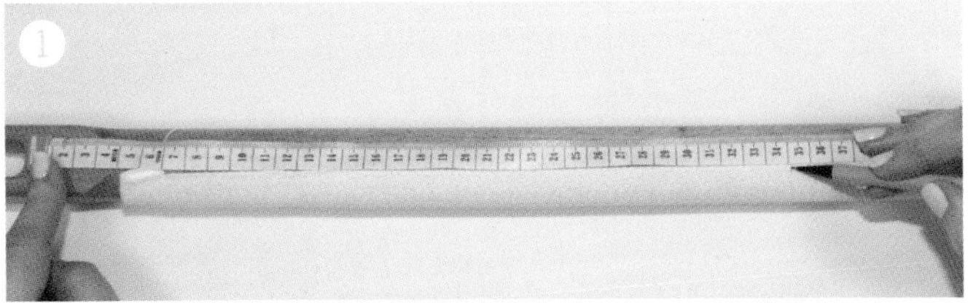

Take each roller bar in turn and mark the middle of the attached webbing by measuring the distance between the holes at either end of the bar.

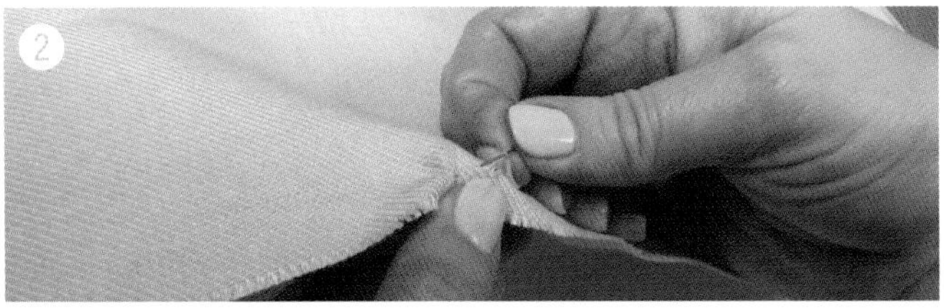

The fabric edges that will be applied to the frame need to be turned under and folded straight along the grain. A good way to do this is to extract a horizontal thread from the fabric approximately 1cm/1.2in in from the edge. Slide a needle under one of the horizontal threads and pull it up. Keep pulling gently on the thread to ease it out of the fabric across the entire width.

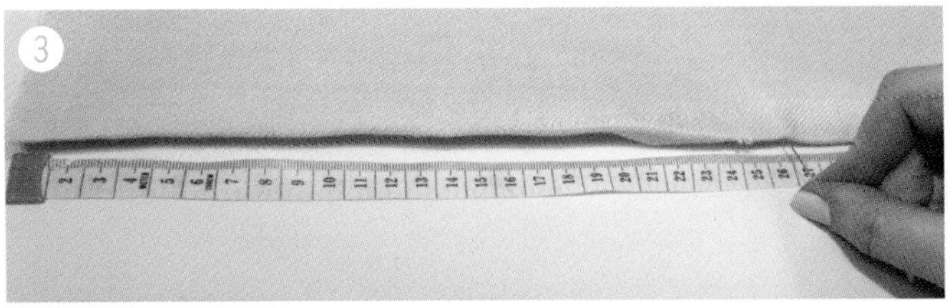

Turn the fabric under and press the fold into place with your thumb and forefinger following the line created by the extracted thread. When this is completed, measure the width of the fabric and mark the centre with a pin on opposite edges of the fabric.

Match the pin to the centre mark on the webbing on the roller bars, making sure that the turned edge sits between the webbing and the surface of the fabric. Pin the two layers together.

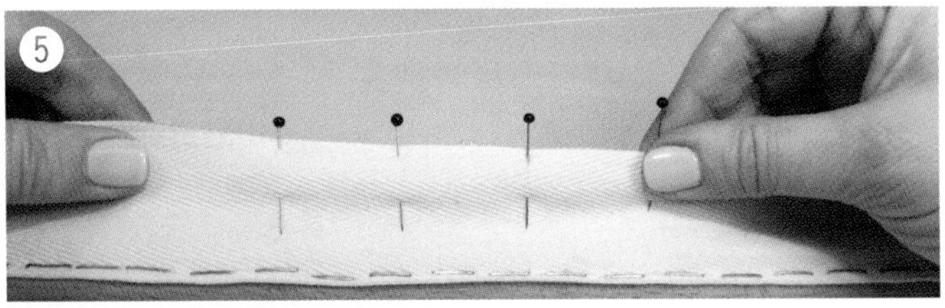

Starting at the central pin and working outwards, smooth the layers together, adding pins approximately every 2.5cm/1in to the end of the fabric. Repeat the process on the other side, until the fabric is pinned along the length of the bar.

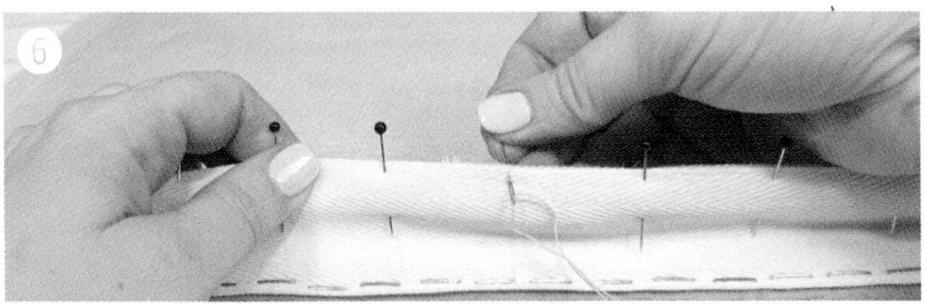

Thread the needle with a length of button thread and knot one end. Remove the centre pin and take the needle through the layers a couple of times to anchor the thread.

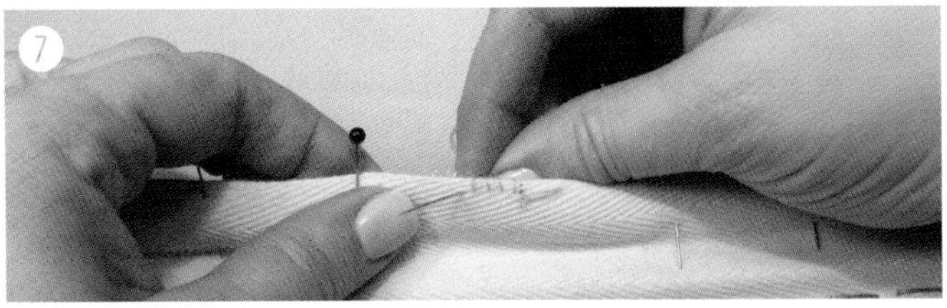

Oversew the edges by making small stitches that are both 3–4mm/⅛in apart and deep, working from the centre to the outside edge. Remove the pins as necessary.

Best practice tip

When stitching fabric on to the roller bars it is preferable not to start and end threads part way along the bar. The best way to estimate how much thread you need is to measure the thread against the roller bar and add 15–20cm/6–8 in.

Continue sewing along the length of the fabric. When you reach the end, stitch back along the worked fabric approximately 2.5cm/1in. Take the needle back and forth through the layers to cast off and trim the thread ends. Go back to the centre with a fresh piece of thread and repeat. Then repeat along the opposite edge.

Before adding the arms to the frame, check to make sure that the holes are mirrored. This will help to keep the frame and fabric square.

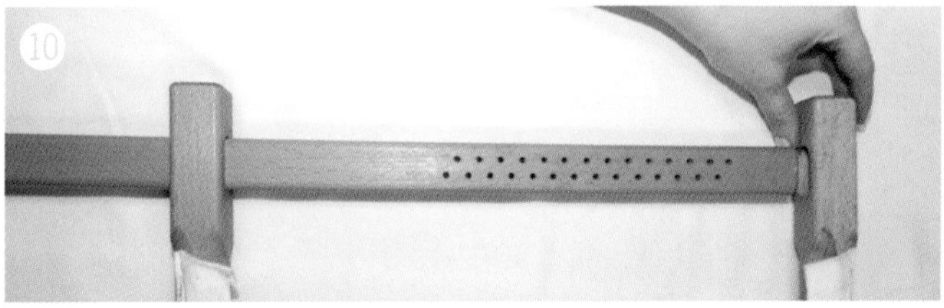

Slide the arms into the roller bars. If the piece of fabric is very large, the excess fabric can be rolled around the outside of the bars before the arms are inserted.

With both bars in place, put a split pin into one of the holes on one arm. Mirror this position on the opposite side of the frame so that one roller bar is held in place. Pull gently on the opposite bar to put a little tension on the fabric and put a split pin into one of the holes. Repeat on the other side. Tissue can be taped to the roller bars (not the fabric) at this stage, particularly if there is a large amount of fabric that has to be rolled in.

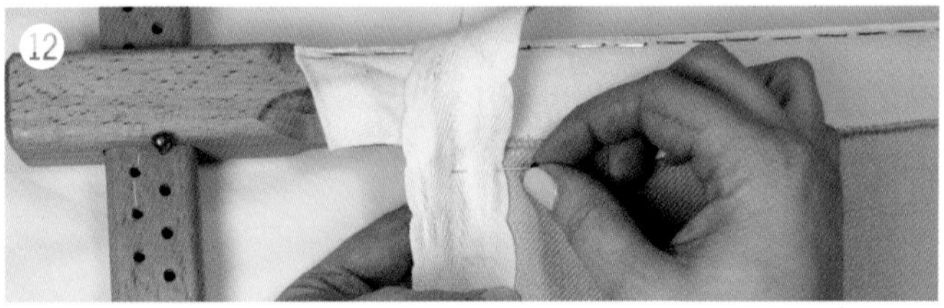

Cut a piece of herringbone tape slightly longer that the width of the frame. Place it on the edge of the fabric so that it runs parallel to the arms. The herringbone tape should sit with at least half its width on the fabric. Pin the tape onto the fabric, placing pins approximately every 2.5cm/1in.

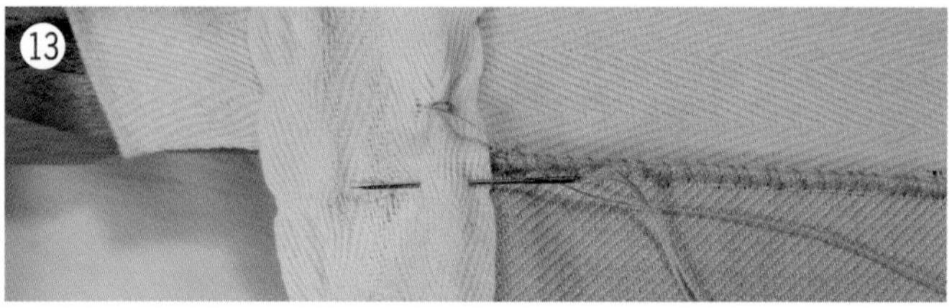

Thread the needle with a length of button thread and tie a knot in the end. Cast on the thread by oversewing the herringbone tape to the webbing on the roller bar. The stitches should be approximately 1cm/$\frac{1}{3}$in wide.

Best practice tip

Herringbone tape can be reused after the project is finished. Ironing is not essential, but can help to draw the fibres back together.

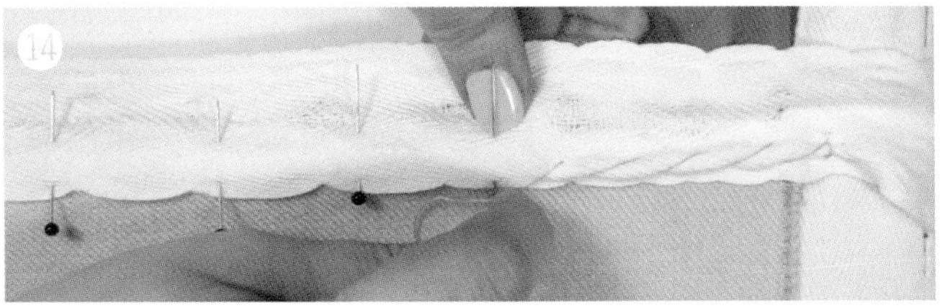

Work a basting stitch down the length of the herringbone tape by taking the needle horizontally through the tape, leaving a diagonal stitch on the surface. Placing your hand on the open side will allow you to hold and guide the tape into place. The stitches should be no more than 1.5cm/½in long. When working the basting stitch, pull each one firmly to create a ridge in the herringbone tape. Cast off the thread when the stitches reach the webbing on the opposite edge of the fabric. Work the other side in the same way.

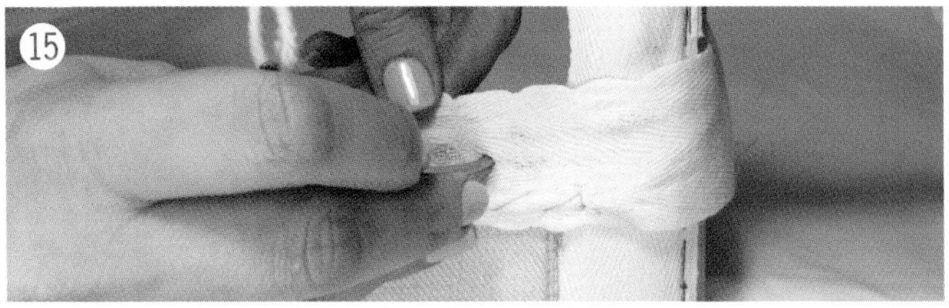

Thread a bracing needle with parcel string. Do not cut the string before the lacing is finished; instead work directly from the reel. Start at one side of the frame by plunging the needle down through the webbing. Take care not to catch the fabric as you work. Bring the needle up on the outside of the arms and take the needle back down through the webbing approximately 2cm/¾ in away from the last stitch. Continue working your way down the webbing. If necessary, pull more string through from the start. Leave the ends long in order to tie off. Repeat on the other side.

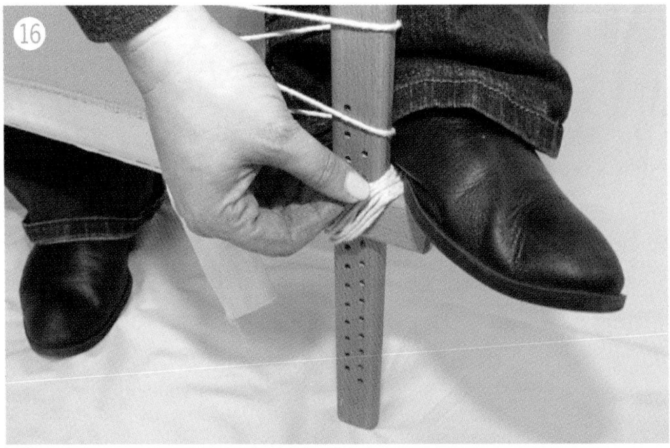

Stand the frame upright and place it on the floor. Place a foot on the edge of a roller bar and gently push down; the roller bar should move. This will allow you to move the split pin down and increase the tension on the fabric. It is best to do this process incrementally across all four split pins; remember to keep each split pin level with its counterpart. When the bar can no longer be pushed down far enough to reveal the next hole, the fabric is tight enough.

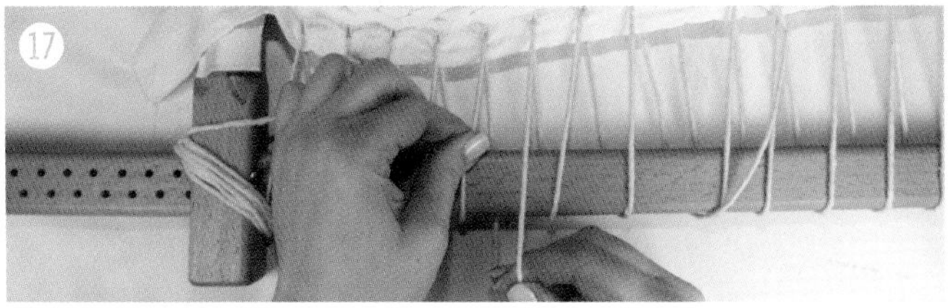

Take one end of the string and wrap it around the roller bar and arm. Tie a knot to secure. Pull each string to take out the slack; work along the bar and at the end wrap the string around the roller bar and arm without tying it off. Work the other side in the same way. As with tensioning the roller bars, it is best to work this process incrementally. This will ensure that the fabric remains square in the frame.

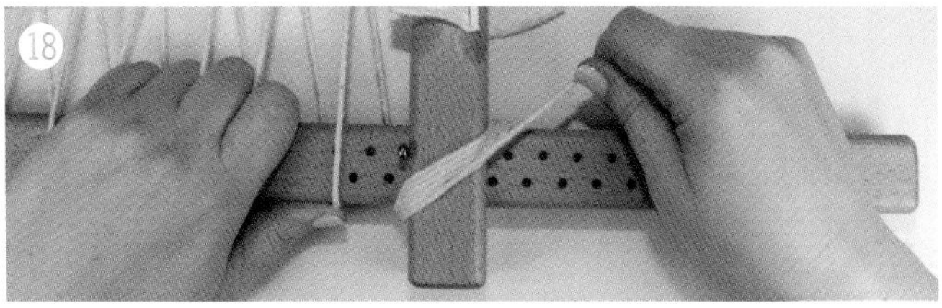

When the strings have been properly tensioned, wrap the excess around the roller bar and arm, then tie a knot to hold it in place. Once the frame has been assembled, tissue paper can be added to protect the fabric.

Best practice tip

When working with a bracing needle, it is important that it is only ever plunged down into the tape. Bringing it up towards you could be dangerous to you or to people around you.

The fabric and strings on a slate frame can stretch over time as a result of moving it from place to place or intense work. It is therefore important to maintain the tension on the frame. Before commencing work, always check the tension; if a finger can be slid between the string and the wooden arm, then they need to be tightened.

Transferring On

There are multiple ways to transfer a design onto fabric. The most common and traditional method used in crewelwork is prick, pounce and paint, which is used due to the nature of the fabrics. Historically fabrics were thicker, which helped to insulate draughty houses, but this means the fabric is not transparent. However, if the insulating properties of a fabric are not a priority, thinner fabrics can be used as an alternative and in these instances designs can be easily traced. On occasion tacking can be used: however, this method is generally used to establish guidelines for painting or tracing on. As paint or pencil lines can fade over time, or be rubbed off if not covered whilst the piece is being worked, tacking on can be used to replace the missing motifs.

Tracing or tacking on are the quicker and less intimidating of the following processes. However, prick, pounce and paint will yield the most accurate results. Before working any of these processes, it is important to start with a finished design that has strong, smooth outlines and sharp points. It is worth taking a moment to go over the design and look for any lines that are irregular or wobbly and re-draw them. Are any of the motifs sitting close together? Often shapes become bigger through the transfer process, leaving them too close to one another, which can disrupt the image. It is also important to ensure that where lines meet there are no gaps. Shapes can become distorted if there is no line to follow when stitching the piece.

When choosing to use an alternative to paint, there are a lot of options. An HB or F pencil work well and are easy to source. There are also water-soluble pens where the ink disappears when wiped with a damp cloth or washed. Vanishing pens, which slowly fade over time, heat erasable pens where the ink will fade when exposed to heat, or more easily sourced options such as a gel or a fine marker pen may be good options, but certain inks can become permanent when exposed to heat (even close proximity to a radiator) or bleed if washed. Washing carries additional problems with crewelwork as the wools can easily felt with a combination of warm water and agitation and is therefore not recommended.

If choosing to use a pen (erasable or permanent), it is important to use a fine tip; ink can easily bleed through a close weave fabric (which is a common attribute with all of the recommended fabrics). This will result in thicker lines that take more work to cover. With the exception of tacking and erasable pens, most transfer methods are permanent. If the options are considered carefully and care is taken at the design and transfer stages, there should be no need to use erasable media or wash a piece.

Tracing On

Tracing on works well for smaller designs worked on thinner fabrics. It is not necessary to frame up the fabric in advance.

For this process you will need the following:

- Fabric
- Design
- HB pencil
- Light box

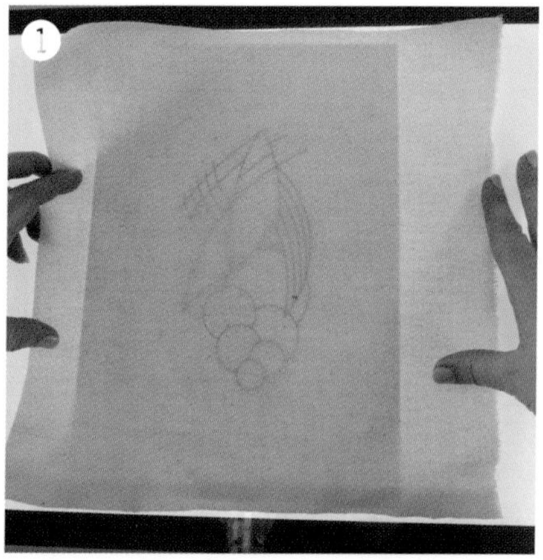

Place the original line drawing onto a light box; sticky tape can be used to secure it in place. Place the fabric over the top, ensuring that the design is in the centre of the fabric and straight to the grain. Again, the fabric can be taped down at the edges to hold it in place.

Using a fine-tipped pen or sharp pencil (HB, F or H), trace the lines onto the fabric, following the design below precisely.

Tacking

Tacking can be used to create a guideline for painting or tracing on. It can also be a useful method for redefining motifs if paint or pencil lines rub off.

When tacking straight lines, make long stitches with small gaps in between. Take care to work along the grain of the fabric as it is easy to wander off grain. Consider using a magnifier as this will allow you to follow the grain more closely.

For this process you will need the following:

- Fabric
- Design
- Tissue paper
- HB pencil
- Machine thread
- Tweezers
- Pins
- Scissors
- Size 26 chenille needle

Lay a sheet of tissue paper over the original design and trace the lines using a sharp pencil. If replacing a section of the design, make sure to include portions of the design that are still visible on the fabric. This will make it easier to line up the design.

Place the tissue paper onto the fabric and, if necessary, match the motifs up to any existing shapes on the fabric or with a straight tacked line. Pin the tissue paper to the fabric, placing pins in the corners and smoothing it as you go. Once the corners are secure, add pins in the gaps approximately every 2.5cm/1in.

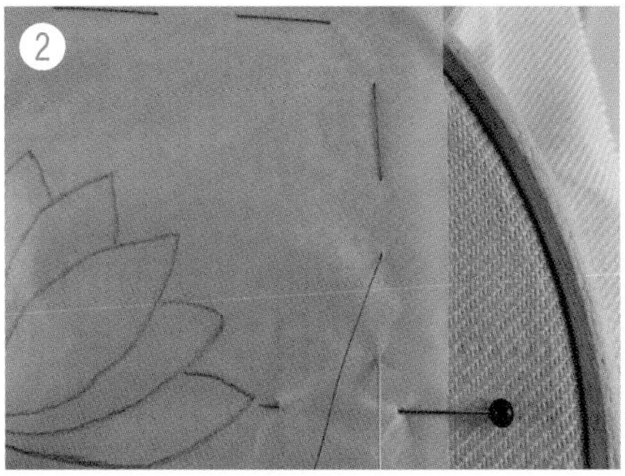

Using a machine thread, work a large Running Stitch approximately 1cm/½in in from the edge of the tissue paper to hold it in place. The pins can be removed after this step is complete.

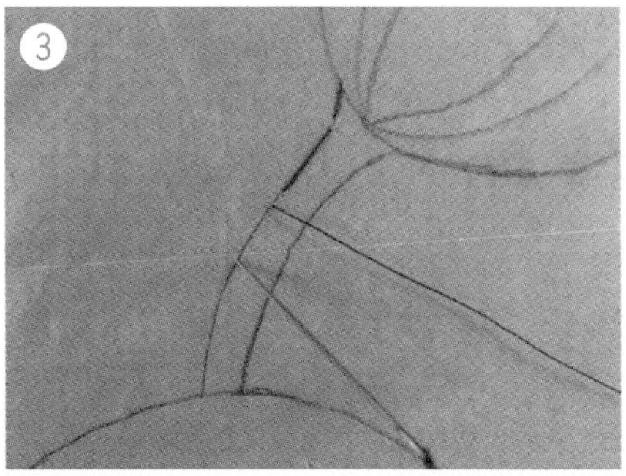

Using a new piece of machine thread and a sharp needle, work smaller Running Stitches along the pencil lines of the design.

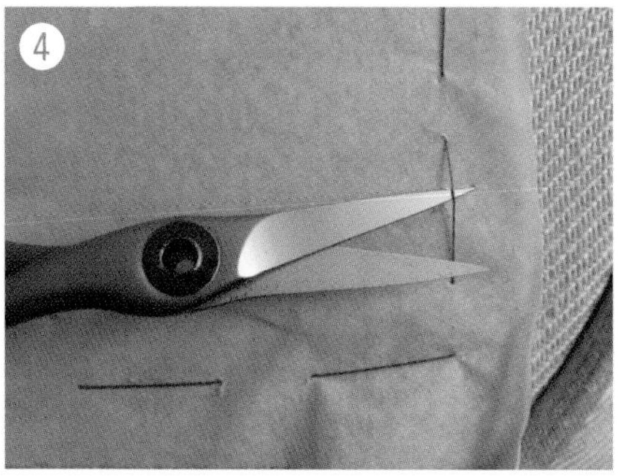

When the tacking is complete, remove the large tacking stitches around the outer edge.

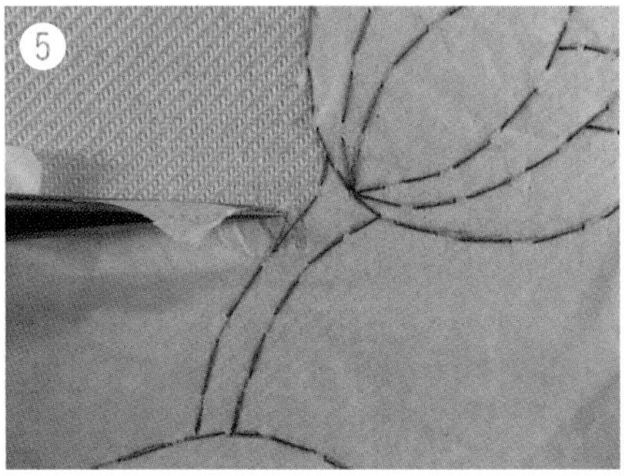

Tear away the tissue paper, leaving behind the outline of the design.

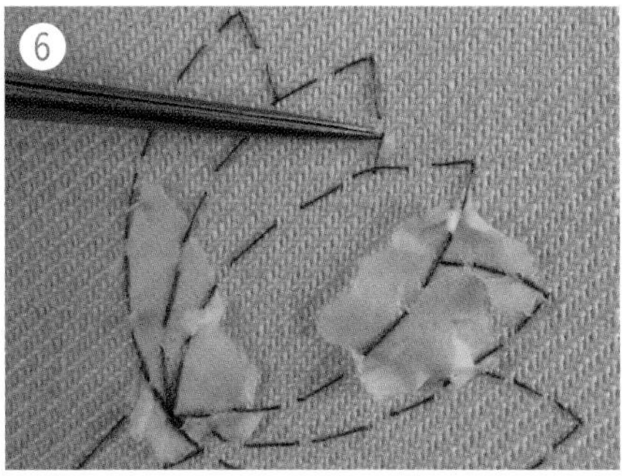

It is important to remove all of the tissue paper; a pair of tweezers can be used to remove smaller pieces.

When completed, the tacking should create smooth outlines and sharp points, just as with painting or drawing on. The tacking stitches can be removed as the shape is worked.

Prick, Pounce and Paint

Start by drawing the outline of the design onto tracing paper. Accuracy at this stage will greatly improve the final piece, so it is important to ensure that the tracing is true to the original design. Using a sharp pencil will create finer lines and more accurate shapes. Lay the tracing on a soft surface such as layers of felt or wadding. Place a fine needle (such as a size 10 embroidery needle) into a pricker.

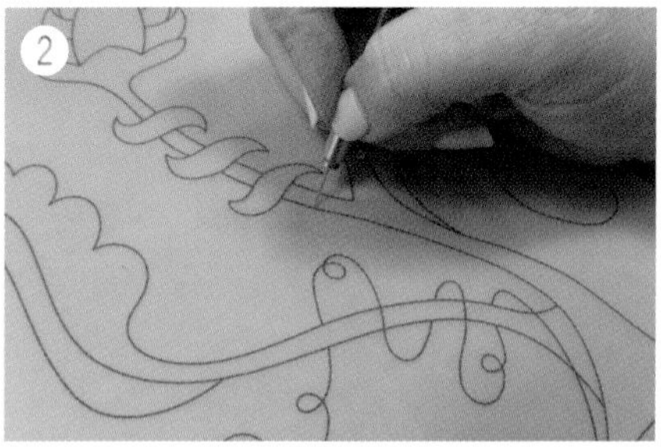

Using the pricker, punch holes through the tracing paper starting with any intersection where the design lines cross, join or end. This ensures that any joins will be neat and points sharp. Once this is complete, work along each design line punching holes approximately 3mm/⅛in apart. In order to create the most accurate replica of the original drawing it is important to follow the design lines precisely. Holding the tracing paper up to the light will allow you to keep track of areas that still need to be worked. When completed, this becomes a pricking.

Lay the pricking on the fabric, ensuring that it is centrally placed and straight to the grain (or lined up with tack lines if present). Place pins into the four corners of the tracing paper by pushing them straight down into the fabric. If the design is quite large, add extra pins to ensure that the tracing paper is stable. Dip the applicator (rolled-up felt or fabric) into the pounce and gently tap off any excess. Rub pounce over the pricking using a circular motion, ensuring that all of the holes are covered. Reload the applicator when necessary. Placing a hand on the tracing paper will help to stabilize it further.

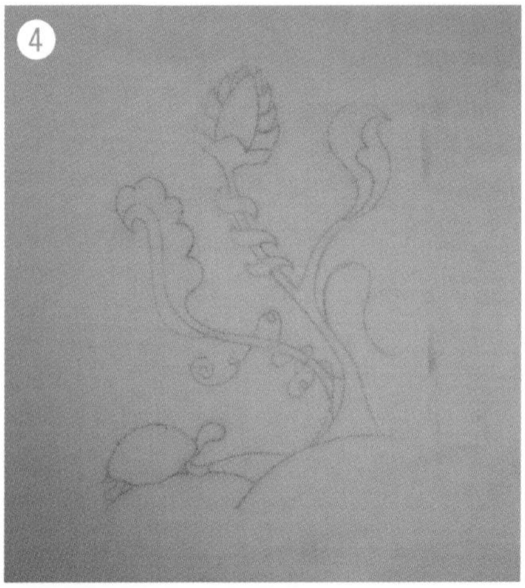

Carefully remove the pins, disturbing the pounce as little as possible, and lift the pricking up off the fabric. Gently blow excess pounce off the fabric. When completed, the pounce will create a series of dots on the fabric that act as a guide for painting on.

The paint colour used should be sympathetic to either the background fabric or the main motif. Most Jacobean pieces use more than one colour, so a colour that is sympathetic to the backing fabric is more suitable. Alternatively, a soft grey that is similar to the colour of pencil lead can also be used. As watercolour paints are strongly pigmented, it is necessary to add a little white to the main colour to reduce its intensity. Mix together the main colour, white and a little water. Test the paint on the edge of the fabric; when mixed properly, the paint should flow like an ink across the surface of the fabric. If the paint is too watery, a grey mark will appear around the paintline where water seeps through the surrounding fabric; add a little more paint to the mix to thicken it up. If the paint clumps on the fabric, it is too thick and more water is needed.

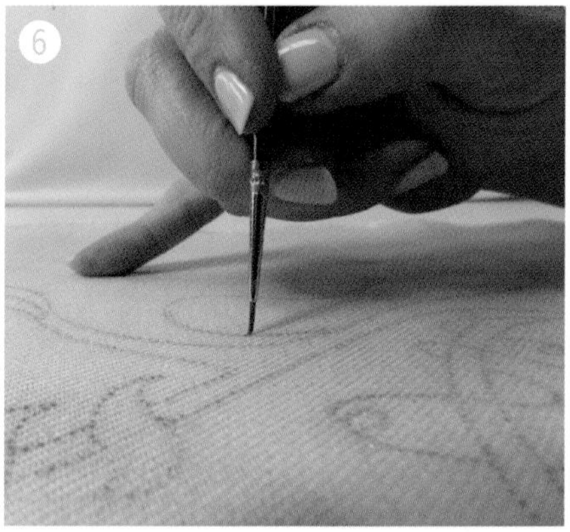

Use a fine paintbrush to carefully paint over the pounce lines. Take care to keep the tip of the brush at a steep angle to the fabric; this will create a fine line that will be easier to cover with stitching. When working across the piece, think about hand placement; if working over a painted area, there is a risk that wet paint could be smeared across the fabric. Similarly, resting a hand on the pounce lines could lift it off the fabric and remove the guide line. The pounce can easily collect on the tip of the paintbrush, so it is important to keep the brush clean. A container of clean water and a piece of tissue can be used to clean it.

Did you know?

The size of the embroidery needle used in the pricker is related to how finely ground the pounce is. A finer powder (similar in texture to talcum powder) will pass more easily through a smaller hole. When using a more coarsely ground pounce, it is better to use a larger needle.

There are a number of pens and pencils available to use when transferring on a design. Take care with any transfer method as marks made on the fabric must *always* be covered.

If there are any circles with in the design, wait until the paint is dry and use a circle template to draw them on with either a pencil or fine-tipped pen. The paint should be fully dry before stitches are added. To test this, gently place a finger over one of the paintlines. If paint is left on your finger, then additional drying time is needed. When the paint is dry, turn the frame over and beat the fabric with the back of a soft bristle brush. On the right side of piece, remove any excess pounce using a sweeping motion whilst lifting the brush up and off the fabric. Take care not to overbrush the fabric as it can cause the fibres to become fluffy.

If using paint seems a little intimidating, a fine-tipped pen or sharp pencil (HB, F or H) could be used instead. Be aware that pencil can fade or rub off as the piece is worked.

Did you know?

Keeping a copy of the original line drawing nearby when painting on can act as a useful guide if the pounce lines are faint or confusing.

Did you know?

Once the fabric is framed up and the design has been transferred on, regardless of the transfer method, the piece should be protected with either tissue paper or a clean piece of fabric. Secure the covering in place with pins, taking care to place them at the edge of the fabric.

CHAPTER 6

FILLING STITCHES

Densely worked filling stitches are often used over large areas, and as a result can become focal points within the design. It is therefore important to consider and plan these areas carefully. It can be tempting to saturate larger areas with too much of one colour, particularly an accent colour. Open filling stitches can create lovely texture; however, the stitches can easily become too long and unstable. An unstable stitch will not lie flat or straight and will draw the eye to it.

Many of the latter stitches in this chapter can be worked either open or closed; as such, careful consideration should be given to their placement. The saturation of colour in an area will change with how open or closed the stitch is, which will affect the overall colour balance. Consider working them from open to closed or shading through more than one colour to create a graduated effect.

Designed and worked by Jessica Aldred, this modern Jacobean motif is worked in a number of dense filling stitches with a contemporary colour palette to create this striking piece.

WORKING WITH WOOL

The repeated action of drawing any thread, particularly wool, through a close weave fabric will cause the thread to wear. It is therefore important to pay close attention to the thread whilst working with it. When the thread starts to wear, the wool will become noticeably fluffy and thin, and the strands may become untwisted, particularly where they pass through the eye of the needle. Continuing to work with a thread in this condition will cause it to snap, which can compromise the stitches already in place. For this reason the length of thread should be kept short – no more than approximately 30cm/12in in length. If the thread shows signs of wear at *any time* when working with it, it should be replaced.

It is also important to ensure the wool is of good quality; before cutting a length for stitching, check to see if the thickness and twist of the thread is consistent. Look for areas of very tight twist or where the twist is indistinguishable and fluffy, as these are areas of particular weakness. A thread that is of inconsistent quality will be more prone to breaking, and this will consequently cause a disruption in the finished stitch.

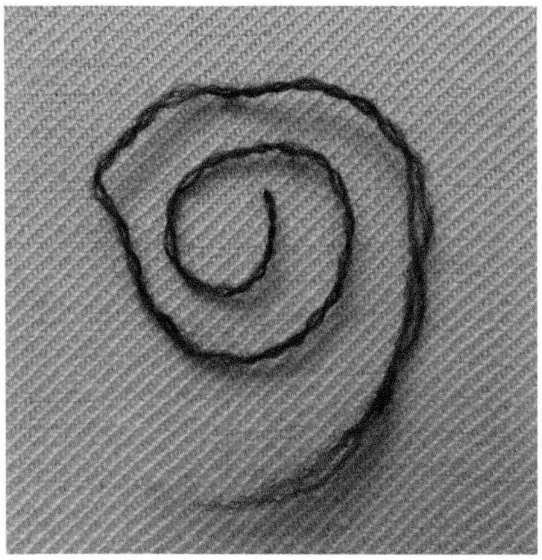

This picture shows areas of wear on the thread. This is particularly noticeable on the right-hand side where the thread has lost its twist and has become fluffy.

Parking the Needle

Often there is a need to work with multiple colours and have several threads cast on. When this is the case, needles can be 'parked', meaning that when not in use the needle can be put to one side until needed.

As needles can leave marks in the fabric, it is important to consider where they are placed; a design line or area intended for dense stitching is the best choice. Take care to pull *all* of the thread through to the front; thread left on the back can become entangled in the stitching, wasting the thread and creating a bulky area on the back. Much like knots, this can create a lump to appear when mounting.

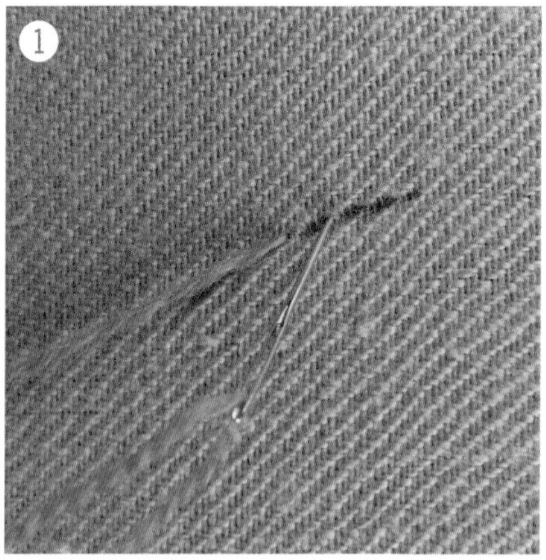

As needles can leave marks in the fabric, it is important to consider where stitches are placed when casting on and parking the needle; a design line or area intended for dense stitching is the best choice. Take care to pull all of the thread through to the front; thread left at the back can become entangled in the stitching, wasting the thread and creating a bulky area on the back. Much like knots, this can cause lump to appear when mounting.

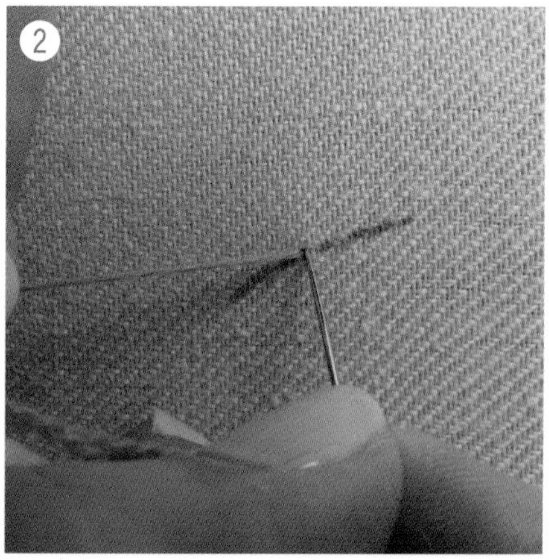

If you find you need to unpick a stitch, pull the thread gently to one side. This should reveal a small hole in the fabric. Slide the needle and thread through the hole to release it.

Casting On

A thread should always be cast on from the front of the piece; knots placed on the back will cause bulk which could, when mounted, cause a lump to appear on the front. This method is discreet and quick to work; however, it is important that stitches are placed in an area that will eventually be covered.

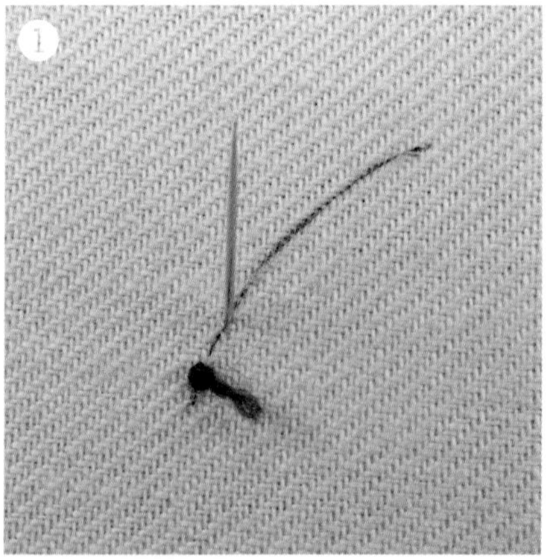

Tie a knot in the end of the thread and plunge the needle on a paintline. Bring the needle up a short distance away.

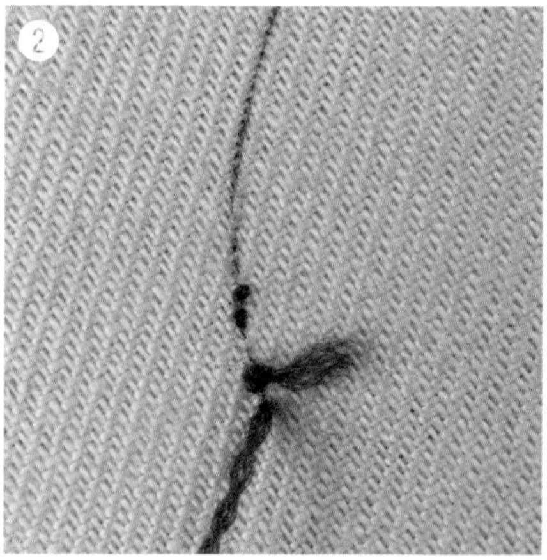

Make two small Back Stitches along the paintline. The smaller these are, the easier they will be to cover. Bring the needle up at the end of the paintline and carefully cut the knot off with a sharp pair of scissors. Ensure that the whole knot comes off and not just the tail.

Casting Off

Working extensively with wool will allow the embroiderer to become more familiar with the fibre, particularly when it starts to stretch or when the thread shows signs of deterioration. When this happens, it should be cast off and replaced with a new thread.

Casting off is worked in the same way as casting on. However, there are times when there is no available paintline, and in this case the stitches should be tucked under a worked area.

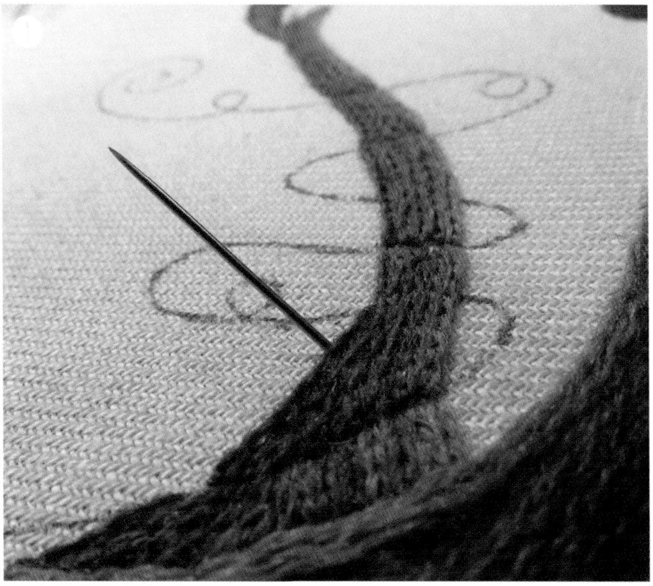

Bring the needle out at a 45-degree angle from underneath a stitched area, taking care not to pass the needle through any of the stitching. Make a small stitch by taking the needle back through the fabric at a 45-degree angle, under the stitched area.

Make another stitch in the same way, then bring the needle back to the surface. Pull slightly on the thread and cut it close to the fabric, taking care not to cut the stitches. There should be no fluff or thread ends showing.

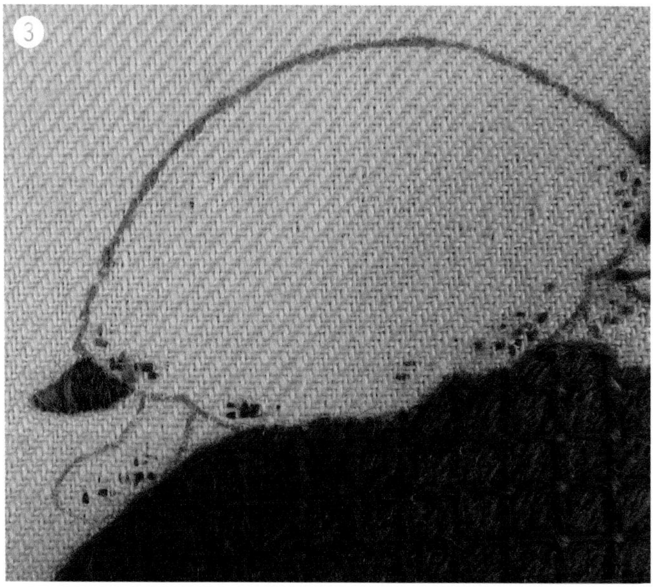

If there is an adjoining area to be worked with solid stitches, it is possible to cast off inside it. Take care when working another colour over the top that fibres from the cast-off thread do not pull through and contaminate the area.

Trellis

Trellis is a series of straight stitches worked evenly across a shape to create a grid. It works well in larger, more open shapes and can be used to bring colour to an area without adding too much density. It can also work well when heavily embellished to create a denser effect. When working trellis, it is best to start in the middle of the shape. Due to the open nature of the edges created by this stitch, you will need to use an outlining stitch to cover the paintlines.

Hints and tips

When working trellis for the first time, following the weave of the fabric can help to maintain the angle at which the stitch lies and regulate the spacing.

Bring the needle up on one side of the shape, then lay the thread across the fabric to the other paintline. At this point the thread can be moved across the fabric until the desired angle is found.

Plunge the needle down on the opposite side of the shape. Bring the needle up on this side a short distance away from the end of the first stitch. From underneath, push the eye of the needle up to the underside of the fabric, causing the needle to lie against the fabric. This gives an indication of where the thread will lie; this helps to regulate the spacing of the stitches. Pull all of the thread through and plunge the needle on the opposite paint line.

Work across the shape spacing the stitches out evenly. It is important to work the stitches consistently across the shape without compromising the spacing and cramming in stitches.

When the first layer of stitching is complete, repeat the process starting in the middle of the shape, placing the stitches at a 90-degree angle to the layer below. This will ensure you achieve a pleasing grid of squares and not rectangles.

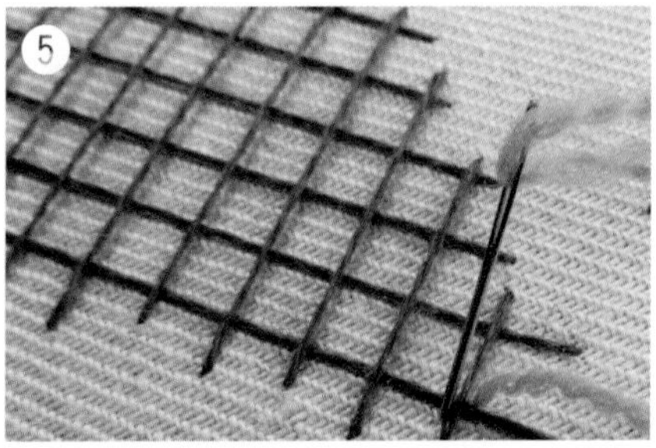

Once the grid pattern is complete, the long stitches need to be secured. Cast on a new thread and wherever two threads cross, work a small securing stitch over the top; it is important to keep these stitches consistent in length. Take care when bringing the needle up and plunging as it is easy to move the threads out of alignment and thereby compromise the grid pattern.

It is best to work the catching stitches in a logical order, working along one thread before moving onto the next.

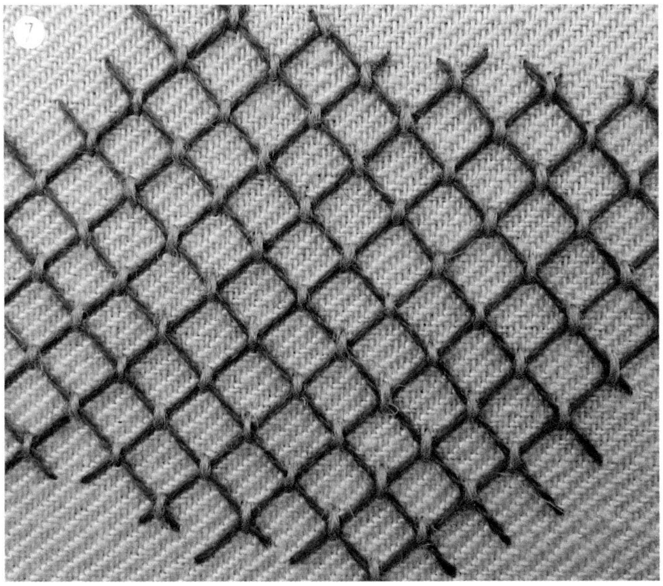

Work across the shape, securing all threads into place. This example shows a small stitch in a contrasting colour; however, this stitch can be worked in a matching or closely matching colour to create a more discreet effect.

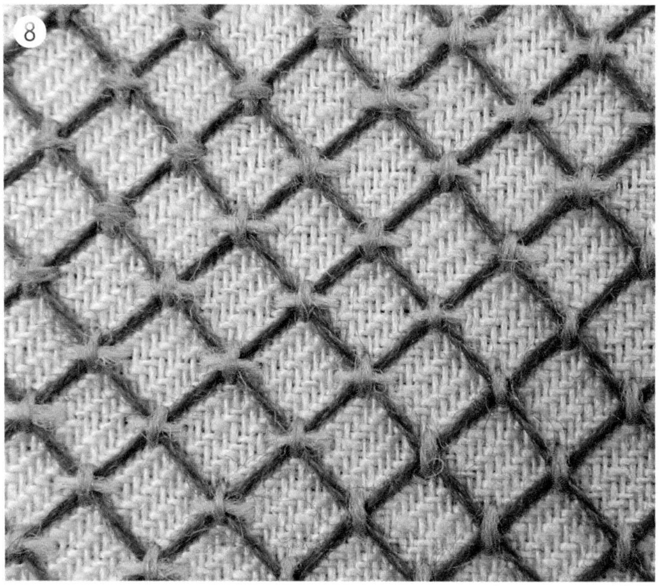

This example shows three different ways of securing the trellis: a simple small stitch over the trellis (bottom right-hand corner), a cross over the trellis, where all of the top stitches go in the same direction (top left-hand corner) and a combination of a Long and Short Stitch in two different colours (middle). Providing the trellis is stable, there are a number of options for combining stitches and colours when adding the securing stitch.

Once the trellis is caught down additional embellishments can be added to the grid, including French Knots, Pistol Stitch, Satin Stitch, Bullion Knots and straight stitches.

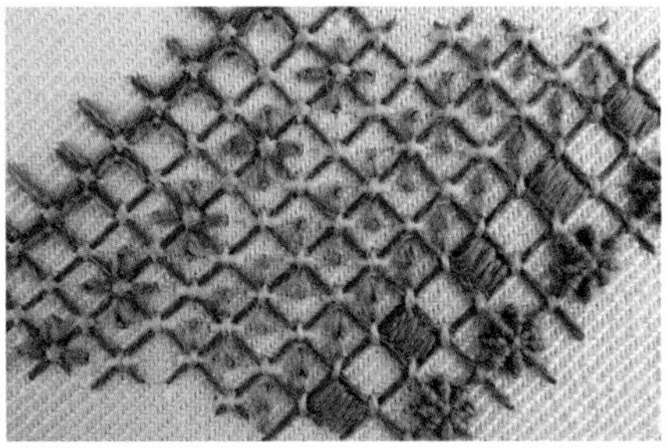

This example shows different types of filling stitches for a trellis. From left to right: single detached Fly Stitch (which could be worked with additional stitches), Detached Chain Stitch, Pistol Stitch, Long Armed Chain Stitch, Satin Stitch and Whipped Wheels. Generally one of these stitches would be worked in a trellis; however, some of them could be worked in combination to create an interesting detail.

This example shows a single French Knot in each square as a simple embellishment.

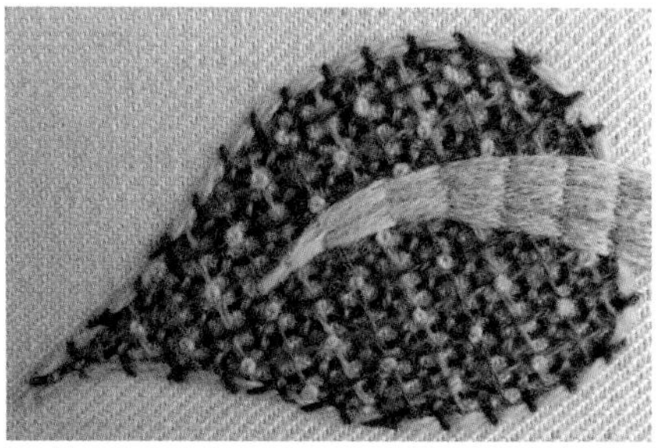

This example shows additional straight stitches (creating the illusion of additional layers of trellis) with French Knots as an embellishment.

Burden Stitch

Burden Stitch can be used to fill large areas, and due to the nature of the stitch, multiple colours can be used to add depth to the work. The example shown is worked in clusters of two stitches; however; it could be worked with single stitches or bigger clusters.

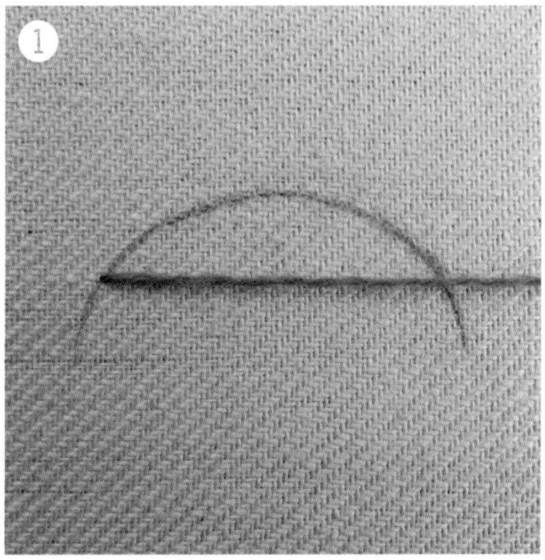

Bring the needle up on the paintline in the middle of the shape. Lay the thread across the shape to establish a straight line and plunge the needle on the paintline.

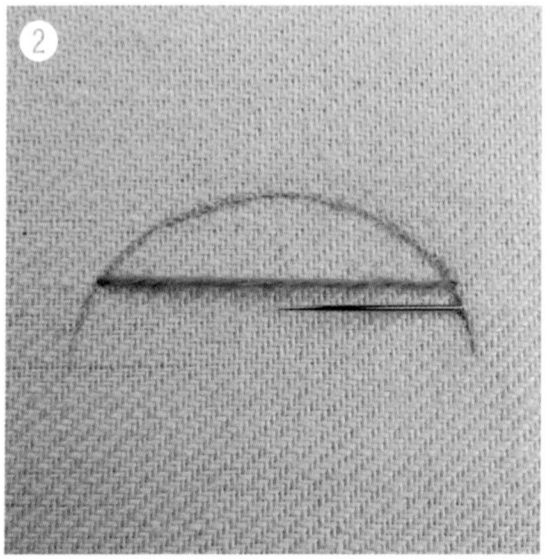

As with trellis, the needle can be used to regulate the spacing of the stitches. Bring the needle up on the same side just a short distance below the initial stitch and plunge onto the opposite paintline, ensuring that the stitch is parallel to the one above.

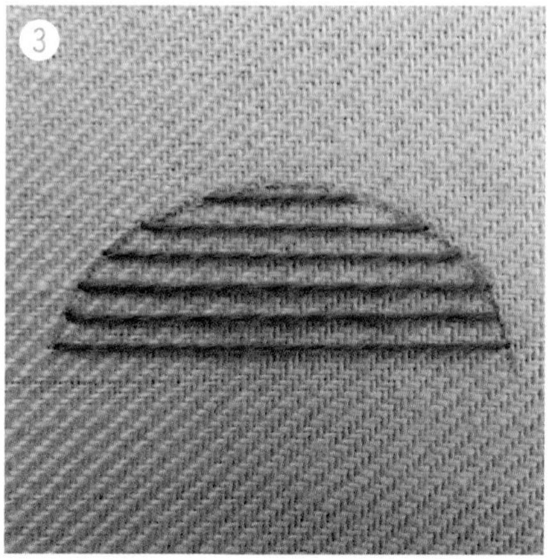

Continue working down the shape, taking care to ensure that the stitches are evenly spaced. Cast the thread off after the last stitch. With a new thread, start in the middle and continue working in the same way until the shape is filled.

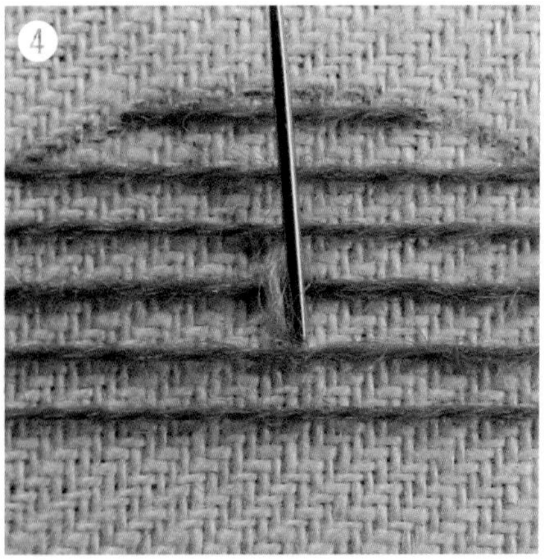

With a new thread (consider using a different colour here), bring the needle up just above one of the horizontal stitches in the middle of the shape. Take the thread over the next horizontal stitch, plunging the needle just beneath the third to make a vertical stitch. There should be no fabric showing between the horizontal and vertical stitches.

Add stitches over the next row in the same way, taking care not to distort the horizontal stitches. In this example a second vertical stitch has been made next to the first. Working two rows in this way will set the spacing.

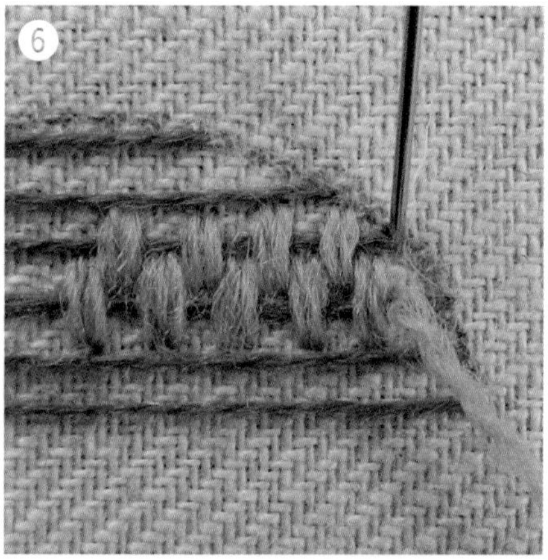

Continue working across the shape, ensuring there is no fabric showing between the stitches. At the sides, as the shape gets smaller, the stitches should be worked to the paintline to ensure there are no gaps.

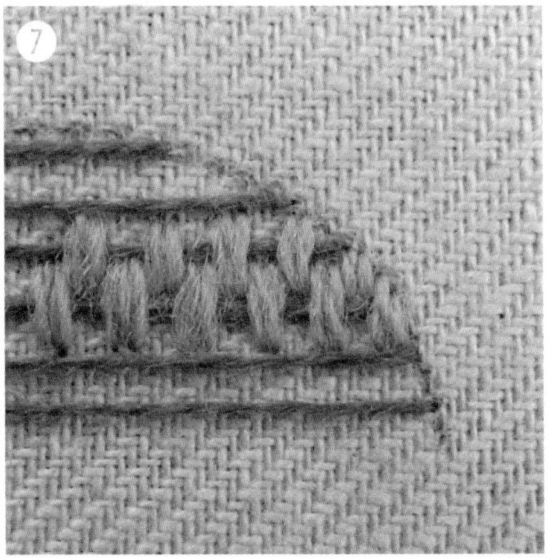

Work stitches right to the edges; any gaps left unfilled will disrupt the pattern and draw the eye.

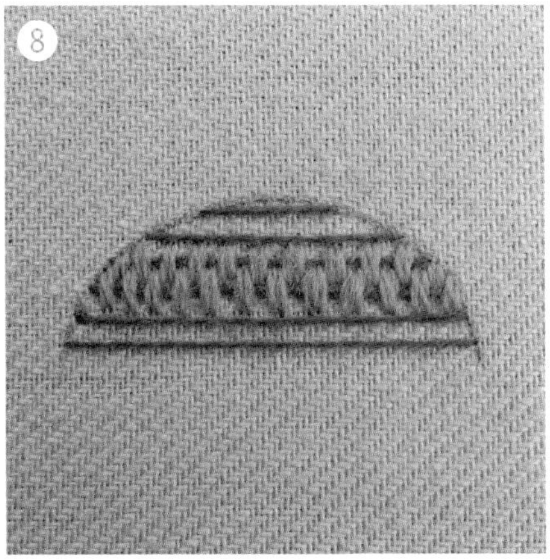

With a new thread, return to the middle and work the stitches to fill in the other side of the shape.

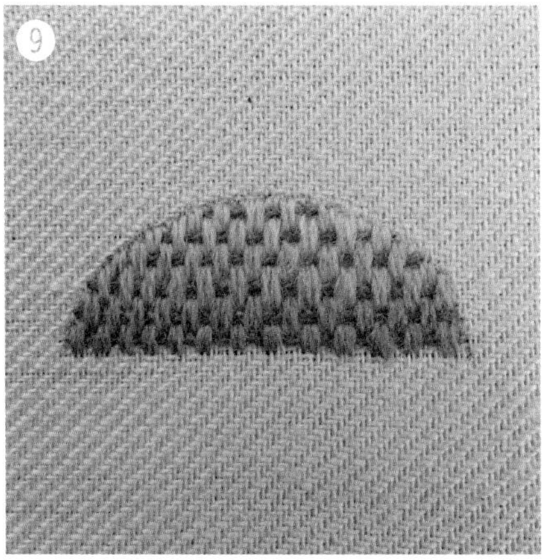

Work the remaining rows, again ensuring that the pattern is continued up to the edges. Along the topmost row, work small stitches from just above the top horizontal stitch to the paintline; this will complete the pattern. This example shows Burden Stitch worked in three colours: two rows of each of dark, medium and light blue.

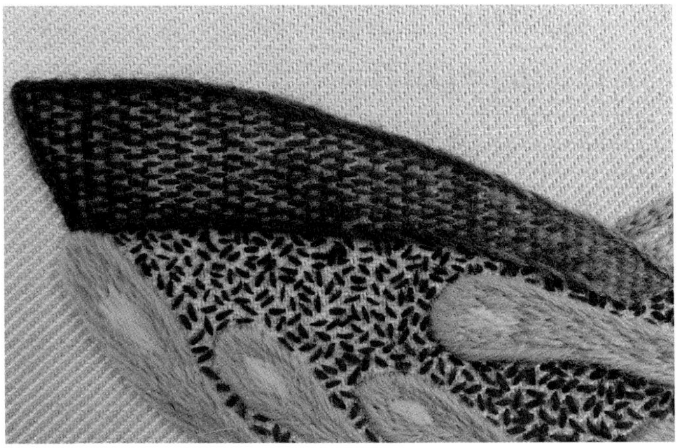

Worked by the author, this detail illustration shows how Burden Stitch can be worked at any angle. In this example the foundation rows are vertical and the top stitches as a result are horizontal. Working the stitch like this can create a water-like effect.

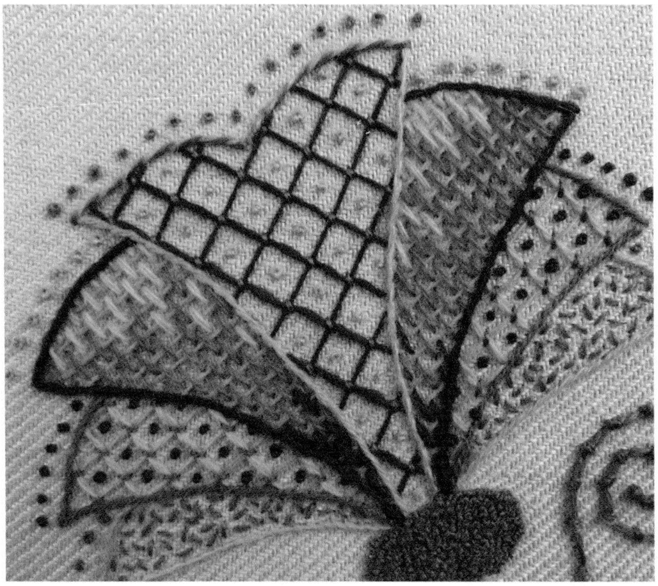

Worked by the author, this detail illustration shows how Burden Stitch can be worked at any angle. Here the foundation rows have been worked in line with the grain of the fabric.

LAIDWORK

This stitch is used to cover larger areas where it is not suitable to use textural stitches such as Feather Stitch or Fly Stitch, or filling stitches such as Satin Stitch. This stitch is designed to make efficient use of the thread, with very little on the back and most of the thread on the front of the fabric.

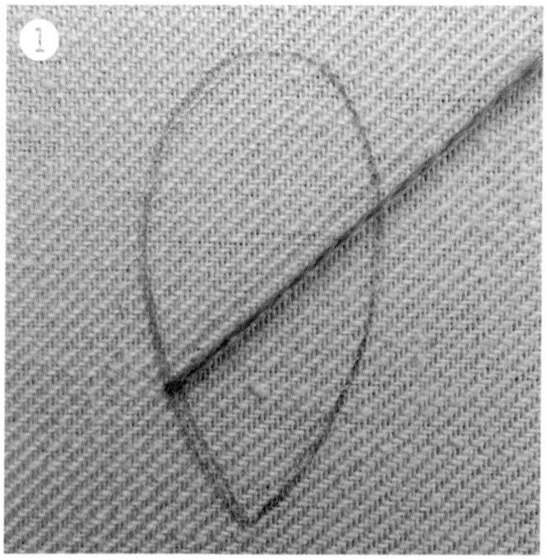

Bring the needle up on the paintline in the middle of the shape. As with trellis, following the grain of the fabric will help you keep the angle of the stitches consistent. Plunge the needle onto the opposite paintline.

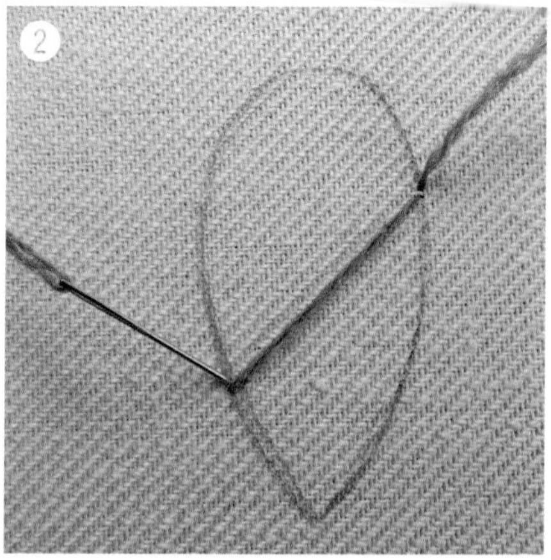

Bring the needle up on the same side where it was plunged next to the previous stitch. Then take the needle down on the opposite paintline. The two stitches should lie well next to each other; there should be no fabric showing between the two stitches, nor should they overlap. Continue making stitches in this way, working back and forth across the shape.

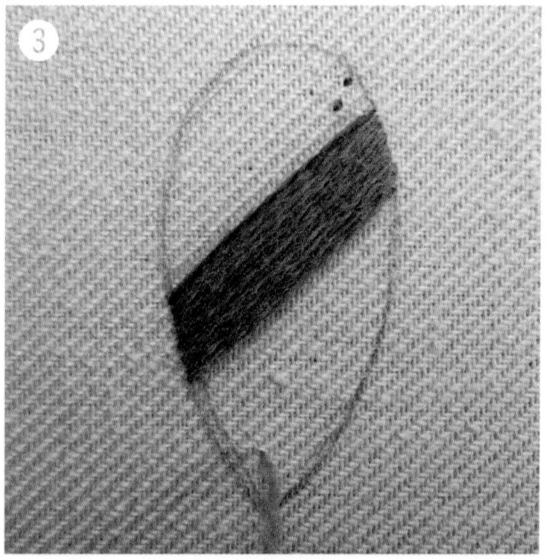

The shape can be filled in this way with the same colour. However, laidwork can also be worked in multiple colours to create depth. Add additional stitches in one colour (A), then add in one stitch of a darker colour (B).

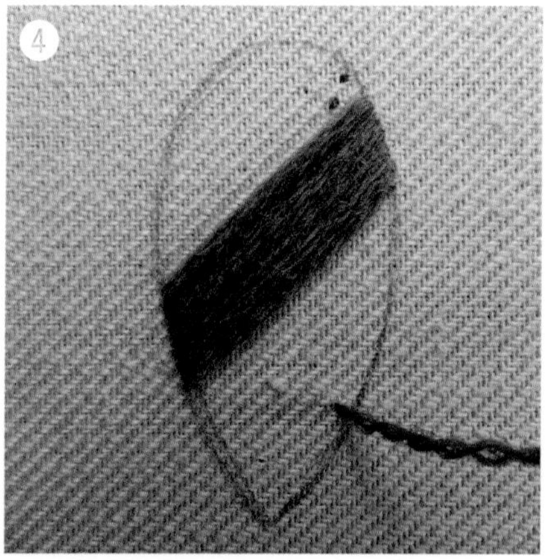

Work a couple of stitches in colour A then one more in colour B.

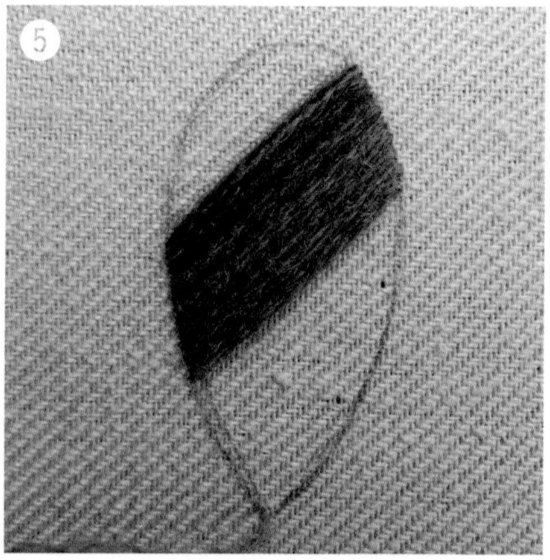

Keep adding stitches, reducing the number of stitches in colour A and increasing the number in colour B.

Keep working in colour B until the shape is filled. Then repeat the process in the lower half of the shape with a lighter colour.

The stitches in laidwork tend to be very long, and quite unstable as a result. Stitches like this can become slack over time and reveal the background fabric, which is undesirable. To counteract this, additional securing stitches should be worked over the top.

Securing stitches should be worked in the opposite direction to the laidwork stitches. Take care when working these stitches as they can disrupt the laidwork and cause some of the background fabric to show through. Make sure that the needle pierces the laidwork stitches to ensure they are not parted. From top to bottom, this example shows Feather Stitch, Couching, Chain Stitch, Stem Stitch and Fly Stitch. Stitches such as trellis and detached chain can also be used.

Worked by the author, this detail illustration shows how trellis can create an interesting effect over laidwork.

Block Shading

Block shading can be used to fill larger areas. Its dense coverage means it works well to create a solid, heavy effect.

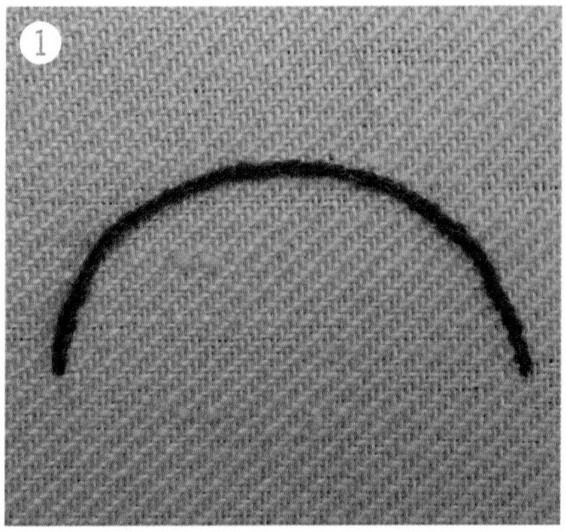

Start by working an outline of Split Stitch. The colour used for the Split Stitch should be the same as the first row of block shading.

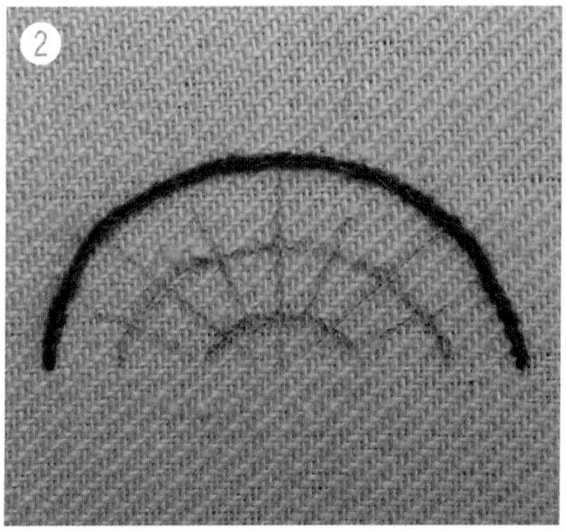

Drawing on guidelines will help regulate the angle of the stitching and the depth of the rows. Avoid trying to cram in too many rows, as the area will look overcrowded. When establishing the angle of the stitches, always start with a line in the middle of the shape that sits at 90 degrees to the shape. Then add in lines at 45 degrees. Once these are placed, add extra lines in between those already marked.

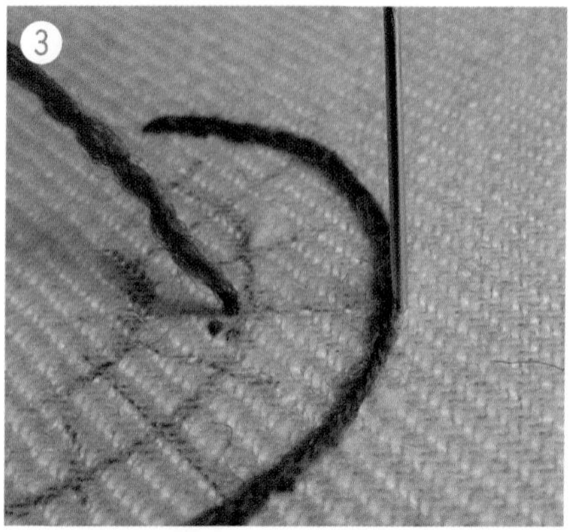

Cast on a new thread and bring the needle up in the middle of the shape on the top-most pencil line. Plunge the needle over the Split Stitch, taking care not to take the stitch too wide or to pierce the Split Stitch. Pull all of the thread through the fabric, taking care not to pull the stitch too tight or leave it loose.

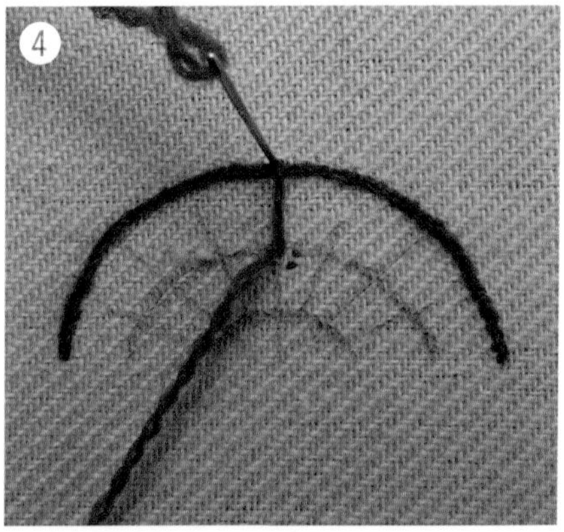

Additional stitches should be worked so that no fabric is visible. Tuck the needle around the Split Stitch and into the last stitch to ensure there are no gaps.

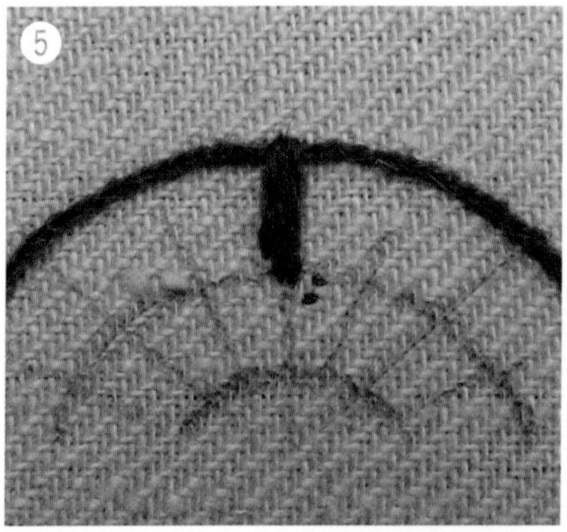

To bring the angle round in line with the pencil marks, a wedge stitch is required. Bring the needle up slightly above the pencil line and plunge over the Split Stitch as described above.

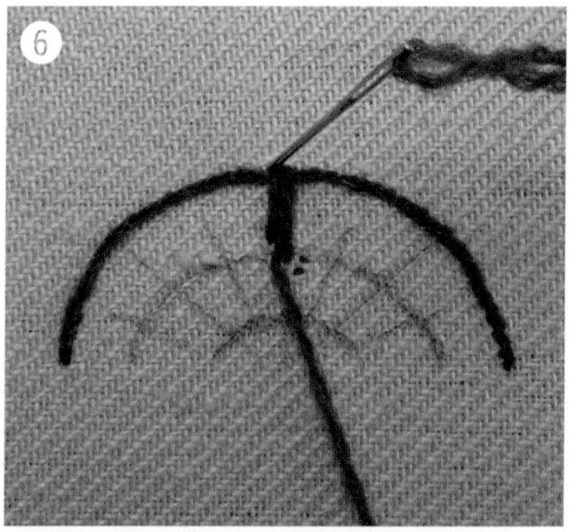

Bring the needle up on the pencil line, directly below the last stitch and plunge the needle next to it over the Split Stitch. This will cause a subtle change in stitch angle. Wedge stitches can be added as frequently as needed in order to bring the angle round in line with the pencil markings. However, working too many wedge stitches next to each other is inadvisable.

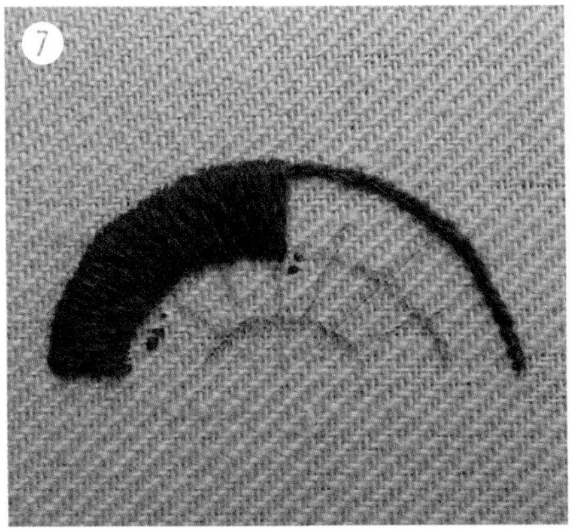

Continue working additional stitches and wedge stitches to complete the row. Take care to always bring the needle up on the pencil line.

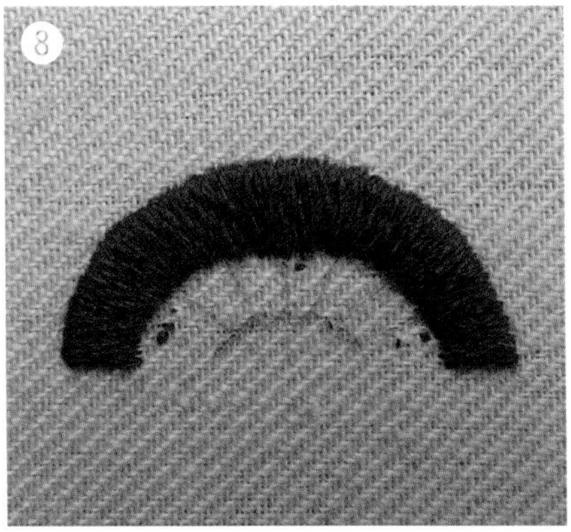

Cast on a new thread and repeat the stitches to fill the other side of the shape. With this row complete, no Split Stitches should be visible.

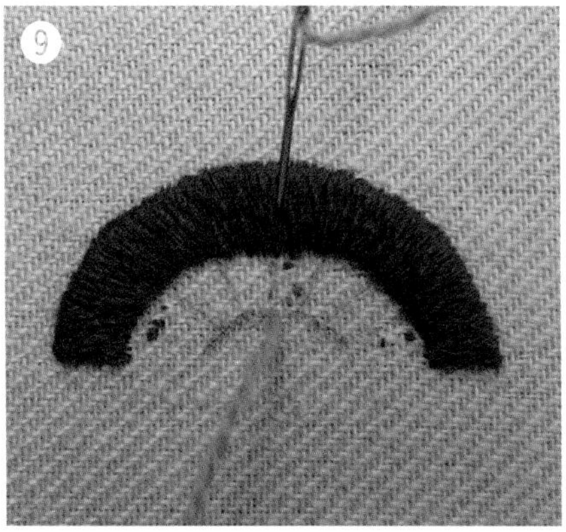

Cast on a different colour and bring the needle up on the second pencil line in the middle of the shape. The needle should be plunged into the existing stitches, cutting into the row above by approximately one third of their height.

Continue working the second row as before, adding wedge stitches where necessary to bring the angle round. The second row of stitches should be plunged evenly to create a smooth and consistent line.

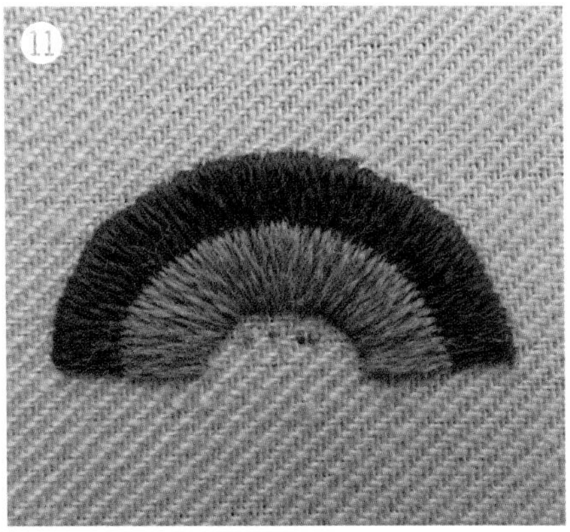

Continue working one side of the row, then cast on a new thread and work the other side.

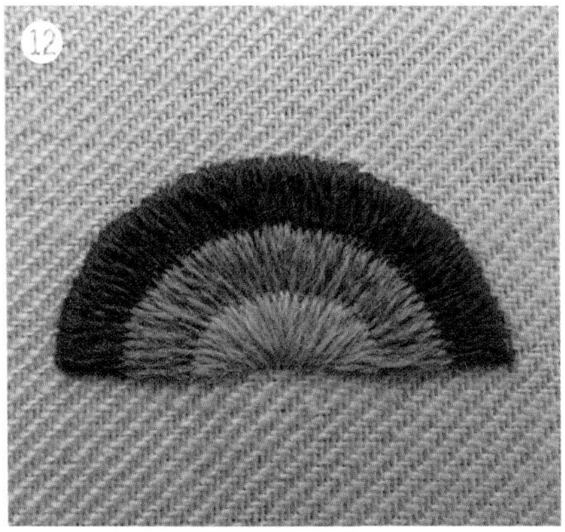

When worked properly, this stitch does not need an outline and should have a series of even rows with a stitch angle that transitions smoothly in line with the shape. This example has been worked in colours that have a strong contrast to demonstrate the stitch; however, it is preferable to use colours that have less contrast to create a more subtle graduated effect.

Satin Stitch

Satin Stitch is a densely worked filling stitch that creates a smooth surface. It is best worked over small to medium-sized shapes. If worked in a shape that is too big, the stitches can become unstable. Adding layers of padding underneath the Satin Stitch can help to create different heights, which can add a sculpted effect. Layers of padding should be worked at opposite angles to the Satin Stitch on top.

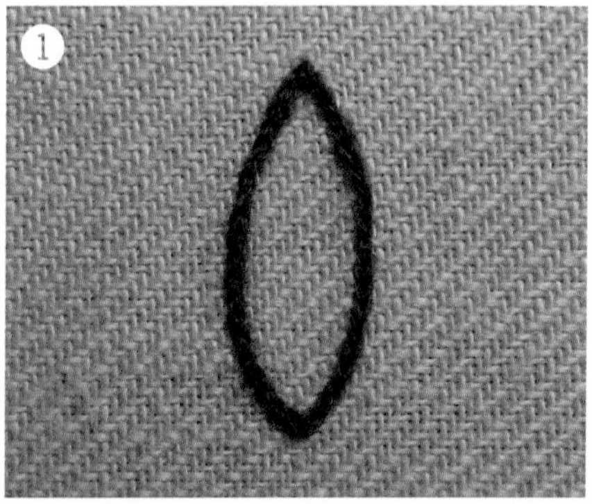

Start by working Split Stitch around the shape.

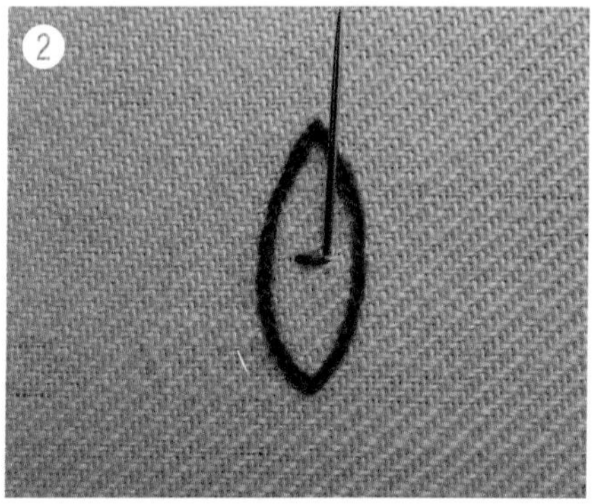

To work the padding, bring the needle up in the centre of the shape and work small stitches back and forth across the shape in a laidwork fashion. It is important to work *within* the Split Stitch outline. Working in this way will reduce the bulk on the back of the piece.

When one side is worked, go back to the middle and repeat to fill the other side. On this side the stitches are worked horizontally and kept well within the shape to leave space for the second layer of padding.

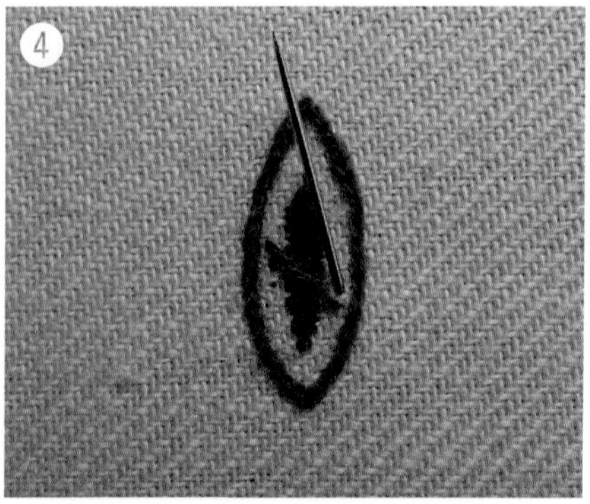

The second layer of padding is worked in the same way, starting in the middle and working out, but on a diagonal from top left to bottom right. This layer is worked closer to the Split Stitch; however, it is still *within* the Split Stitch.

Cast on a new thread and bring the needle up on the left-hand side of the shape on the outside of the Split Stitch. Take care not to bring it up wide of or cutting through the Split Stitch. Plunge the needle down slightly higher up on the other side of the shape, again on the outside the Split Stitch (as for block shading). This should create a diagonal stitch.

Bring the needle up on the left-hand side of the shape below the last stitch. It should be close to the last stitch but without crowding it. Plunge the needle on the right-hand side of the shape, this time tucking it into the previous stitch without stitching through it.

Continue working in the same way, bringing up the needle on the left-hand side below the last stitch.

Tuck the needle into the previous stitch on the right-hand side of the shape. Work down the shape until the padding and Split Stitch are covered. At this stage it is important to keep an eye on the quality of the thread. If there are signs of wear or fluffing, cast off and start a new piece of thread.

When one half of the shape is completed, cast on a new thread and work up the shape. This time bring the needle up on the right and plunge on the left. By working in this way, the angle of the stitch will be easier to maintain.

When completed, the surface should look smooth and the stitch angle should be consistent. The angle of the stitch will turn a little, but this should not be immediately obvious. In this example the Satin Stitch is worked in a different colour to the Split Stitch and padding so that the different elements are easily distinguishable in the illustrations. Generally, Satin Stitch is best worked in the same colour as the layer below.

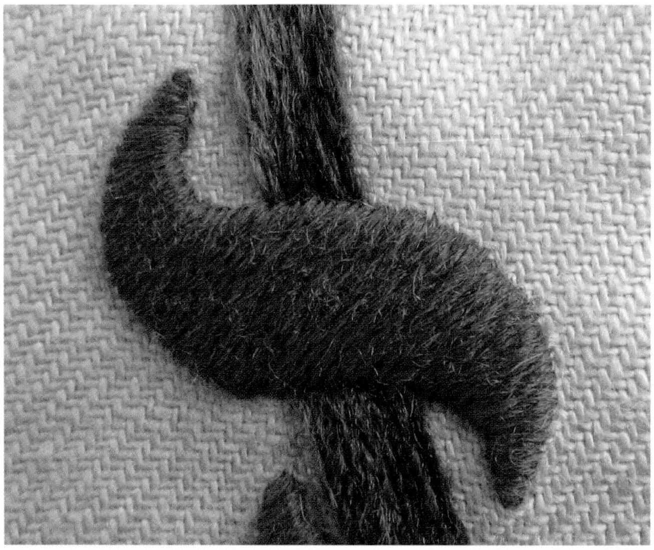

Worked by the author, this detail illustration show how the angle of Satin Stitch can move with the shape. This sweeping angle change creates a sense of flow through the shape and the overall piece.

Long and Short Stitch

Long and Short Stitch is used prolifically in many forms of embroidery. It is a densely worked stitch that creates a smooth surface that can be turned around curves to create a sense of flow and movement through an area.

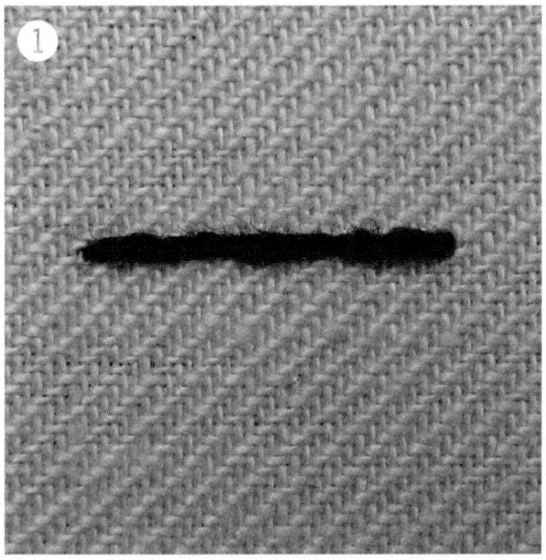

Start by working a Split Stitch outline. Only a short line has been worked in the example; however, unless shapes overlap, a Split Stitch outline should be worked around the entire shape in a colour that is sympathetic to the colours that will go over the top. When working multiple colours, use the middle of the range.

Cast on a new thread, bring the needle up in the middle of the shape and plunge the needle down over the Split Stitch (as for block shading). Bring the needle up next to and slightly longer than the last stitch, and plunge over the Split Stitch.

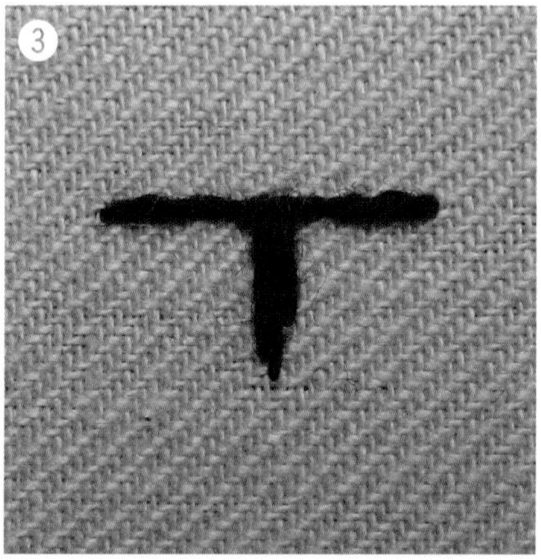

Add additional stitches, taking care to ensure that the stitches are of different lengths. Work one side first, then go back to the centre and work the other side. As with Satin Stitch, pay close attention to the quality of the thread and replace if it shows signs of wear or fluffing.

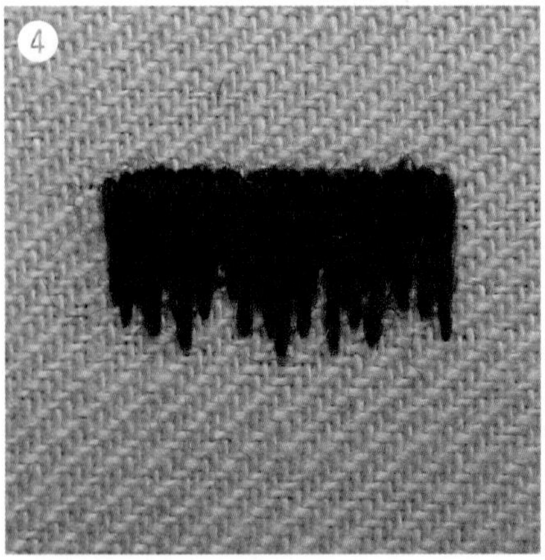

When completed, the bottom of the row should have a serrated, irregular look, which will help to achieve a smooth surface when the stitching is completed. If a group of stitches end in the same place, a slightly ridged effect will be created when the next row is added; this is not desirable.

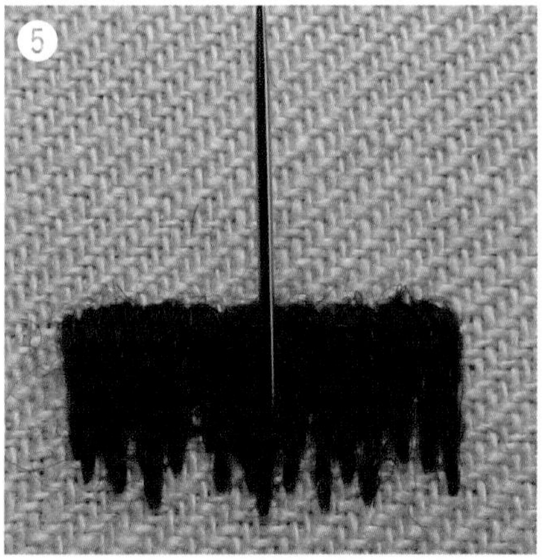

To work the second row, cast on a new thread and bring the needle up in the middle of the shape within the first row. When bringing the needle up, pay close attention to the effect it has on the first row. If the stitches in the first row shift to reveal the fabric, you should rework the first stitch of the second row.

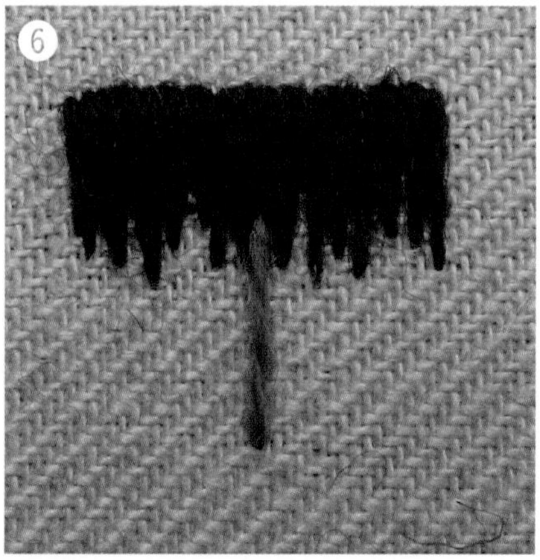

Plunge the needle down below the row to make the stitch. From this point on the stitches should all be the same length. Each stitch should cut into approximately one third of the stitch above it.

Bring the needle back up in the first row, next to the first stitch but at a different height. Varying the point at which the needle is brought up and keeping the stitch the same length will create a serrated bottom edge and smooth surface.

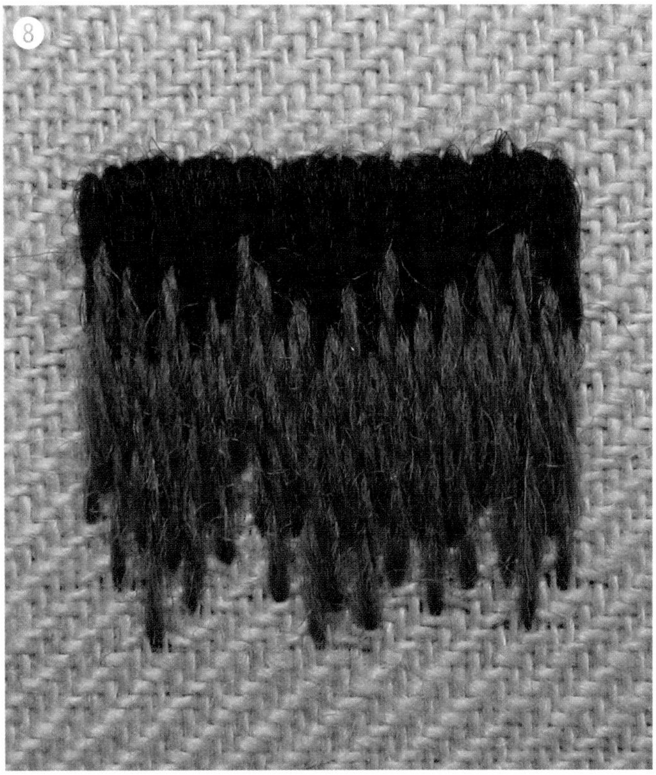

When the row is complete, there should be no fabric visible between the stitches.

Blending Two Colours in Long and Short Stitch

Blending colours is a straightforward process in Long and Short Stitch and can create a lovely, subtle effect that draws the eye through the piece and provides depth.

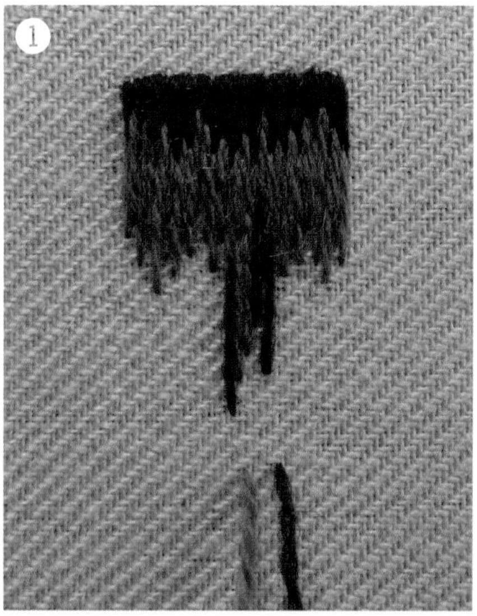

Cast on two threads in the middle of the shape. As these threads will be worked separately, two needles should be used. Work the second row as described above, introducing both colours but working one or two stitches in the original colour then one of the new colour.

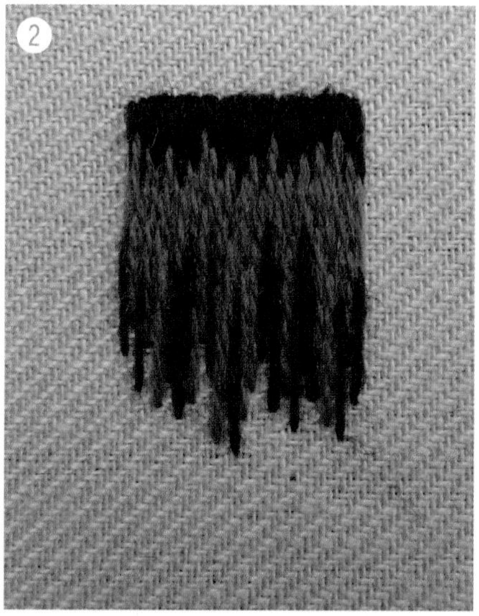

Take care not to alternate the colours too frequently as this will create a stripy effect; similarly, working too many stitches of the same colour will create a block of colour that will detract from the overall effect. Work across the shape and repeat to fill the other side.

Add in a third row in the second colour to complete the effect. This example has been worked in colours that have a strong contrast to demonstrate the stitch. When working this technique, it is better to have less contrast between the colours to create a more subtle effect.

Working Long and Short Stitch around a Curve

Working around gentle curves can create a sense of flow through the piece.

Start by working a Split Stitch edge and an initial row as previously described.

Cast on a new thread and bring the needle up in the first row in the middle of the shape. Lay the new thread on the fabric in line with the angle of the initial row, then pull the thread slightly to one side – in this example to the right – to change the angle. This should be a very subtle move so the angle changes only fractionally.

Work the second row as previously described, taking care to ensure that the stitches are staggered to create a smooth surface. Work from the centre out, then go back and fill in the other side.

Repeat this process on the third row, again slightly altering the angle, using the previous row as a guide.

Work additional rows to bring the angle round further. If necessary, lines can be drawn on with pencil to act as a guide.

When complete, the angle of the stitches should transition smoothly. If the eye is drawn to a particular area, it could be because the angle has been changed too sharply.

Raised Stem Band/ Raised Outline Band

This stitch works well in long shapes, particularly if they curve, such as stems or branches. It is worked on a foundation of straight stitches with the top stitches packed closely together, creating a domed effect.

Hints and tips

For clarity in the illustrations, the foundation row of this stitch is worked in a contrasting colour. However, this stitch it is best worked in the same colour as the top stitching. If using multiple colours, always choose the middle of the range.

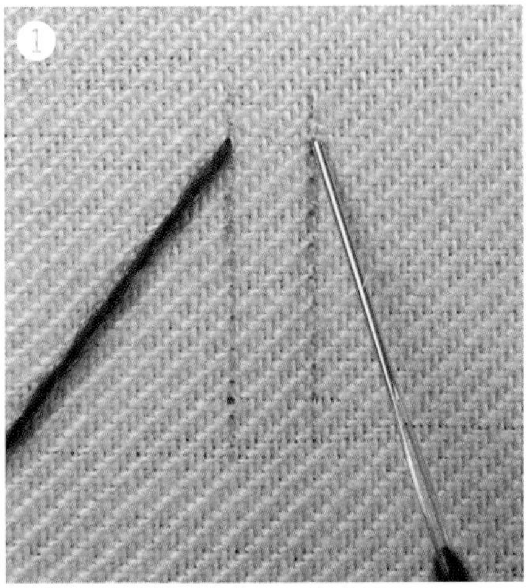

Bring the needle up on one side of the shape just below the top and on the outside of the paintline. This will ensure the paintlines are covered. Plunge the needle down on the other side of the shape, again just on the outside of the paintline, to create a straight stitch.

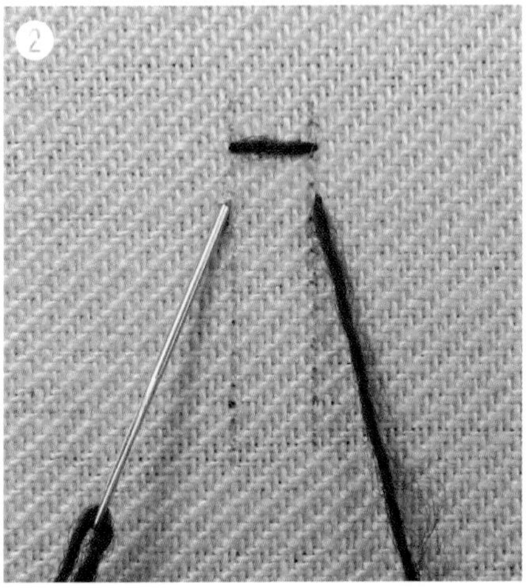

Bring the needle up on the same side and plunge the needle on the opposite side, again creating a straight stitch. Continue working down the shape, keeping an equal distance between each of the stitches and ending just before the bottom of the shape.

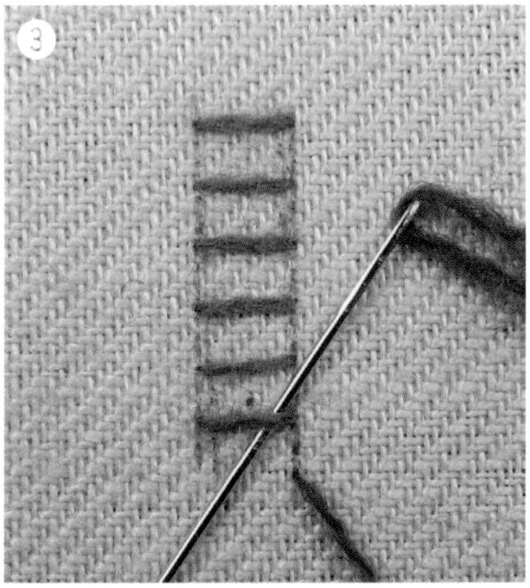

Cast on a new thread on the right-hand side of the shape and switch to a tapestry needle. Take the thread over the first bar and slide the needle underneath, angling it towards the bottom left.

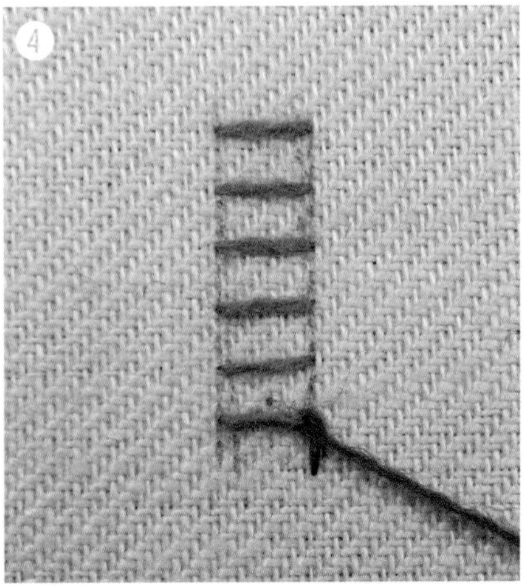

Pull all of the thread through, creating a wrap around the bar. Take care not to distort the bar.

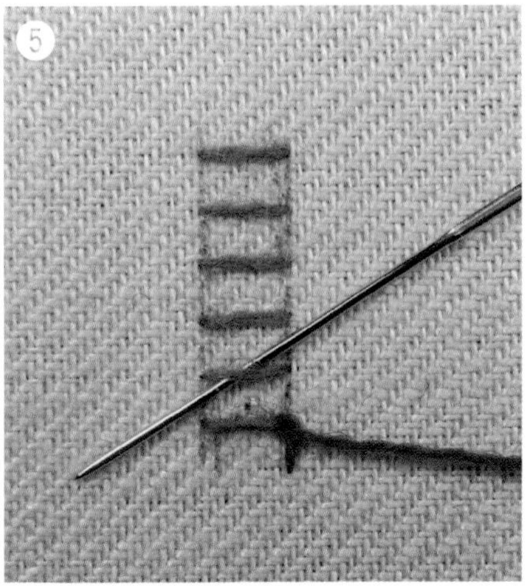

Take the thread over the next bar and slide it under to create the next wrap. Again, take care not to distort the bar.

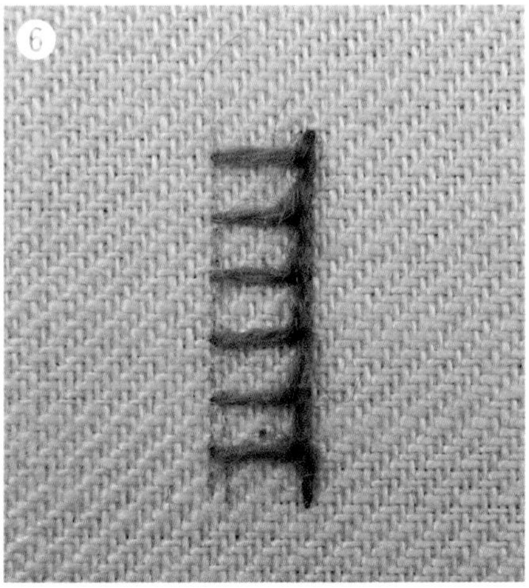

Work up the shape until the row is complete, then plunge the needle on the top paintline.

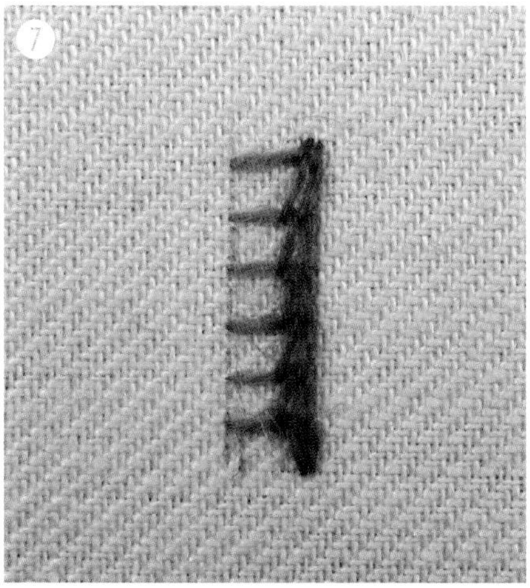

Add additional rows to fill the shape; there should be no fabric showing between the rows. Additional colours can be added at this point to shade the shape.

Keep adding rows until the shape is full. The foundation bars should be kept straight and should be fully covered, as should the paintlines. Take care when adding the final rows not to put too much stress on the foundation bars.

As with Stem Stitch, raised stem band can be worked in the opposite direction to create raised outline band. The process is identical except that the stitches will lie from bottom right to top left. As a result, the top stitches should be started on the left-hand side.

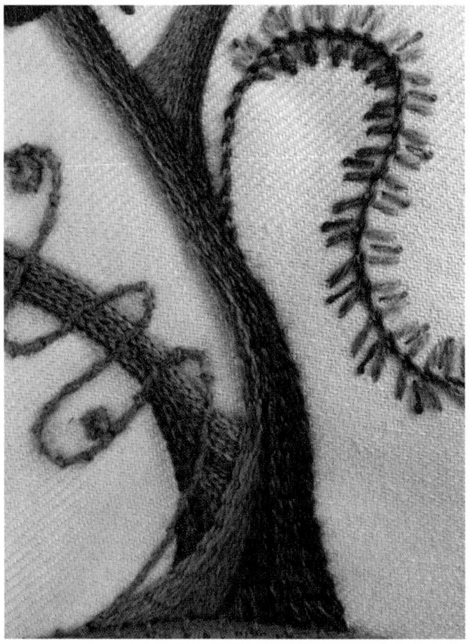

Typically, the curve this stitch is worked around is long and graceful. It creates a long, lean effect that is quite elegant.

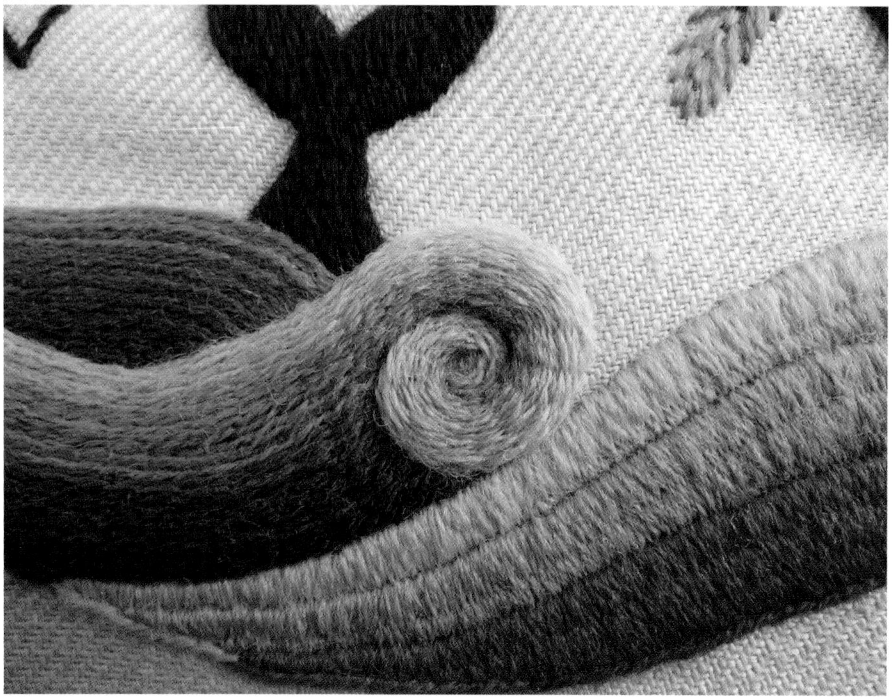

This stitch, if carefully worked, can go round much tighter curves that can add a sense of movement and drama to a shape.

Raised Chain Band

This stitch creates a highly textured effect that works well in long, curved shapes. However, working a steep curve in this stitch would be tricky. This stitch is not as dense as raised stem band and small amounts of fabric are be visible when the stitch is complete.

Hints and tips

For clarity in the illustrations, the foundation row of this stitch is worked in a contrasting colour. However, this stitch is best worked in the same colour as the top stitching. If using multiple colours, always choose the middle of the range.

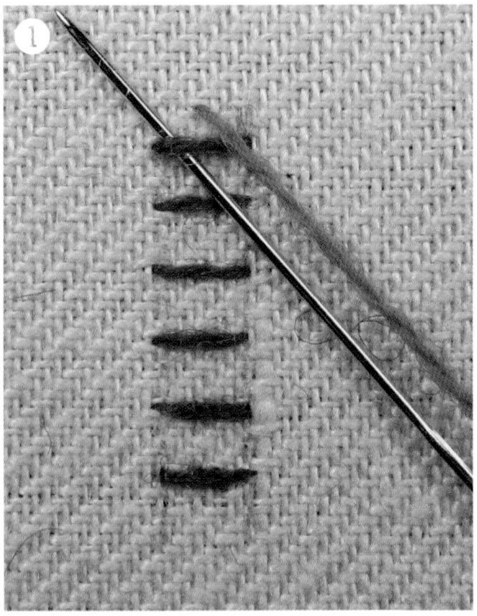

Start by working a row of foundation bars, as described for raised stem band. Cast on a new thread in the middle top of the shape and switch to a tapestry needle. Pull the thread down over the first bar and slide the needle underneath it from bottom to top. Pull the thread through without distorting the bar.

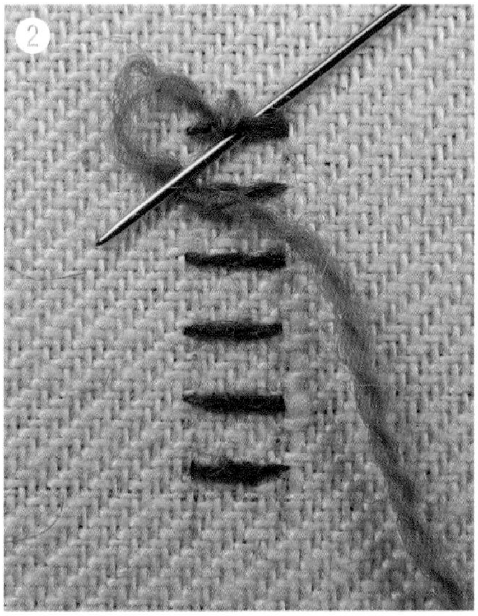

Take the thread back over the first bar and slide it underneath the bar again, this time from top to bottom. Pull the thread through and bring the needle up through the loop created.

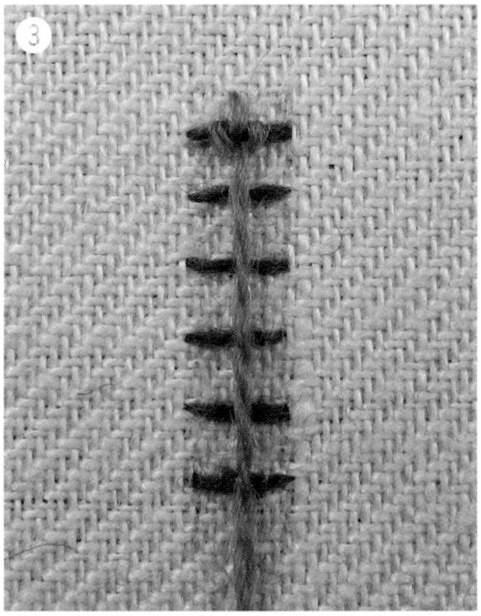

Pull the thread through completely to create a Chain Stitch over the bar. The Chain Stitch should not be loose.

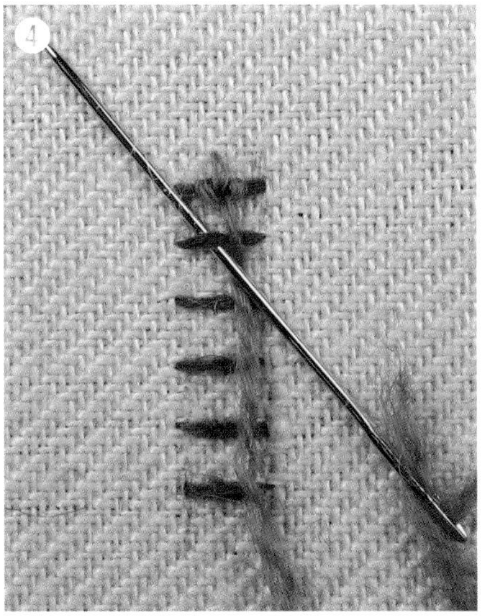

Repeat this process by taking the thread over the next bar and sliding the needle underneath it from bottom to top. Pull the thread through completely without distorting the bar.

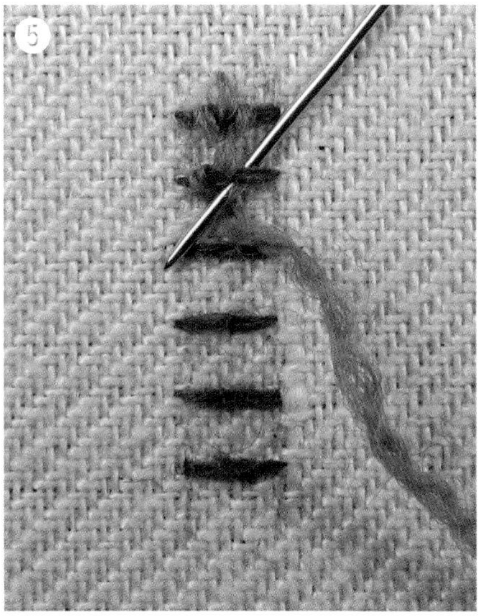

Take the thread over the bar and slide the needle underneath it from top to bottom on the other side of the second stitch. Pull the thread through completely without distorting the bar but not leaving the thread loose.

In a particularly narrow shape, one row of chain would be sufficient. This will leave the area with a little texture and colour, but will also reveal some of the fabric to create a semi-open area. You would then need to work an Outline Stitch to cover the paintlines.

In larger areas, multiple rows of Chain Stitch can be added to create a denser, more textured effect. If the paintlines are still showing after the shape has been filled, you will need to work an Outline Stitch.

RAISED BUTTONHOLE BAND

This stitch creates a slightly textured effect that works particularly well in long, narrow shapes.

> **Hints and tips**
>
> For clarity in the illustrations, the foundation row of this stitch is worked in a contrasting colour. However, this stitch is best worked in the same colour as the top stitching. If using multiple colours, always choose the middle of the range.

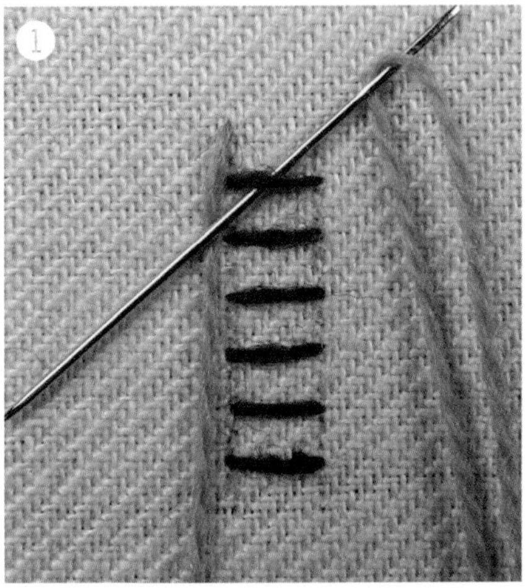

Work a foundation row of straight stitches as described in raised stem band. Cast on a new thread and bring the needle up at the top of the shape on the left-hand side. Take the thread over the first bar and then slide the needle under the first bar from top to bottom. Pass the needle through the resulting loop and pull the thread through.

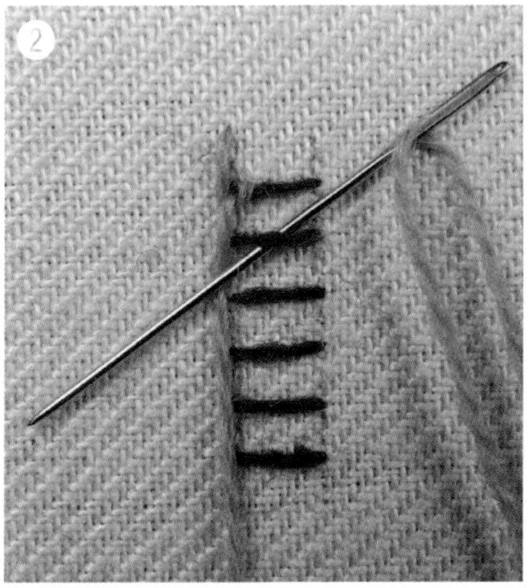

The first stitch should be worked firmly, without distorting the bar or leaving the stitch loose. Work the next stitch in the same way, taking the thread over the second bar and sliding the needle under it, then bringing the needle up in the resulting loop. Work down the shape and plunge the needle on the bottom paintline.

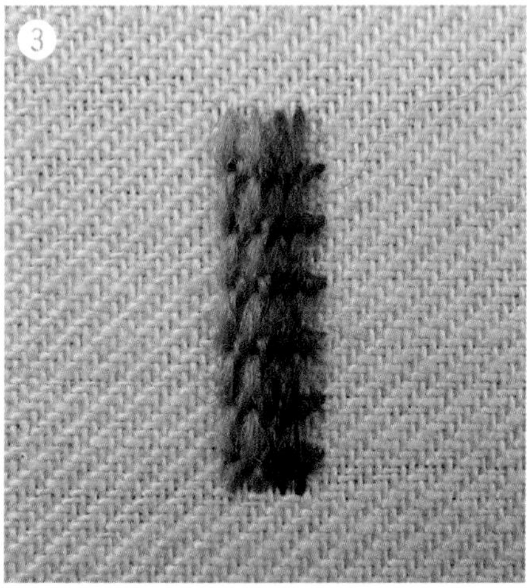

Work additional rows in the same way, changing colour if desired. This stitch will not cram together in the same way as raised stem band.

The nature of this stitch may result in some of the bars still being visible, so you will need to work an outlining stitch if this is the case.

FEATHER STITCH

Feather Stitch creates a lovely texture that can be used to fill a small shape, or create feathers or a fern-like tendril. The component stitches are angled, so it can be tricky to cover paintlines with this stitch, and you will need to finish with an outlining stitch if you use Feather Stitch to fill a shape.

Bring the needle up through the fabric and take it down approximately 5mm/½in away from and level with the point where it was brought through. Do not pull all of the thread through; instead, leave a loop on top.

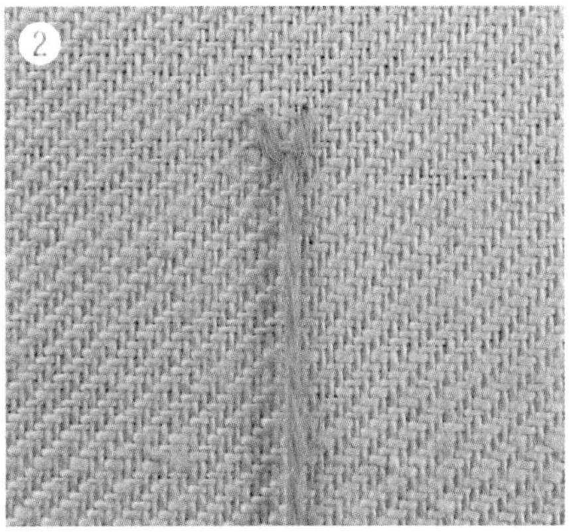

Bring the needle back up through the loop, a short distance below and in the middle of the first stitch. Pull the thread through the fabric to form a 'V' shape. The stitch should lie flat on the surface without pulling on the fabric or leaving the thread loose.

Plunge the needle to the right of the first stitch. Take care to ensure that the plunge point is level with where the needle was just brought through and the width of this stitch is the same as the first. Do not pull all of the thread through; instead, leave a loop on top.

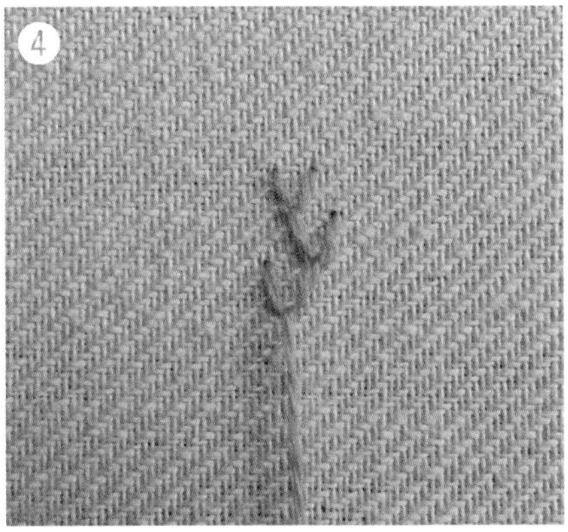

Bring the needle back up a short distance below and in the middle to create another 'V' shape. Pull all of the thread through, ensuring that the stitch lies flat against the fabric. Plunge the needle to the left and repeat the process.

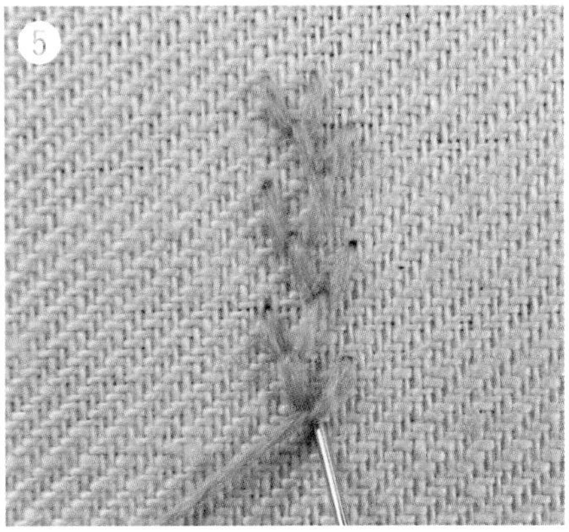

Continue making stitches in this manner, alternating between plunging the needle on the right and on the left. At the end of the row, take the needle down over the last stitch to secure it in place.

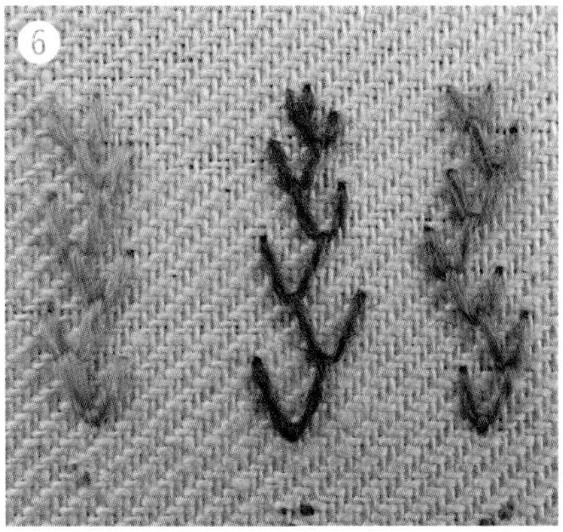

The example on the left of the illustration shows the stitch as described above with the stitches consistent in width and depth. The middle example shows how the stitches can be gradually increased in size; this can be useful when filling a shape. The right-hand example shows the stitches worked with two on each side.

Fly Stitch

Fly Stitch creates a lovely texture that can be used to fill a small shape, or create feathers or a fern-like tendril. It can be worked open (revealing some of the fabric) or closed (covering all of the fabric). The example that follows shows open Fly Stitch, which will require you to work an outlining stitch when it is used to fill a shape.

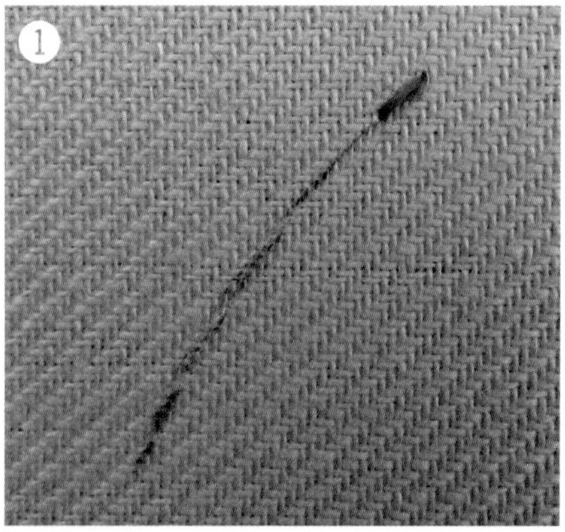

Start by making a straight stitch along the paintline.

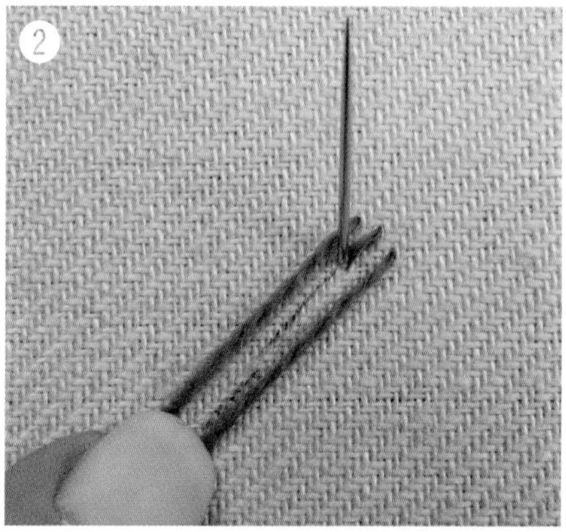

Bring the needle up on one side of the straight stitch and plunge on the other side; the straight stitch should be in the middle of these two points. Do not pull all of the thread through; instead, leave a loop on top. Bring the needle up at the base of the straight stitch and through the loop; this will create a 'V' shape.

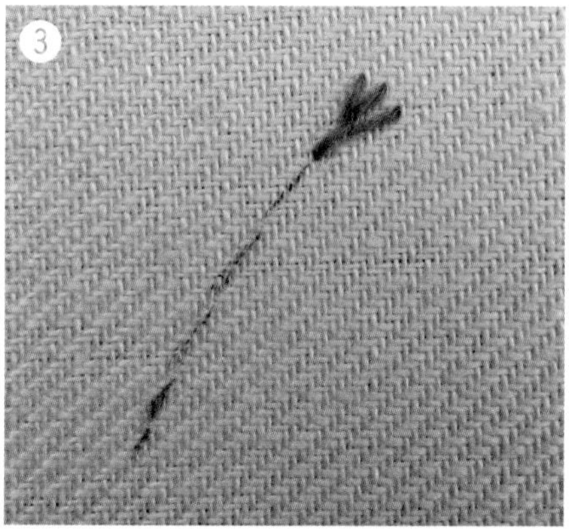

Plunge the needle down on the paintline creating a straight stitch and securing the 'V' in place.

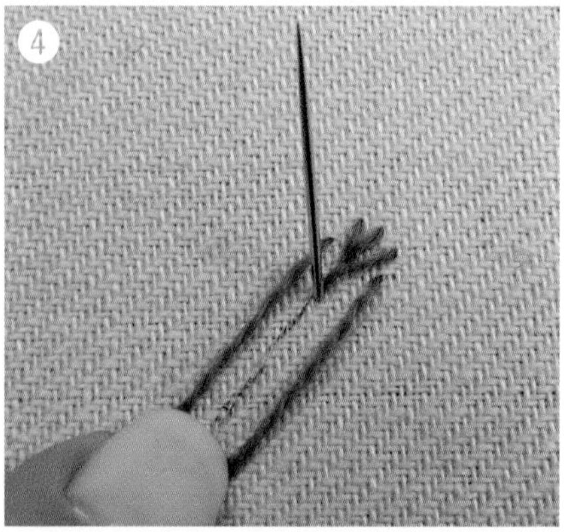

Bring the needle up on one side of the straight stitch and plunge on the other side, taking care not to catch the previous stitch. Do not pull all of the thread though. Bring the needle up at the base of the straight stitch and pull the thread through to create the next 'V'. Make a straight stitch to secure the 'V' in place.

Continue working stitches in this manner, keeping the straight stitches consistent in length. Finish the row with a straight stitch and cast off. The angle of the stitches will flatten out, although they should still have a distinct angle at the end of the row.

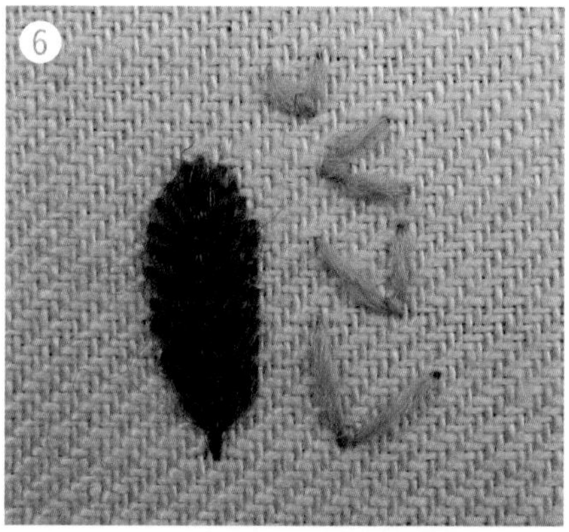

The example on the left of the illustration shows closed Fly Stitch; the stitches are packed closely together and the width of each stitch has been expanded to fill the shape. When worked properly, there should be no need to outline it. Fly Stitch can also be worked as individual stitches, known as detached fly, as shown in the example on the right. These can be scattered through an area as a form of seeding or worked in various sizes to embellish other stitches.

CRETAN STITCH

Cretan Stitch works well in leaf-like shapes and can be worked over a slightly wider area, due to the way the stitches tie each other down. It is made up of a series of offset 'V's, which can be worked in an open or closed manner. When worked in an open manner, you will need to finish the shape with an outlining stitch.

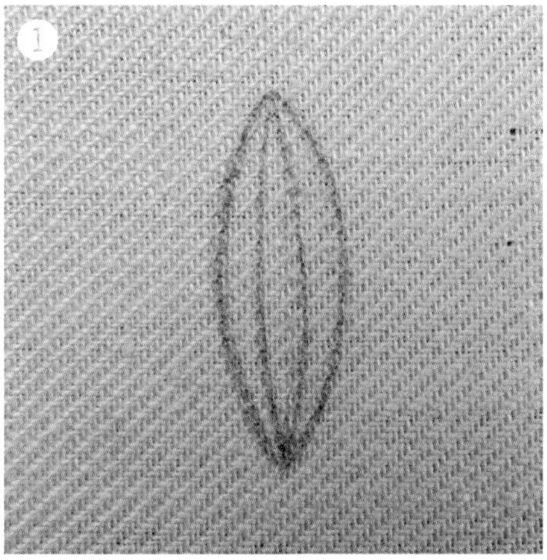

When working this stitch for the first time, it is best to draw on some additional guidelines in pencil. This stitch works better if these lines are slightly curved to echo the shape. Take care not to extend these lines outside of the shape. The additional guidelines have been drawn on quite heavily in this example, so they are clear in the illustrations. This has resulted in them being quite visible when the stitch is finished. When working this stitch in an open fashion, it is preferable to work by eye and omit the guidelines.

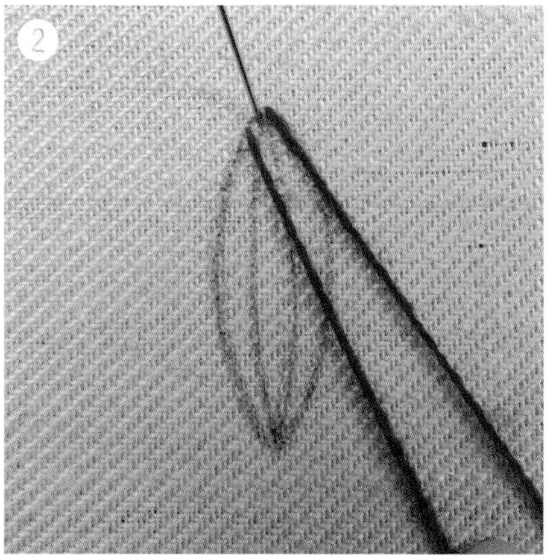

Bring the needle up at the middle top of the shape. Plunge the needle along the left paintline, but do not pull all of the thread through; instead, leave a loop on top. Bring the needle up between these two points on the left-hand pencil line. Pull all of the thread through to create a 'V'-shaped stitch.

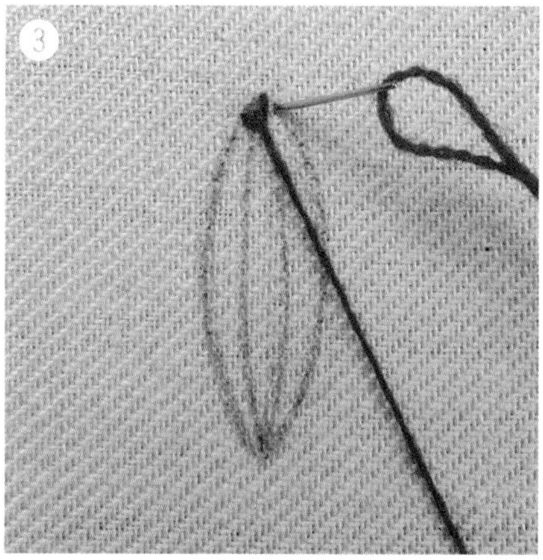

Plunge the needle down on the right paintline leaving a small gap between the plunge point and the last stitch. Do not pull all of the thread through; instead, leave a loop on top.

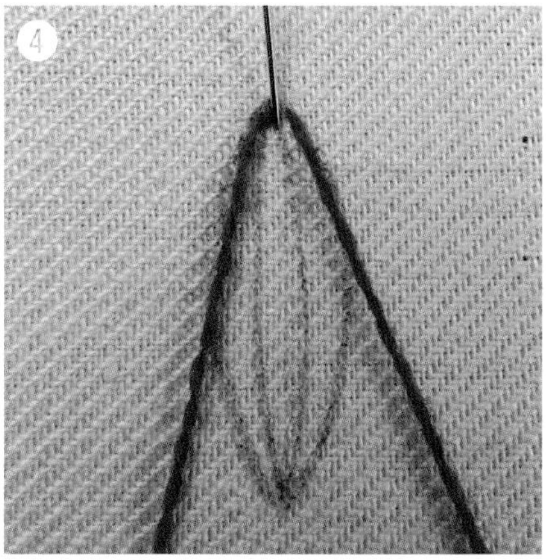

Bring the needle up on the right-hand pencil line and pull all of the thread through to create another 'V' shape.

Continue working down the shape making stitches in this way. As the shape broadens, the texture will become more apparent.

To finish, plunge the needle down over the last stitch on the bottom paintline and cast off.

Herringbone Stitch

Herringbone Stitch creates an unusual texture, using an offset Cross Stitch that can be worked in an open fashion. You will need to finish with an outlining stitch when using this stitch to fill a shape. When worked closed, Herringbone Stitch becomes quite padded, which can add an extra dimension to the piece.

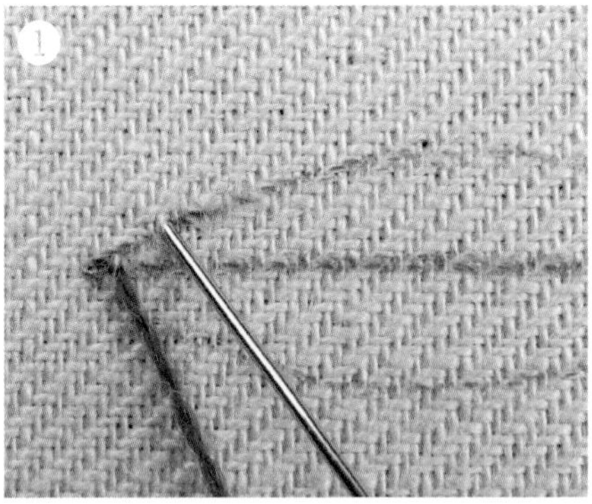

Bring the needle up on one side of the paintline and plunge on the other, slightly further along the shape, creating a diagonal stitch.

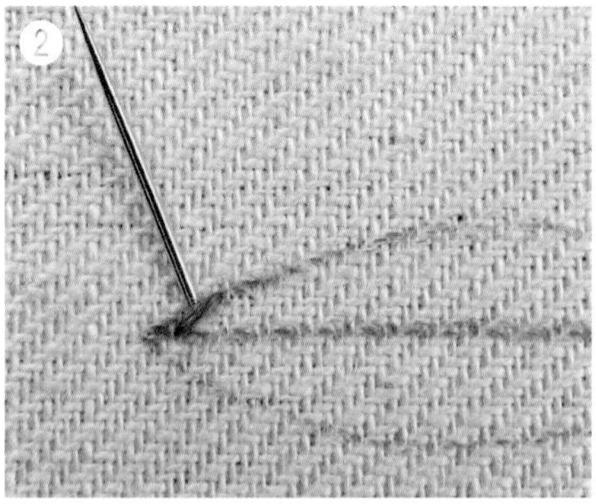

Bring the needle up on the same paintline, behind where the needle was just plunged, leaving a gap of fabric visible. Plunge the needle on the opposite paintline, again creating a diagonal stitch.

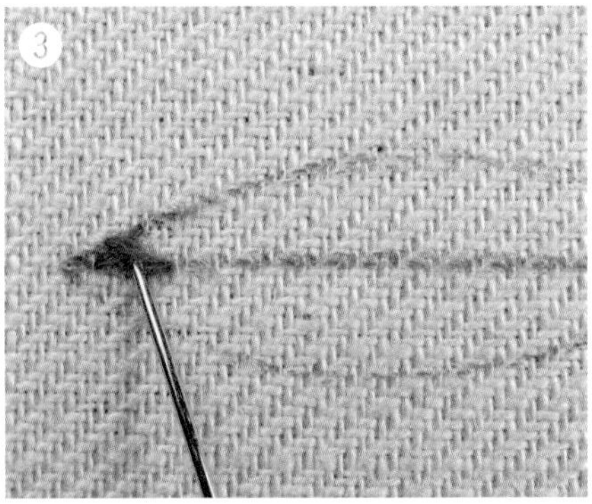

Bring the needle up on the same paintline behind where it was just plunged.

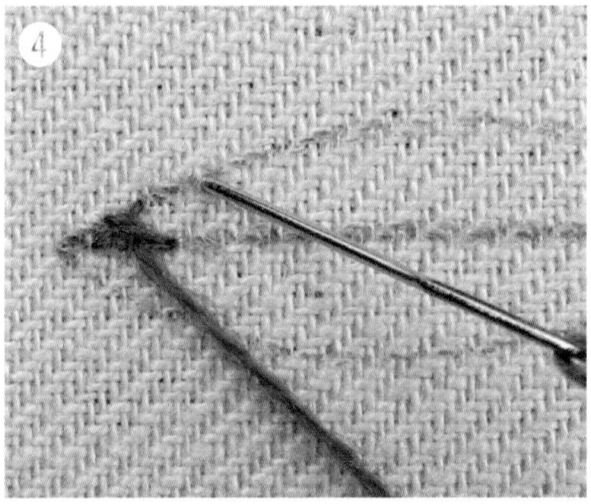

Make a diagonal stitch across the shape by plunging on the opposite paintline.

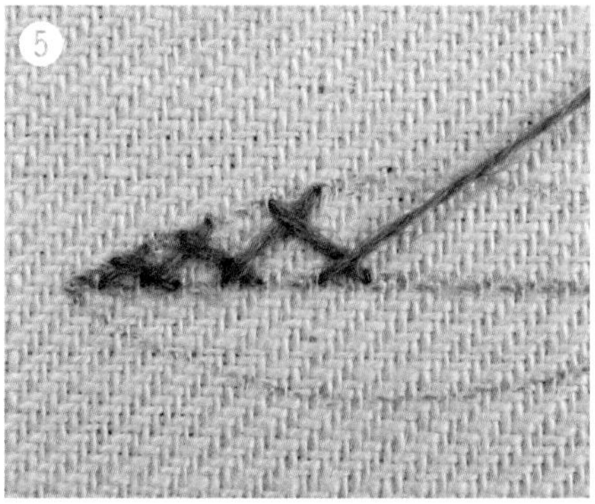

Continue working along the shape, trying to keep the spacing of the stitches consistent. Laying the thread across the shape is a good way of deciding the plunge point and keeping the angle/spacing consistent.

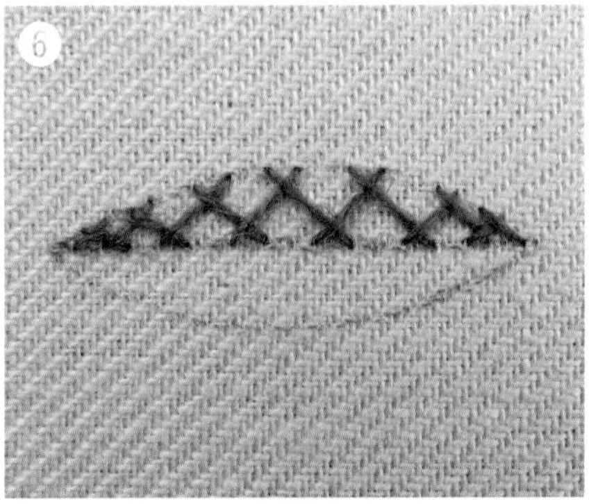

When completed, the stitches should progress evenly. If any section draws the eye, it will likely be because the angle or spacing has changed too suddenly. Try working the stitch from closed to open and then back to closed; this will emphasize curved shapes.

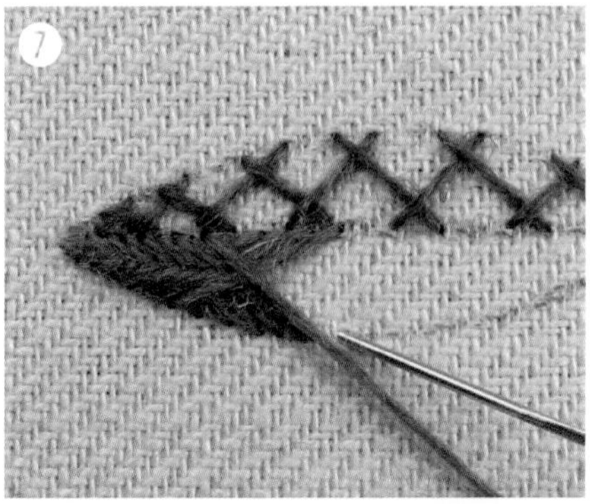

Closed Herringbone Stitch is worked in the same way; however, the stitches should be much closer together so that none of the fabric is visible. Take care to keep the edges neat and smooth by tucking the needle into the previous stitch without catching it.

When worked together, closed and open Herringbone Stitch can create a striking effect, with closed Herringbone Stitch creating a central vein down the middle of the shape and sitting higher than open Herringbone Stitch.

Van Dyke Stitch

Van Dyke Stitch creates a ladder-like texture with a plaited effect down the middle. It is ideal for use in both small, narrow shapes and curves. When working it round a curve, remember to make the gaps narrower on the inside and wider on the outside of the curve. You will need to work an outlining stitch due to the open nature of Van Dyke Stitch.

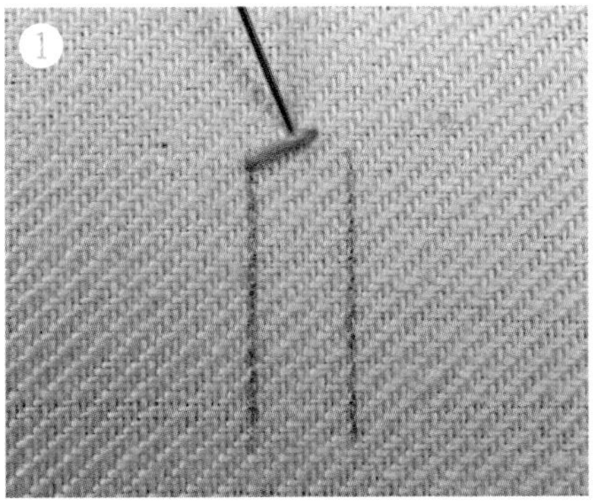

Bring the needle up slightly to the right of the middle top of the shape and plunge on the left-hand paintline just below where it was brought out, creating a diagonal stitch.

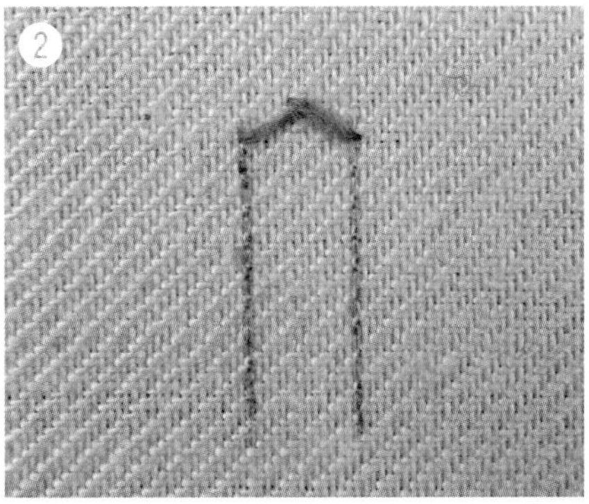

Bring the needle up just to the left of centre and plunge the needle on the right-hand paintline level with where it was plunged on the left-hand paintline.

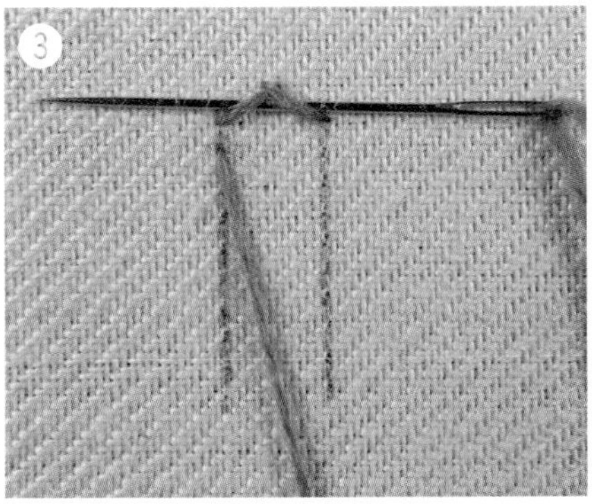

Bring the needle up on the left-hand paintline just below the first stitch. Take the needle across to the right-hand side and slide it under the point where the two stitches cross over.

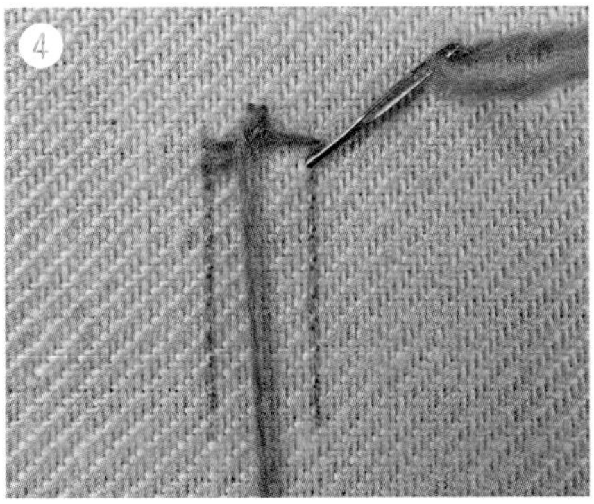

Plunge the needle on the right-hand side, level with where it was brought through on the left-hand paintline. The stitch should lie flat on the fabric; however, take care not to pull the thread too tightly as the plait will start to shift to the right.

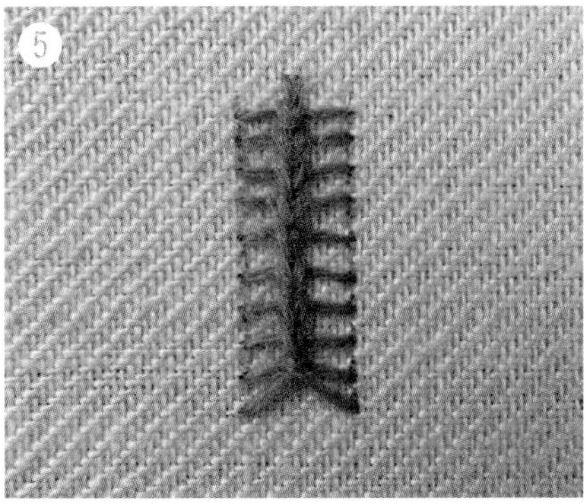

Continue working stitches in this manner, always bringing the needle up on and plunging on the same sides. Each stitch should pull the bars of the previous stitch straight.

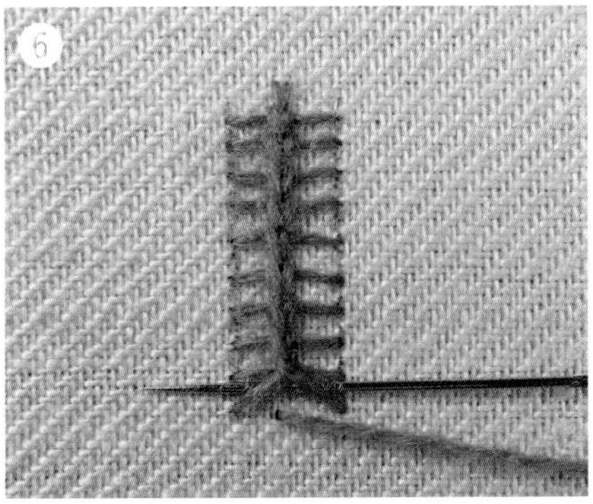

At the bottom of the shape bring the needle up just to the left of middle underneath the plait. Take the needle over to the right-hand side and slide it under the last stitch.

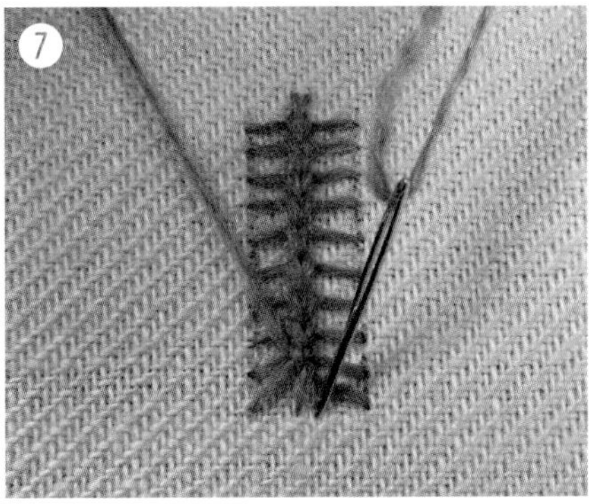

Plunge the needle down to just right of the centre underneath the plait and cast off. This last stitch should pull the final stitch straight to complete the ladder.

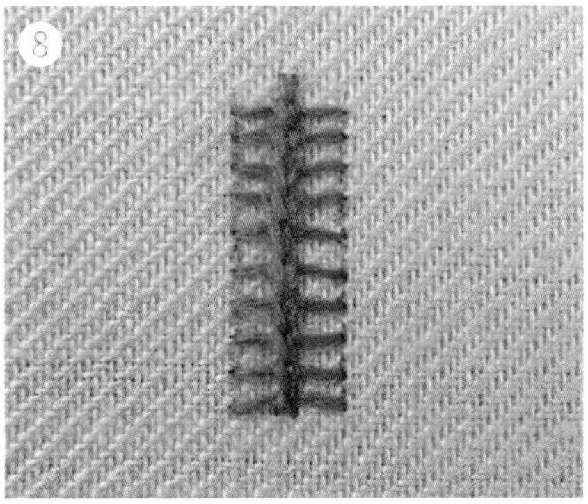

Take care to ensure the distance between the stitches is consistent and the plait is central in the shape.

Loop Stitch

Much like Van Dyke Stitch, Loop Stitch creates a ladder-like effect that works well in long, narrow areas. You will need to work an outlining stitch due to the open nature of Loop Stitch.

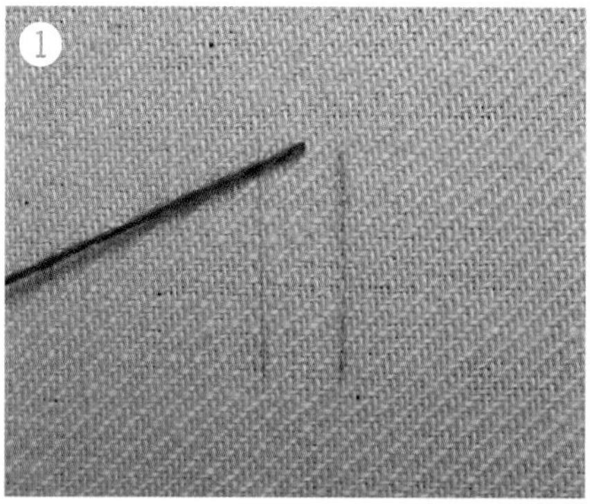

Bring the needle up in the middle top of the shape.

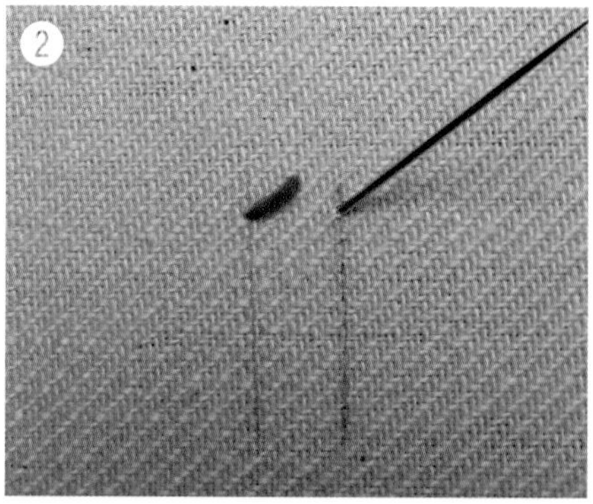

Plunge the needle on the left-hand paintline below the point where it was brought out, creating a diagonal stitch.

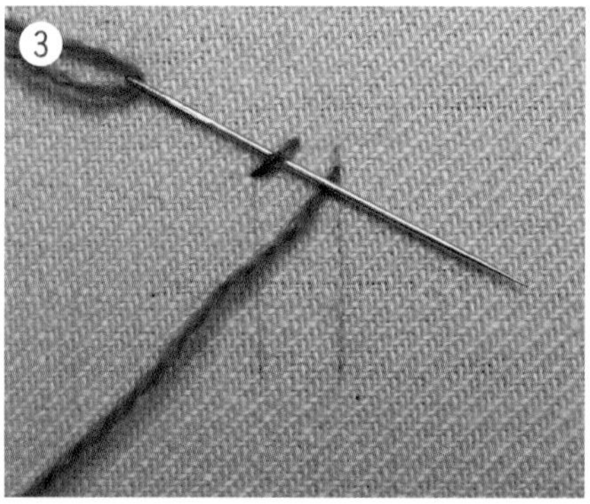

Bring the needle up on the right-hand paintline level with the point where it was just plunged on the left-hand paintline. Take the needle over to the left-hand side and slide it under the first stitch.

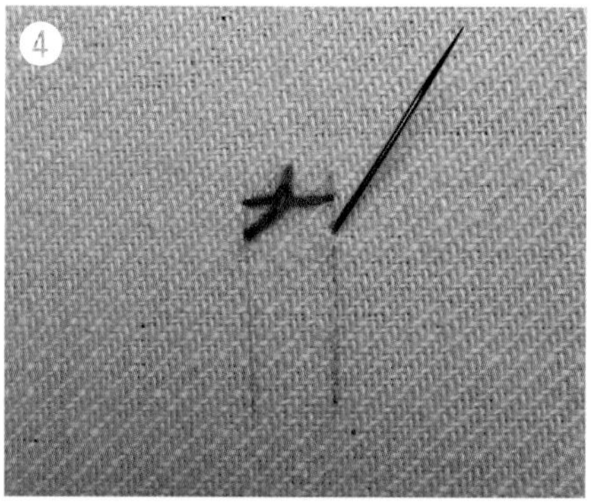

Plunge the needle on the left-hand side below the first stitch, leaving a small gap in between. Bring the needle back up on the right-hand side, level with the point where it was just plunged on the left-hand paintline.

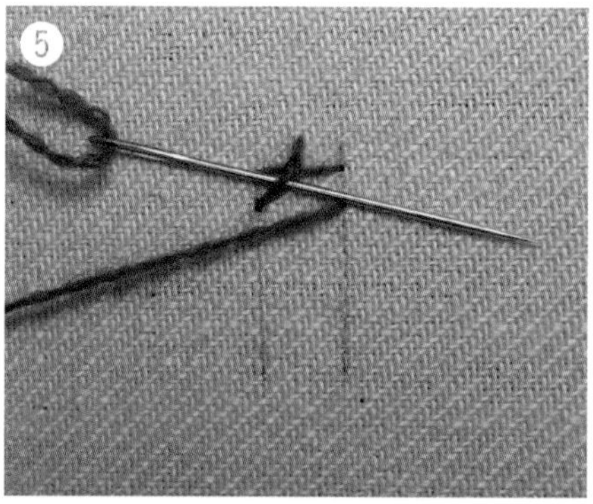

Take the needle over to the left-hand side and slide it under the last stitch. Continue making stitches in this way, keeping the spacing consistent until the shape is filled. Try to keep the central line in the middle of the shape.

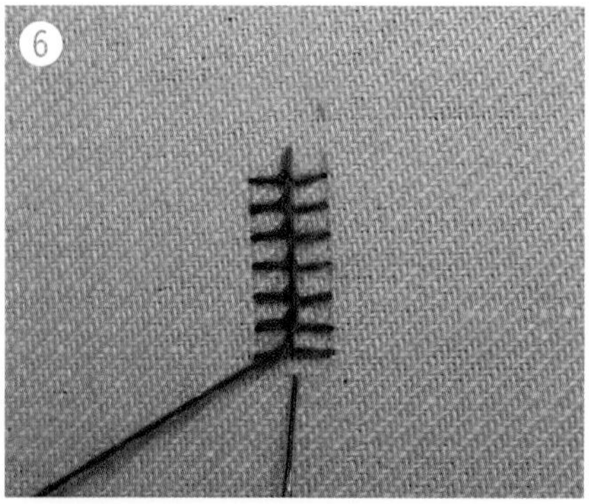

To finish the stitch, take the needle over to the left-hand side and slide the needle under the last stitch. Plunge the needle in the middle of the shape just below the last stitch and cast off.

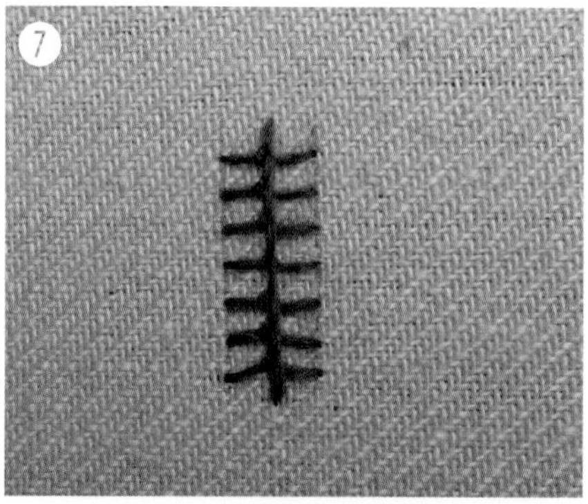

When working this stitch around a curve, remember to make the gaps on the inside of the curve slightly smaller than the those on outside of the curve.

SEEDING

Seeding is a useful stitch as it can be used to introduce touches of colour without solid stitching. This stitch can be worked in multiple colours and other stitches can be used in the same way to create a different texture. You will need to work an outlining stitch due to the open nature of seeding.

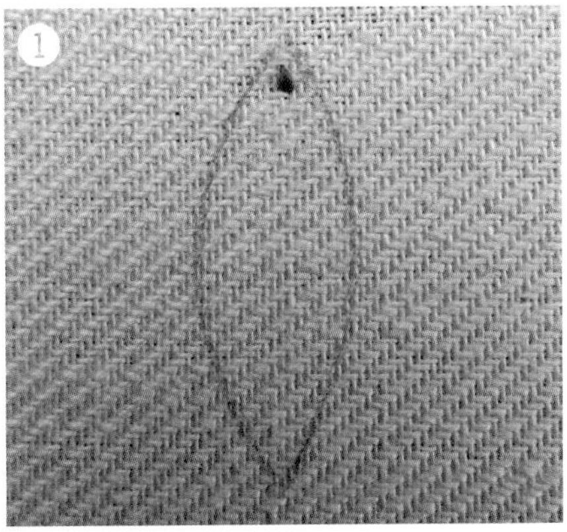

Bring the needle up within the shape and work a small straight stitch. The stitch should not touch the paintline.

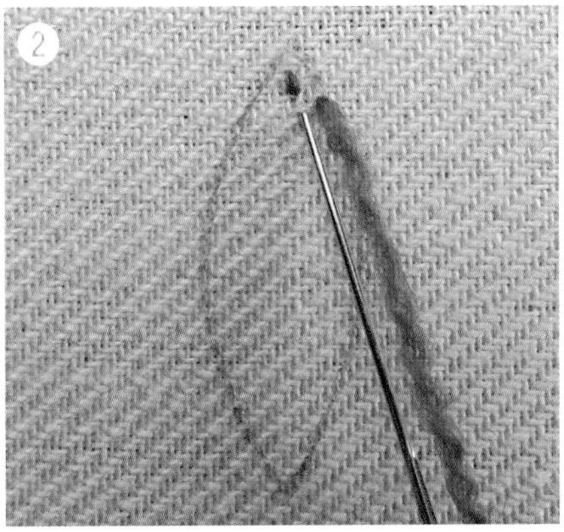

Bring the needle up nearby and make another small straight stitch, equal to the length of the first but at a different angle.

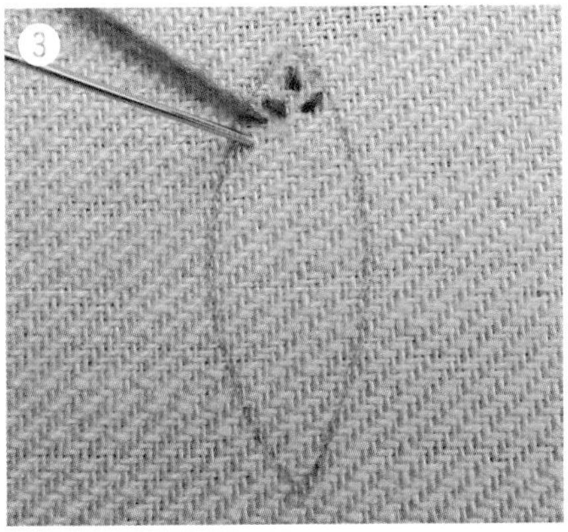

Work additional stitches in this manner, ensuring that the stitches are all of equal length but sitting at different angles to one another.

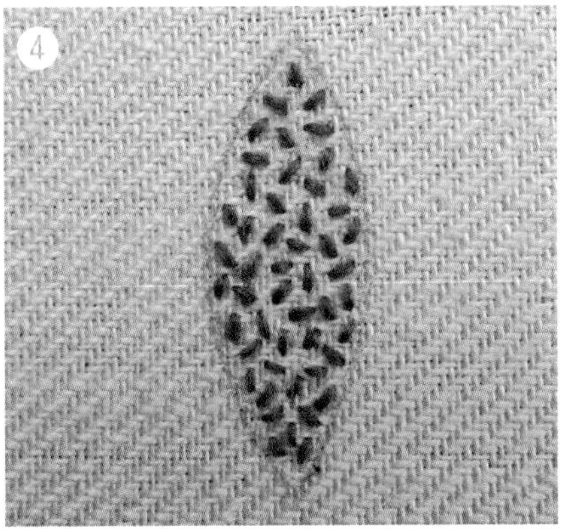

Continue until the shape is full, ensuring that the stitches do not touch the paintlines or each other. The stitches can be worked quite densely or with more space between them. Stitches such as detached Fly Stitch, Detached Chain Stitch, Pistol Stitch, French Knots and Bullion Knots can also be used as a form of seeding.

Turkey Rug Stitch

This stitch adds a lovely texture to any piece. As it is generally worked with two threads, it is possible to work in multiple colours to add depth. In larger areas, consider sculpting it to create different areas of height.

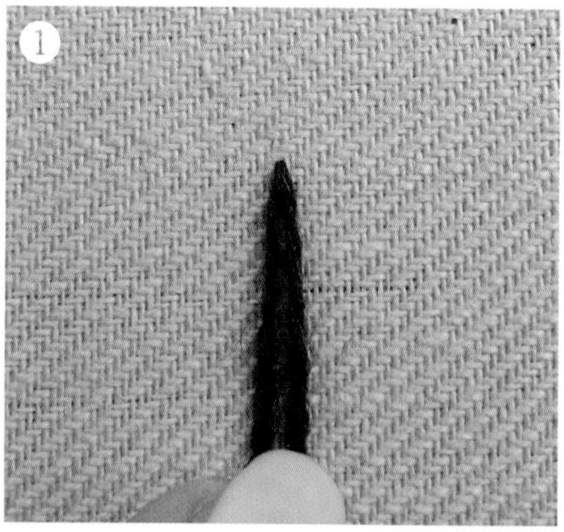

Plunge the needle into the fabric leaving a tail on top (there is no need to knot the thread) to cast on.

Bring the needle up next to the thread on one side.

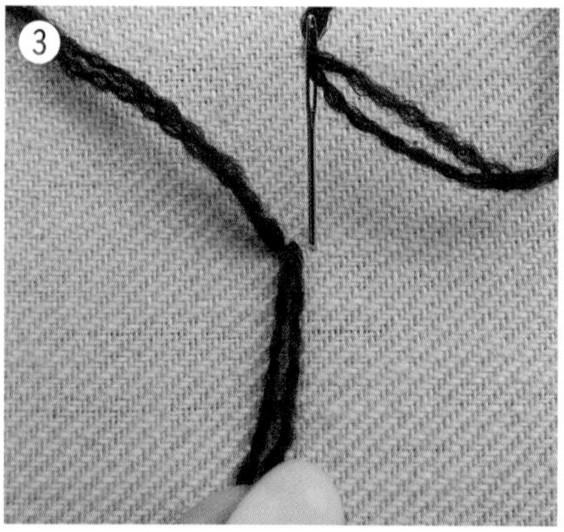

Plunge the needle on the other side, making a small straight stitch twice the width of the thread over the base of the tail.

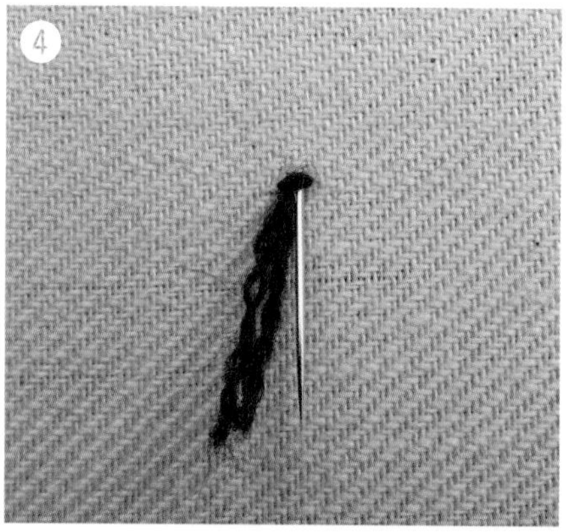

Bring the needle up under the last stitch. Try not to pierce the thread.

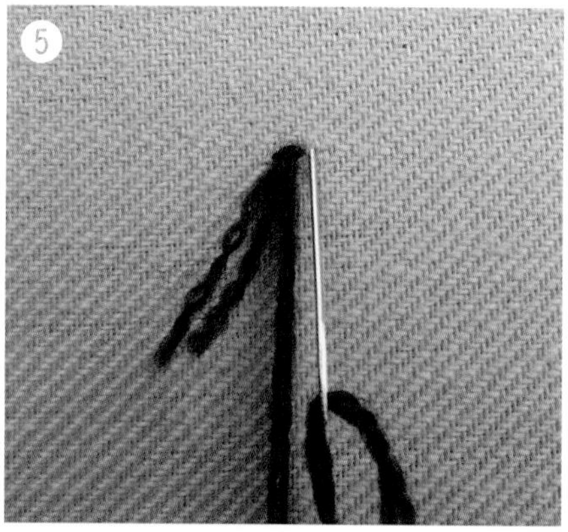

Plunge the needle down next to the straight stitch, leaving a loop of thread on top.

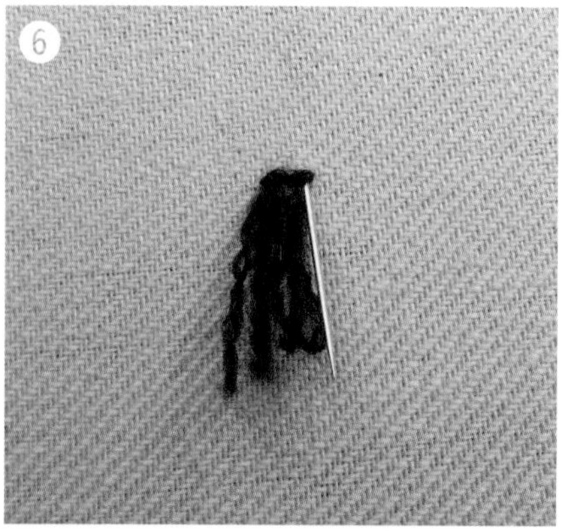

Bring the needle up on one side, making a straight stitch to secure the loop in place. The two straight stitches should sit next to one another with no fabric showing in between.

Bring the needle up from underneath the last straight stitch, taking care not to pierce the thread. Continue making stitches in this manner until the shape is filled or the thread runs out.

To end a thread, bring the needle up from underneath the last straight stitch, pull all of the thread through and trim the ends level with the other loops. Continue working stitches until the shape is full.

Trimming Turkey Rug Stitch

Once the area has been filled, the stitches should be trimmed to shorten the pile and create a velvet-like effect.

Start by cutting all the loops. This will give a clear idea of the overall height of the pile.

Hints and tips

Periodically pinching the threads between the thumb and forefinger will help to both lift the pile and expose any threads that are too long or short, and remove any fluff.

Trim the ends of the threads conservatively by holding the scissors horizontally on top of the threads. Keep snipping until the pile is of a consistent length and the shape is better defined. *Do not* angle the point of the scissors towards the fabric.

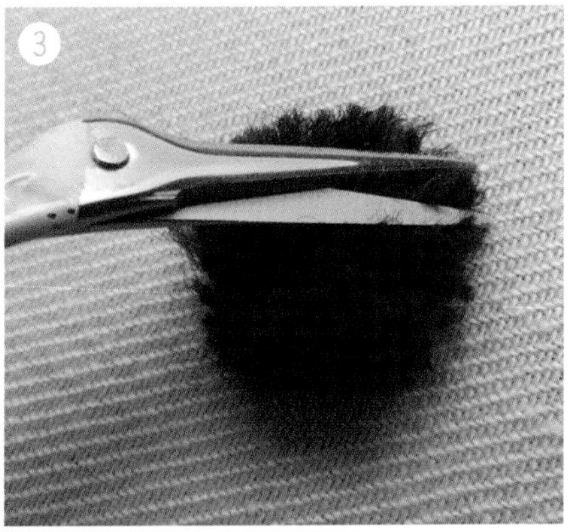

Working from the top of the pile, snip small amounts of the top of the threads to create a domed effect. Take care not to pierce the fabric when doing this.

When completed, Turkey Rug Stitch can be carefully steamed over a kettle or pan of boiling water. This will cause the threads to lift, exposing any that may be inconsistent length. This step is optional.

CHAPTER 7

OUTLINING STITCHES

As their name suggests, outlining stitches are used to outline areas, cover cast-on stitches and, most importantly, cover *all* design lines or other marks on the fabric. These stitches are usually worked last and, with careful consideration, can be used to balance the colours across the piece.

RUNNING STITCH

This stitch appears as a dashed line. It can be used to introduce colour to an area and is best worked without a paintline.

Bring the needle up through the fabric and make a short straight stitch approximately 4mm/⅛in in length.

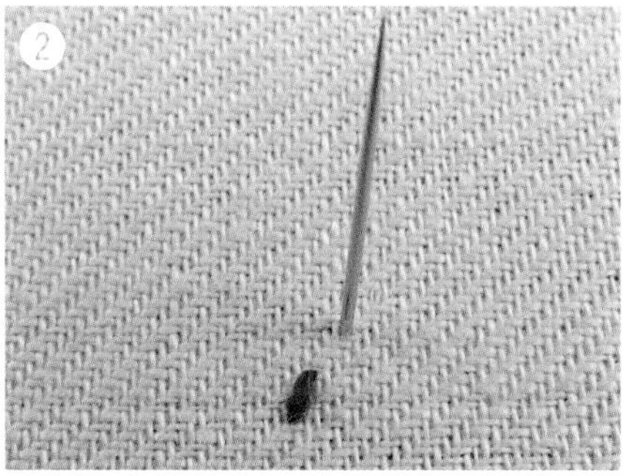

Leave a gap the same length as the first stitch and bring the needle and thread up through the fabric.

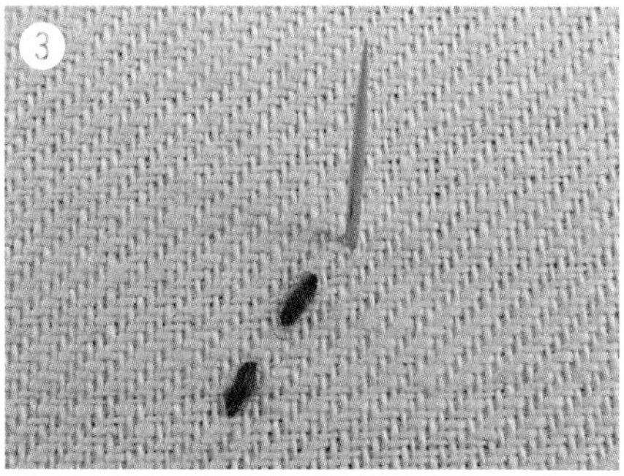

Make another stitch the same length as the first and again leave a gap that is equal to the length of the stitch.

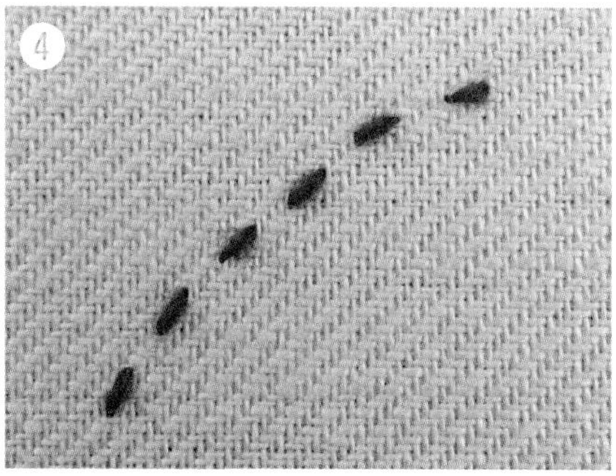

Continue making stitches and leaving gaps of the same length until the desired distance has been covered. When completed, the stitch should create a dashed effect; however, due to its sparse nature, stitches or gaps that are too large or too small will draw the eye.

Designed and worked by Shelley Cox, this section of a larger aquatic-themed piece uses a number of outlining stitches to add detail.

Back Stitch

Back Stitch is a simple stitch that can be used to outline an area or form the basis of an accent stitch.

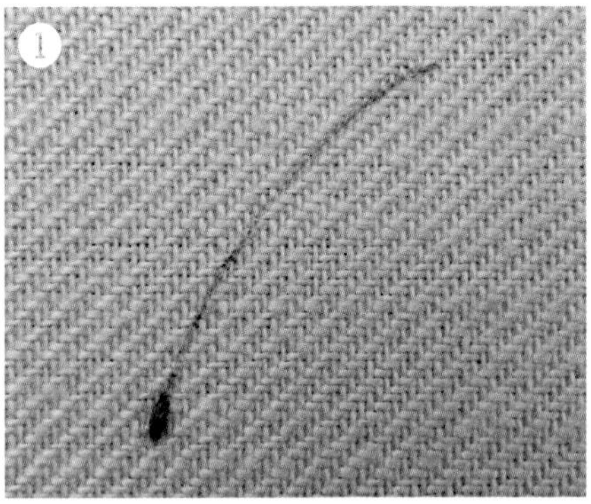

Bring the needle up at the start of the paintline and make a short straight stitch along the line.

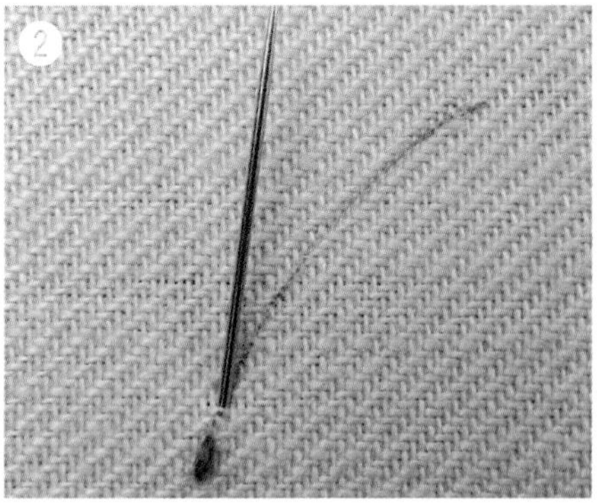

Bring the needle up on the paintline a short distance away, the same length as the first stitch.

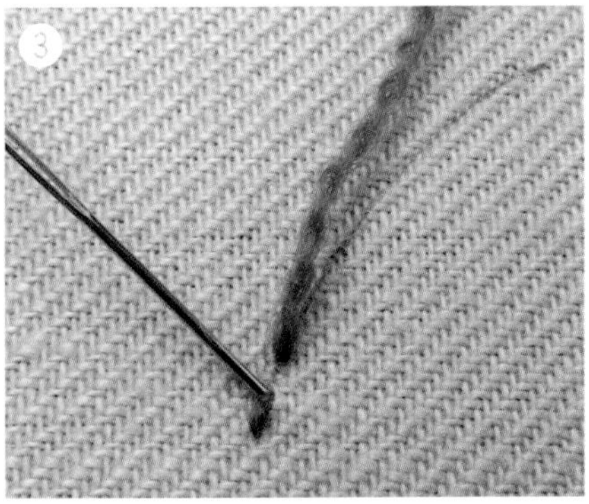

Plunge the needle down at the end of the first stitch. There should be no fabric showing between the two stitches, nor should the needle pierce the stitch.

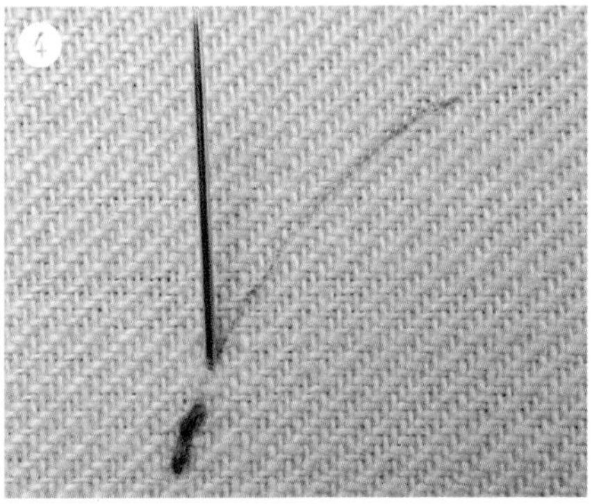

Bring the needle up a short distance away, the same length as the first stitch, and plunge next to the stitch last worked.

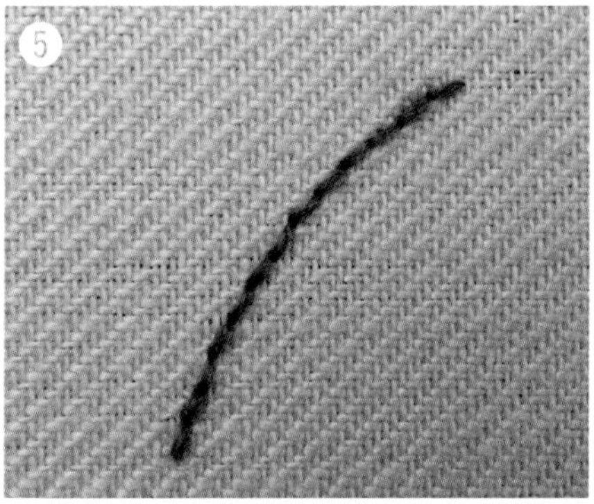

Continue working along the paintline until it is covered. The stitches should be equal in length with no fabric showing between them.

Stem Stitch

Stem Stitch is so called because it is commonly used to create the stems of plants and can be used in many forms of embroidery. This stitch creates a fine line with a twisted effect. The direction of the twist should lie from bottom left to top right. It is perfect for working around curves and for use as an outlining stitch.

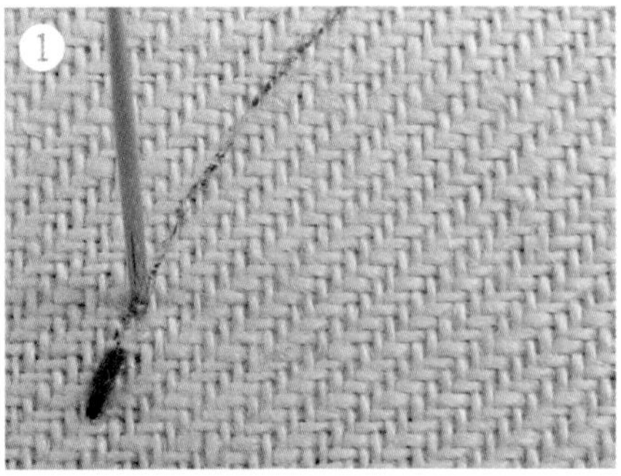

Bring the needle up at one end of the paintline and make a short straight stitch, plunging the needle on the paintline.

Bring the needle back up at the start of the line and make a stitch that is twice the length of the first. Do not pull all of the thread through the fabric; instead, place the loop to one side, in this example to the right. Bring the needle up on the paintline in the middle of this new stitch (which should be at the end of the previous stitch). There should be no fabric showing between the previous stitch and where the needle is brought up.

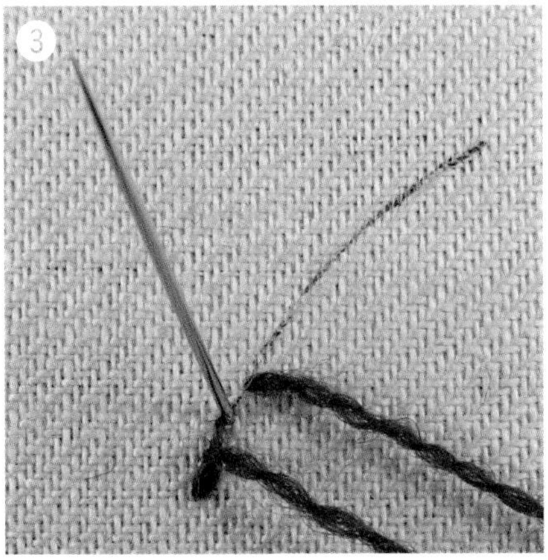

Make another stitch the same length as the previous stitch (note that the stitches should overlap each other by half their length each time) and repeat the process. The stitches should now be worked to a consistent length until the end of the paintline is reached.

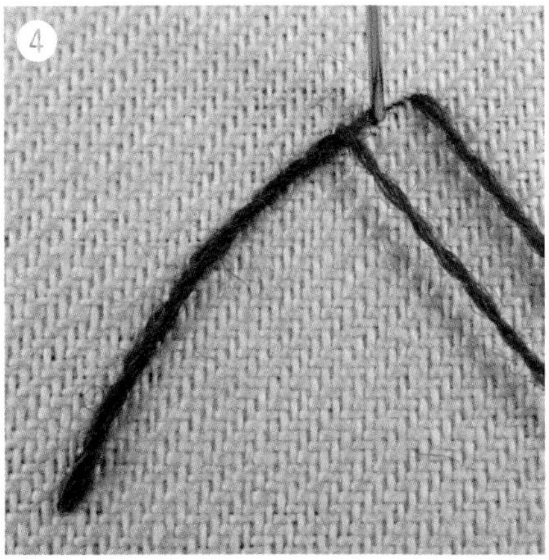

The penultimate stitch should be worked as above up to the end of the paintline. Then bring the needle up in the middle of the stitch and plunge the needle at the end of the paintline. This is in effect a half stitch that will complete the twisted effect and cover the paintline.

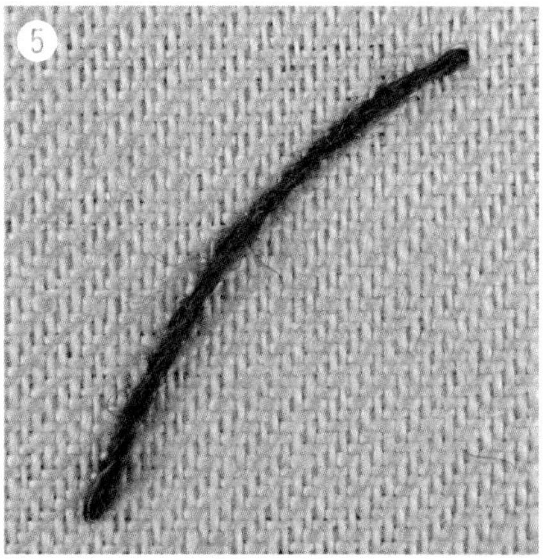

The completed stitch should follow the paintline smoothly; this is achieved by always bringing the needle up and plunging it on the paintline.

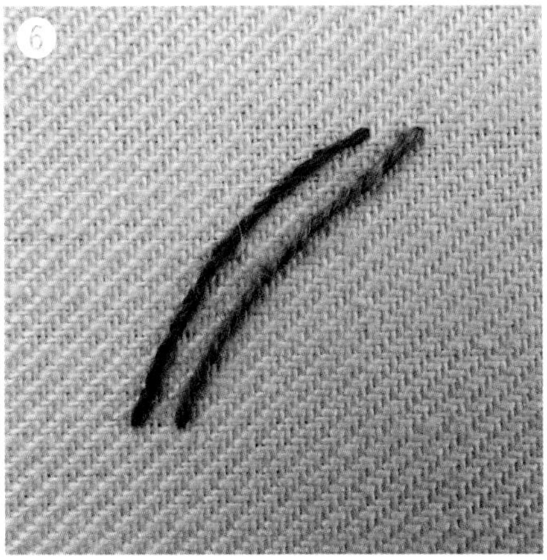

At first glance Stem Stitch and Outline Stitch appear to be the same. However, there is a subtle difference. As explained above, the direction of the twist in Stem Stitch is from bottom left to top right. In Outline Stitch the direction of the twist is from bottom right to top left, the opposite of Stem Stitch. This can be used to the stitcher's advantage when working two sides of a shape; working the twist both ways creates a subtle effect of the two stitches mirroring each other.

Hints and tips

If the line of stitches appears irregular, it could be that the length of the stitch is too long for the curve it is following. Shortening the stitch length should correct this.

If the twisted effect is lost, this could be because the stitch is not brought up in the correct place, for instance leaving a section of fabric between the end of one stitch and the beginning of the next. Closing this gap will give more support to the overlying stitch and create the twist.

Sharp points can be achieved. However, it is important to end one row and restart the stitch on the adjoining line. Working a continuous row of Stem Stitch around a sharp point does not work.

SPILT STITCH

Split Stitch is very versatile: it can be worked to create a fine line that has the appearance of a very small Chain Stitch, it can be worked as padding under Satin Stitch, and it can be used as an Outline Stitch that creates a smooth and stable edge for stitches such as Long and Short Stitch or Satin Stitch.

Bring the needle up at one end of the paintline and make a short straight stitch, plunging the needle on the paintline.

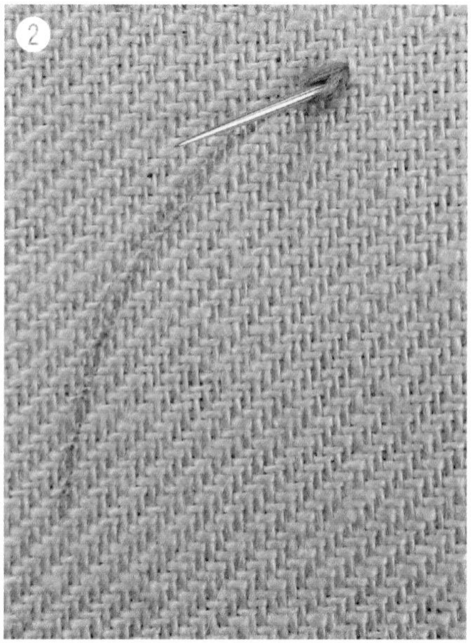

Bring the needle up in the middle of the stitch. This will split the fibres of the wool, hence the term Split Stitch. Pull all of the thread through.

Plunge the needle on the paintline, creating a stitch the same length as the first.

Bring the needle up in the middle of the length and width of the last stitch. Continue working along the paintline.

When worked consistently, Split Stitches should overlap each other by half the length; the resulting line should be smooth with a slightly textured effect. If working this stitch in conjunction with Long and Short Stitch or Satin Stitch, it is important that the Split Stitch is firm and consistent. This can be achieved by working very small stitches that are all the same length. When using this stitch decoratively, the stitch length can be a little longer.

CHAIN STITCH/ LAZY DAISY STITCH

Chain stitch is a series of loops worked in a continuous line. The effect is slightly broader than Stem Stitch or Split Stitch.

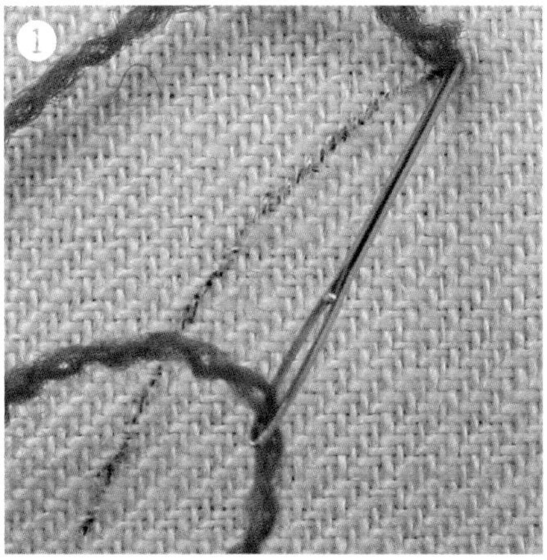

Bring the needle up at the start of the paintline and take it back down in the same place. There should be no gap between the two threads. Do not take all of the thread through the fabric; instead, leave a loop on top and lay it along the paintline.

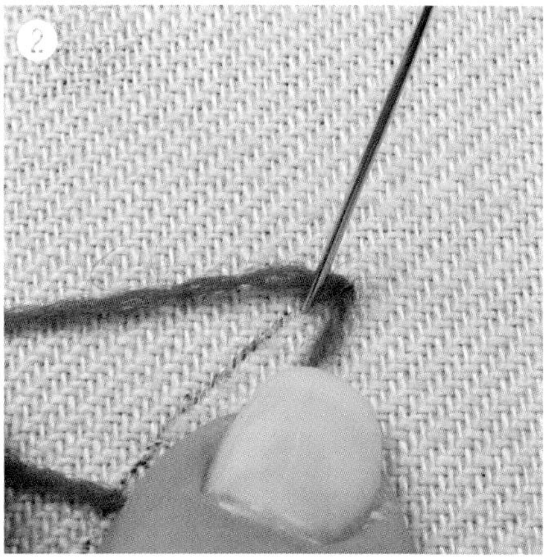

Bring the needle up on the paintline 3mm/⅛in away from where the needle was plunged, ensuring that it is brought up *within* the loop of thread. Pull all of the thread through and settle the stitch into place, taking care not to pull the thread too tight. The thread should be arranged in a teardrop-like shape, which will be distorted if the stitch is pulled too tight.

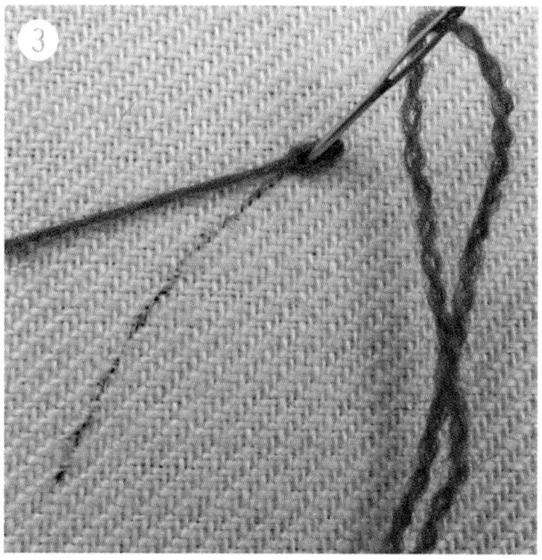

Take the needle down through the fabric next to where the thread comes out, again *within* the loop. Do not take all of the thread through; leave a loop on top and bring the needle back up on the paintline 3mm/⅛in away from where it was last plunged.

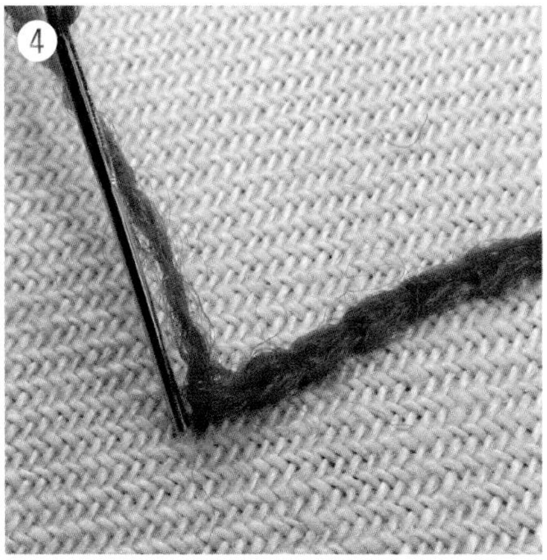

Continue stitching in this way until the paintline is covered. When the thread is pulled through in the final loop, plunge the needle over the edge of the final loop, catching it in place.

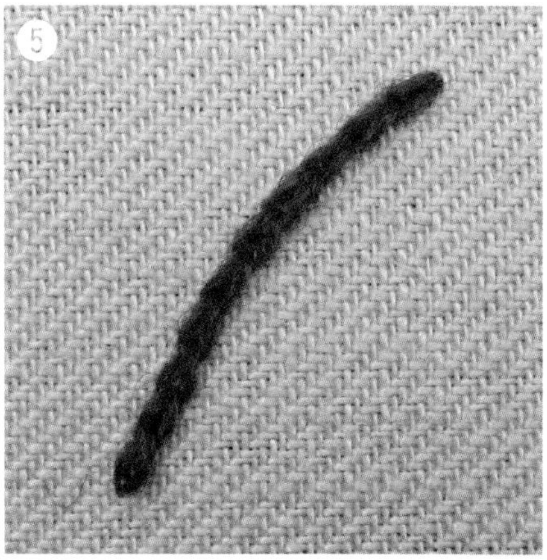

Once complete, the stitch should create a bold, textured effect. Try to keep the stitch size consistent as this will create a neater finish; making the stitch size too large could result in the stitches being unstable and looking untidy.

Chain stitch does not have to be worked in continuous rows. Each stitch can be worked individually in a random way or in organized patterns; this is often referred to as Lazy Daisy Stitch.

COUCHING

Couching is a stitch that is found in a number of embroidery techniques, most notably goldwork. However, the same principles can be applied to crewelwork. This stitch is particularly effective when working around curves as the threads can be moulded to the shape. This stitch uses threads that are laid on the fabric (couched threads) and are secured to it using a second working thread (couching thread). In this example three couched threads have been used; more could be added to create a heavier outline, but using less than two threads is inadvisable.

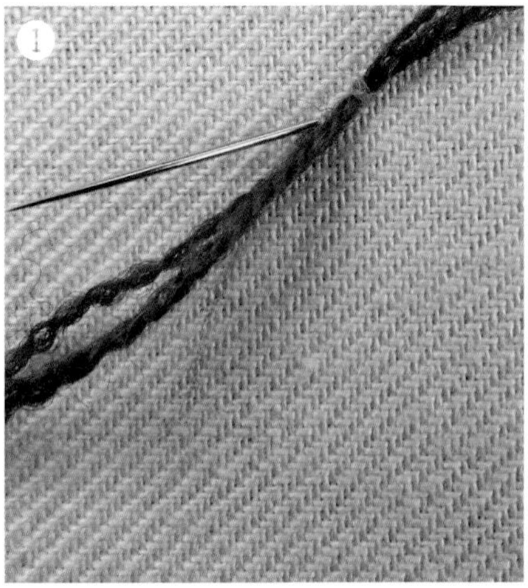

1. Lay the couched threads along the paintline. Bring the needle up on one side of the couched threads and plunge the needle on the other side. When making the stitch, try to keep it at a 90-degree angle to the couched threads. There can be a temptation to angle the needle under the couched threads; this will have the effect of 'pinching' them, which will cause the threads to bulge.

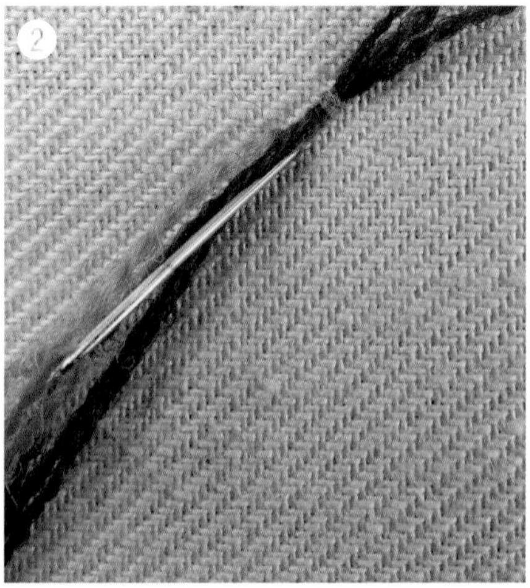

2. Bring the needle up 3–4mm/⅛in along the paintline and repeat the Couching Stitch.

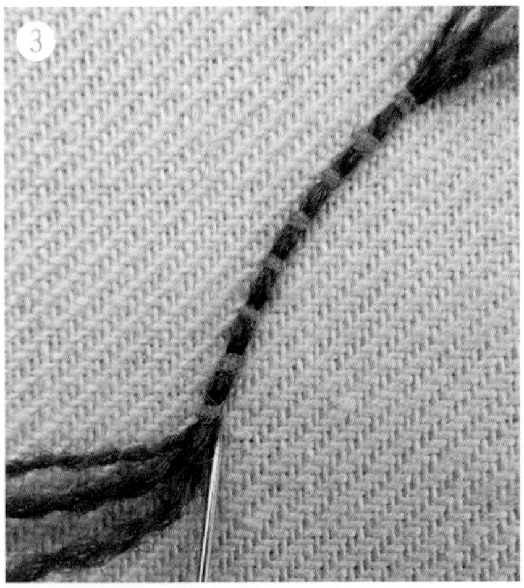

3. Continue working along the paintline, keeping the spacing of the stitches consistent. When the line is complete, cast off the couching thread and use the needle to plunge the couched threads one or two at a time at the end of the paintline. Turn the frame over and run the needle and threads through the back of the stitches.

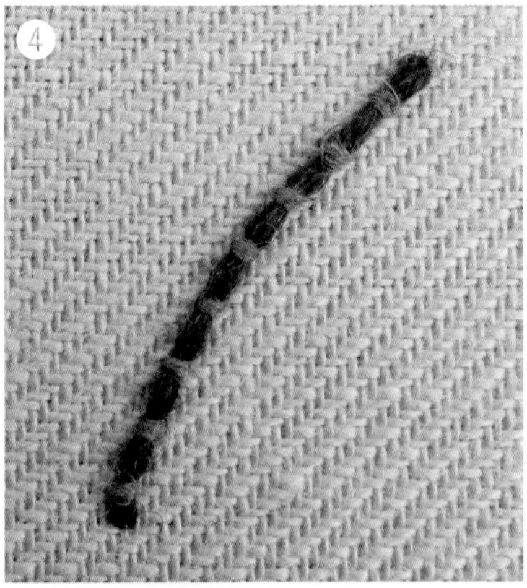

4. Sharp points can be worked in this technique. However, one row of couching should be finished and a new one started at the point. This example has been worked in contrasting threads to demonstrate the stitches. If the spacing was inconsistent, it would be very noticeable and draw the eye.

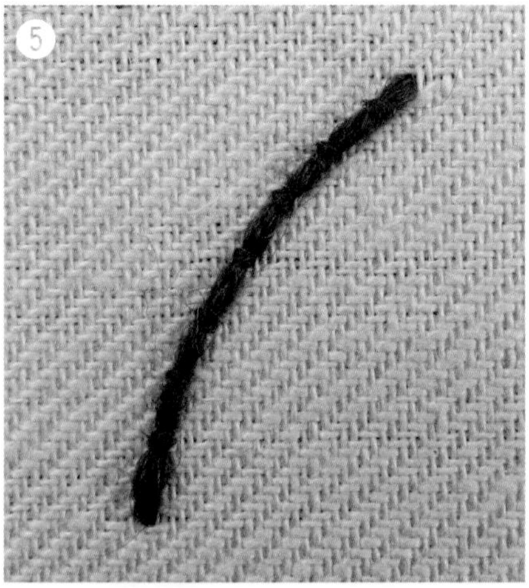

5. It is preferable to use matching colour threads as inconsistencies will be less obvious.

Scroll Stitch

This stitch is a series of loops with a scalloped effect. It works very well as a wandering tendril.

Bring the needle up at one end of the paintline and draw the thread round in an anti-clockwise direction to create a loop. Plunge the needle on the left-hand side of the paintline taking care not to cross over the thread. Do not pull all of the thread through; instead, leave a loop on top.

Bring the needle up on the right-hand side of the paintline within the loop. Use a finger to hold the thread stable.

Pull all of the thread through to create a knot.

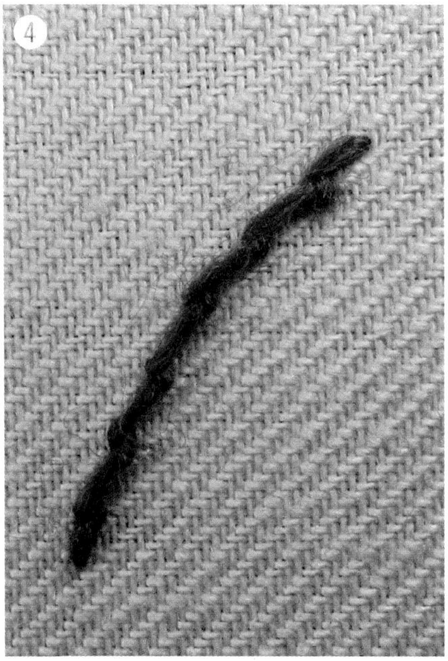

Continue working along the paintline, leaving gaps of equal length between each knot. At the end of the line, plunge the needle and cast off.

Coral Knot Stitch

This stitch has the appearance of knots connected with straight stitches and is best worked with two strands of thread.

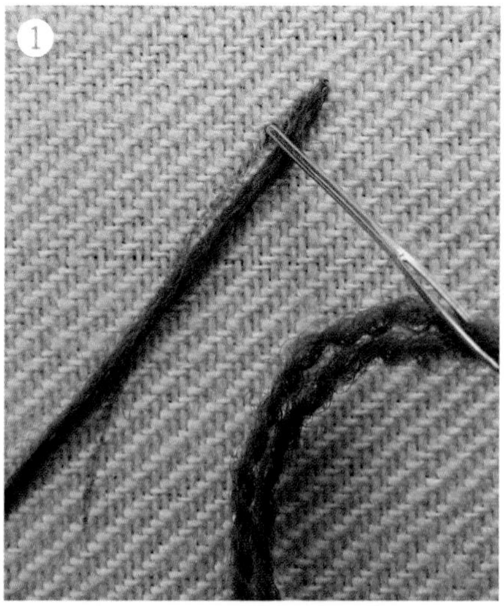

Bring the needle up and lay the thread along the paintline. Plunge the needle on one side of the paintline, crossing over the laid thread, but *do not* pull all of the thread through.

Bring the needle up on the other side of the laid thread through the loop. Hold the laid thread in place with a fingernail placed next to the needle.

Pull the needle and thread through to form the knot.

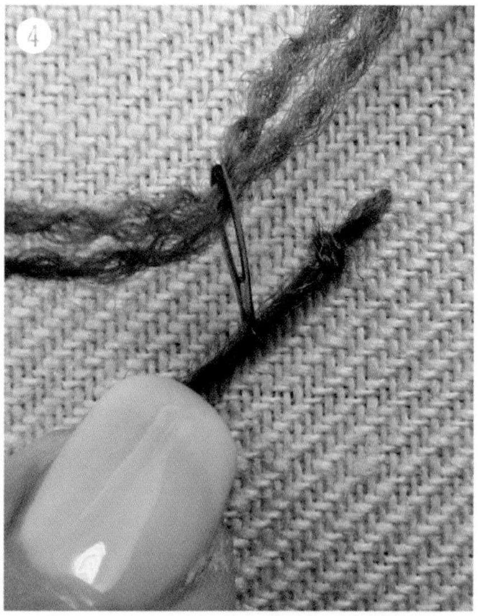

Repeat this process until the paintline is covered, ensuring the gaps between the knots are consistent in length.

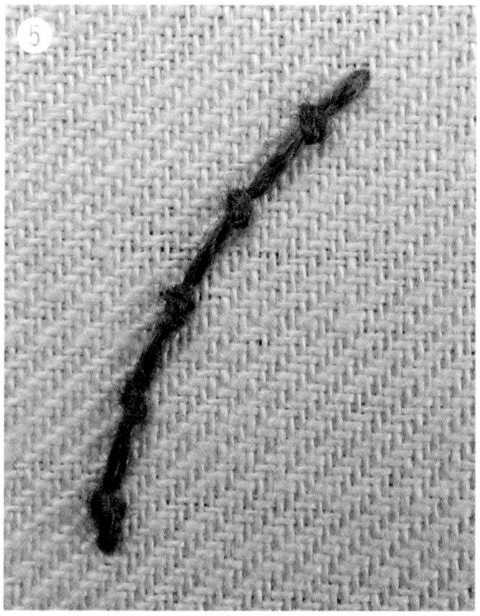

When working round a curve, it is better to have a shorter stitch between each knot and it is therefore advisable to work a shorter stitch from the start.

Portuguese Knotted Stem Stitch

This is a lovely textured stitch with a shell-like effect creating quite a heavy line. It works well as an outlining stitch or wandering tendril. The following example has been worked in two threads.

Bring the needle up at the base of the paintline and make a straight stitch, plunging the needle on the paintline. Do not pull all of the thread through; instead, leave a loop on top and throw it to one side, in this example to the left. Bring the needle up on the paintline in the middle of the stitch. Pull all of the thread through.

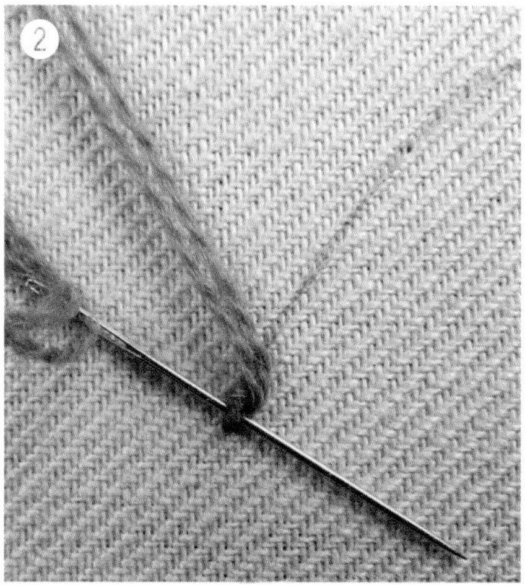

Take the needle over the top of the first stitch and slide the eye of the needle under it, pulling all of the thread through. Repeat this action, moving towards the start point, so the initial stitch is wrapped twice.

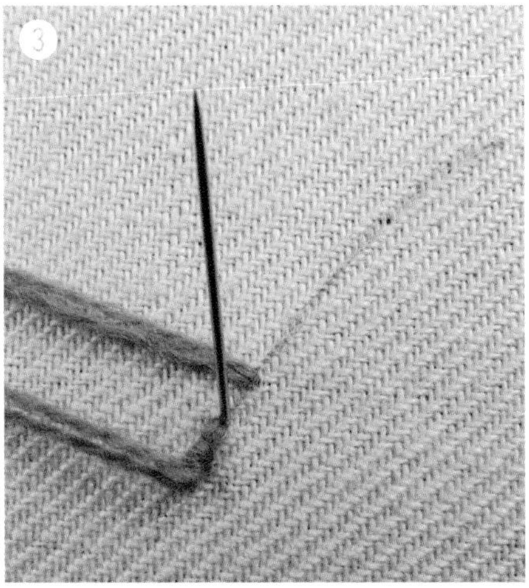

Plunge the needle on the paintline, taking care to keep the length of this stitch the same as the previous one. Do not pull all of the thread through; instead, throw the loop to the same side as before, in this example to the left. Bring the needle up in the middle of this stitch, which (just like Stem Stitch) should be at the end of the previous stitch; there should be no fabric visible.

Where the two stitches overlap, take the thread over the top and slide the eye of the needle under the stitches twice. This wrapping action should be made towards the start point. Repeat this process along the length of the paintline. After creating the last knot, plunge the needle down to create a half stitch and complete the row.

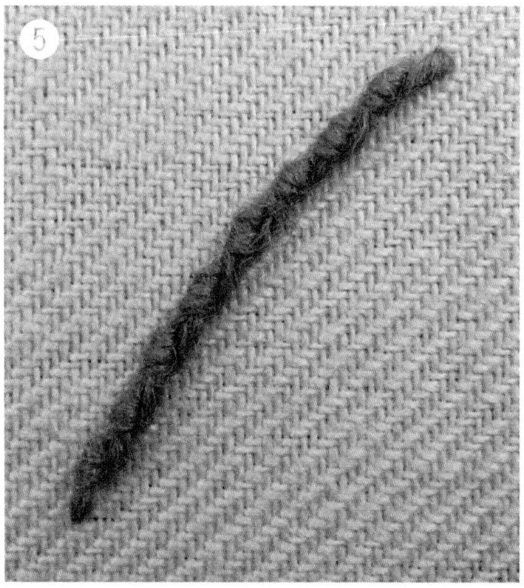

When completed, the row of stitching will have a heavily textured effect.

Buttonhole Stitch

This stitch is commonly used to edge buttonholes (hence the name). It can also be used to edge textiles, when it is often referred to as blanket stitch. It creates a lovely textured edge and can be worked open (with fabric showing between each stitch) or closed (with no fabric showing between the stitches).

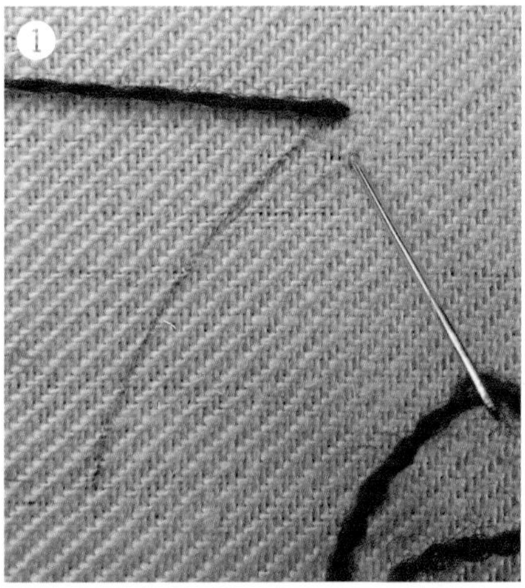

Bring the needle up on the paintline and plunge it into the fabric a short way away from the start point and a little to one side. Do not pull all of the thread through; instead, leave a loop on top.

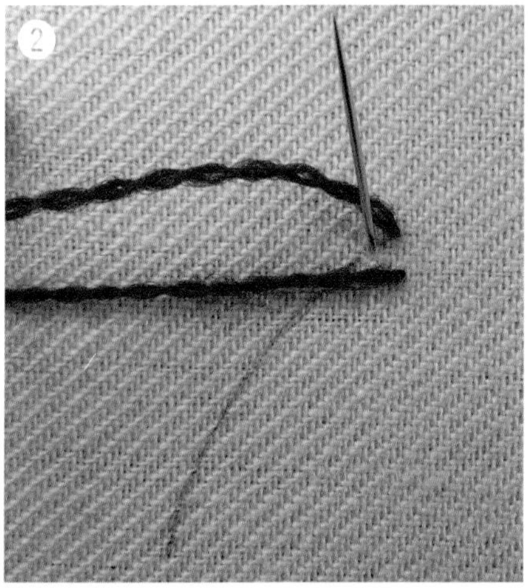

Bring the needle up on the paintline and through the loop, level with where it was just plunged. Pull all of the thread through; this will catch a length of thread on the fabric creating an 'L' shape.

Repeat this process by plunging the needle level with the previous plunge point, leaving a small gap between the two stitches. Do not pull all of the thread through; instead, leave a loop on top.

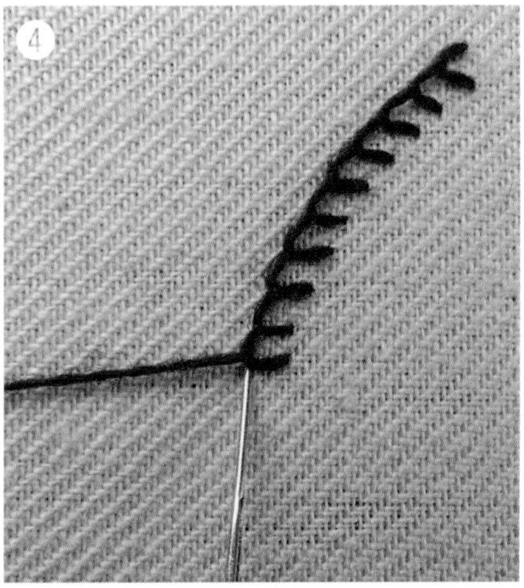

Continue working along the paintline until it is covered. To finish the line, make the last stitch, then plunge the needle on the outside of the final stitch and cast off the thread.

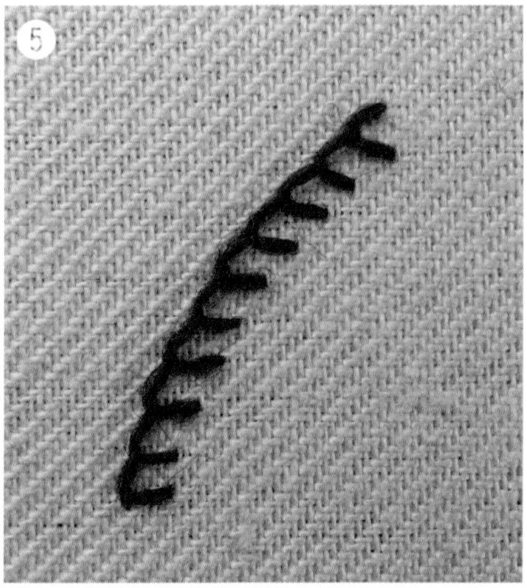

When completed, open Buttonhole Stitch has a serrated appearance.

If worked more densely, this stitch is referred to as closed Buttonhole Stitch. It should cover the fabric completely and has a slightly textured edge on one side.

Rope Stitch

Rope Stitch is a self-padding stitch that creates a heavy outline. Try working it across a broader shape as a substitute to Satin Stitch.

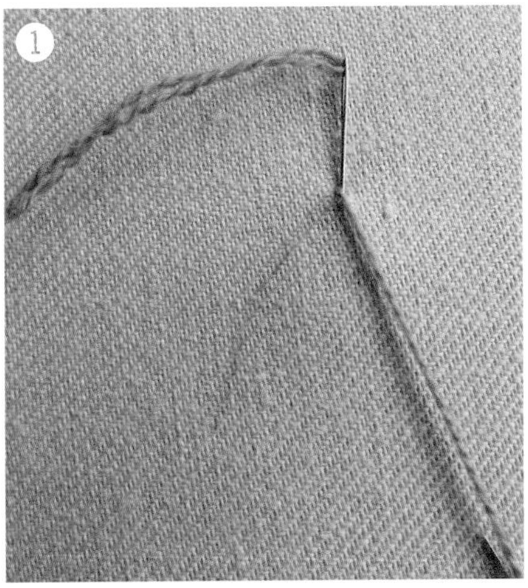

Bring the needle out just in from the end of the paintline. Take the thread round anti-clockwise and plunge the needle at the end of the paintline. Do not pull all of the thread through.

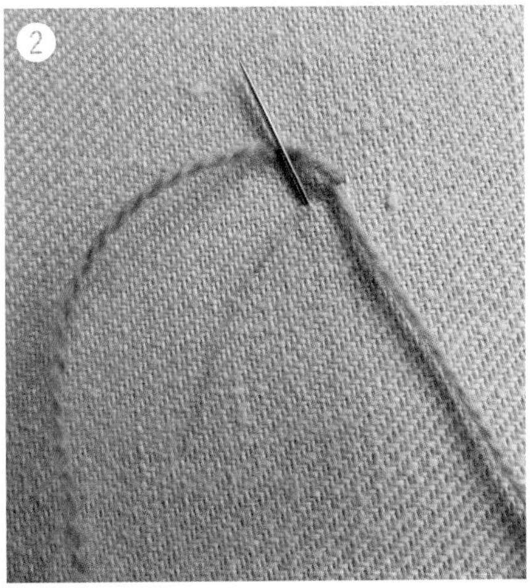

Bring the needle up on the paintline 3–4mm away and in the loop. Pull the thread through and settle the stitch into place. The stitch should not be loose.

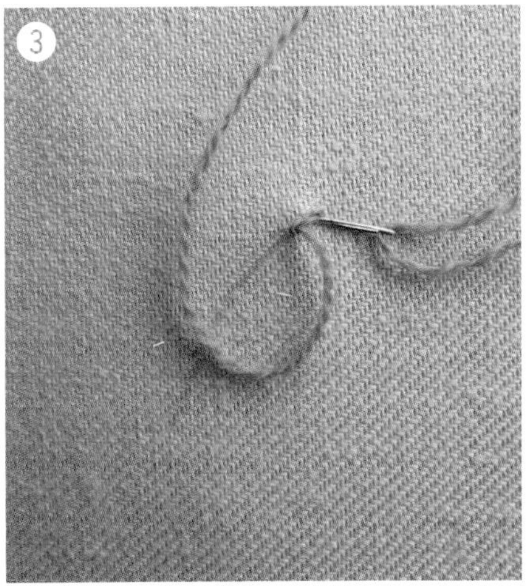

Take the thread round anti-clockwise and plunge the needle on the right hand side, tucking it in at the top of the previous stitch. Do not pull all of the thread through.

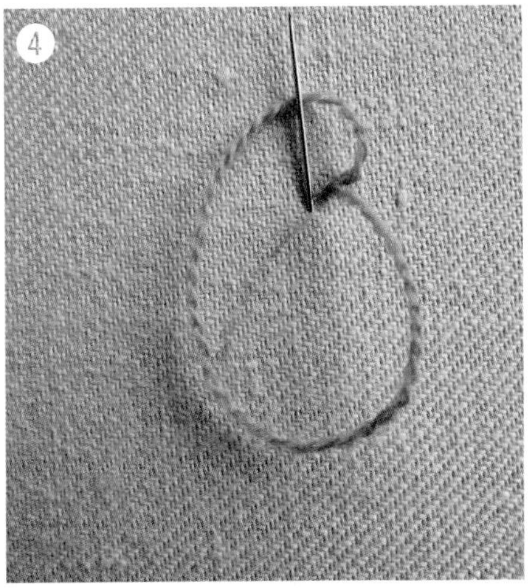

Again bring the needle up in the loop just below the previous stitch and the all of the thread through.

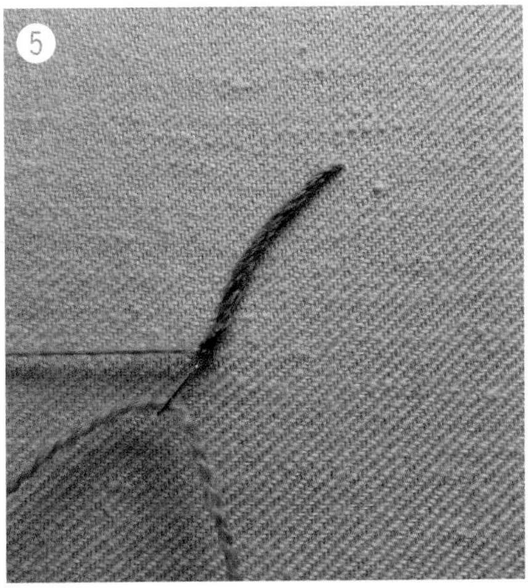

Continue making stitches in this way, ensuring that the line is smooth and the stitches lay flat. At the end of the paintline, plunge the needle over the last loop to catch it in place.

Chapter 8

Accent Stitches

Accent stitches are used to add a splash of colour or a fine detail within a piece. They are usually the last stitches to be worked and can be used to balance the placement of colour. Some of the following stitches can also be used as a form of seeding or to embellish trellis, or can be worked closely together to fill an area and create an interesting texture.

Beetle Stitch

This stitch creates a raised area that can be used to represent small insects such as beetles or ladybirds. With the addition of a diagonal stitch in green, it can be turned into a small flower bud.

Working with two threads in the needle, make a short straight stitch in the fabric.

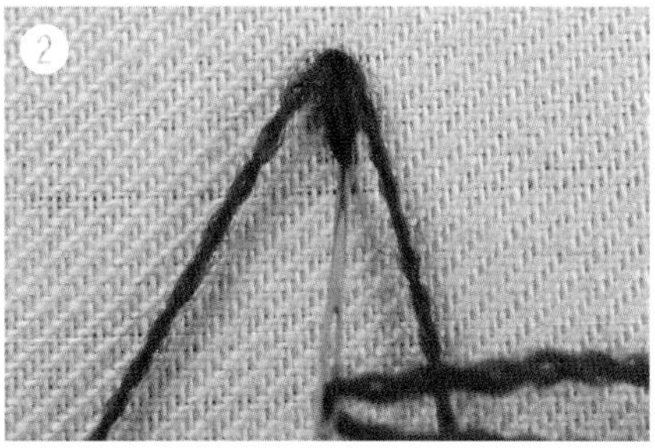

Bring the needle back up at the top of the stitch and plunge at the base. As the thread is pulled through to the back, separate the strands and guide them to either side of the first stitch.

Repeat this stitch several times, bringing the needle up at the top of the stitch, plunging at the base of the stitch and guiding the strands around the previous stitches.

Keep adding stitches until the desired size and shape is made, ensuring that holes do not form at the top and base of the stitch due to the large number of threads coming up through the fabric.

Designed and worked by Helen Richman, this piece uses accent stitches to create detail and texture.

French Knots

French Knots are a great accent stitch. They can be used to embellish trellis or make fine detail such as eyes on an animal. This example is worked in a single strand of thread; working in multiple strands will result in a bigger knot.

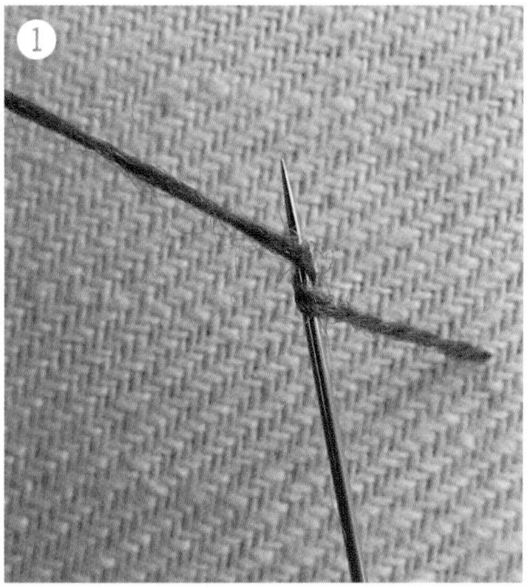

Bring the needle up through the fabric and wrap the thread around the needle once.

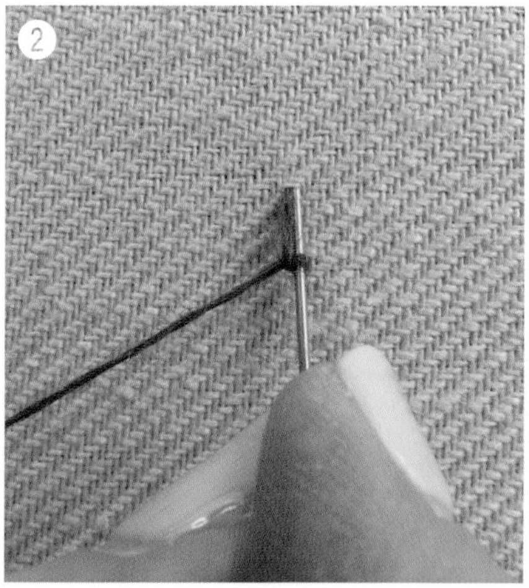

Plunge the needle back through the fabric next to where the thread comes out. Do not plunge back through the same hole.

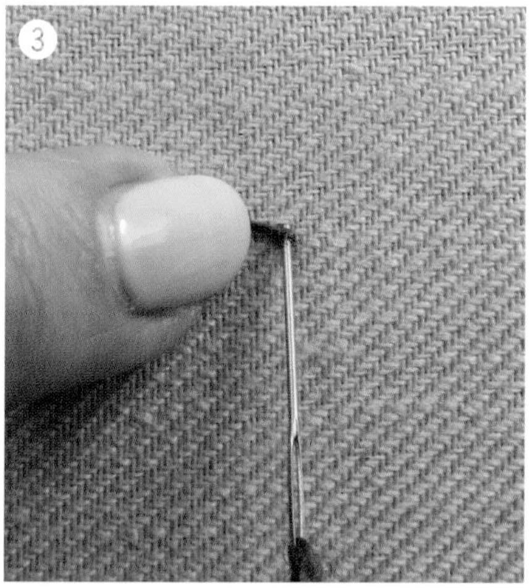

Pull the wrap tight and place a fingertip on the thread up against the needle to hold the tension in place.

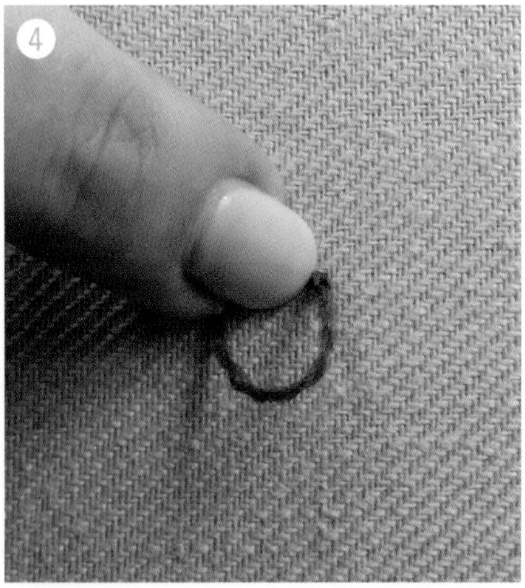

Gently pull the thread through the fabric to form the knot. Do not release the tension until the knot is properly formed.

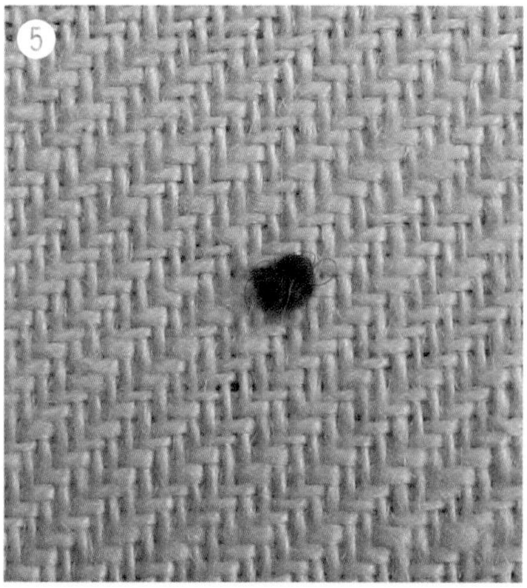

Take care not to pull too hard on the thread as this may cause the knot to disappear to the back of the fabric. When completed, there should be no loose threads.

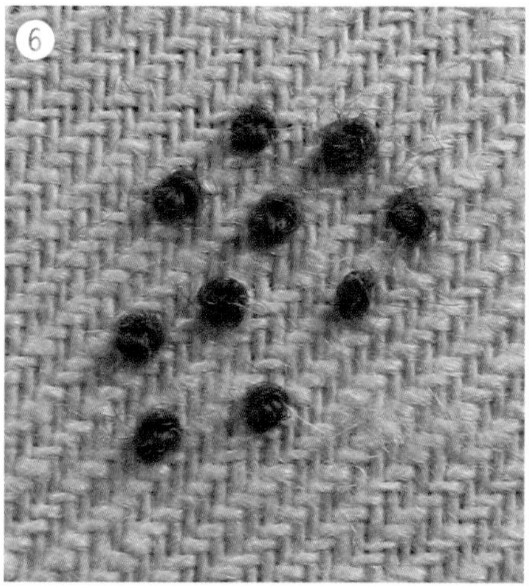

French Knots create an interesting texture when clustered together, or can be scattered about as a form of seeding.

Bullion Knots

Bullions Knots are another option for embellishing trellis. They can also be worked over very small shapes or packed together to make an interesting texture. This example is worked with a single strand of thread; working with multiple strands will result in a bigger knot.

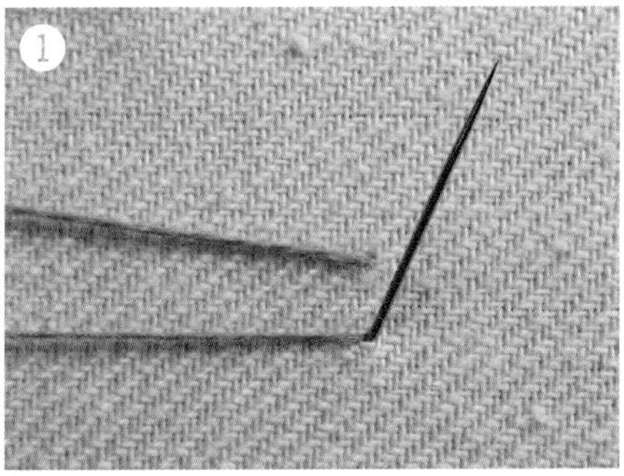

Bring the needle up in the fabric and plunge a short distance away. Do not pull all of the thread through; instead, leave a loop on top. Bring the needle up at the start point but do not pull it all the way through the fabric.

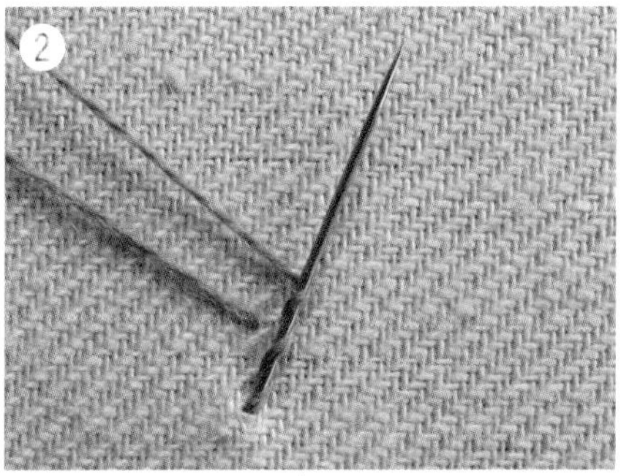

Wrap the thread around the needle multiple times.

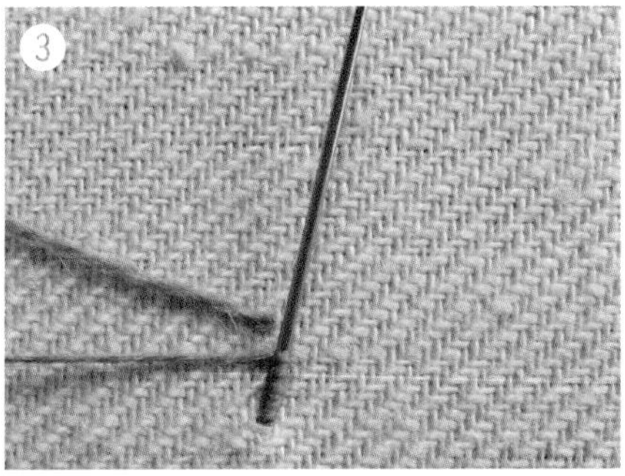

To check there are enough wraps on the needle, push the eye of the needle up to the fabric. This will cause the needle to lie flat on the fabric and you will be able to compare the depth of the wraps made to the distance they need to cover.

Add more wraps if necessary and check again.

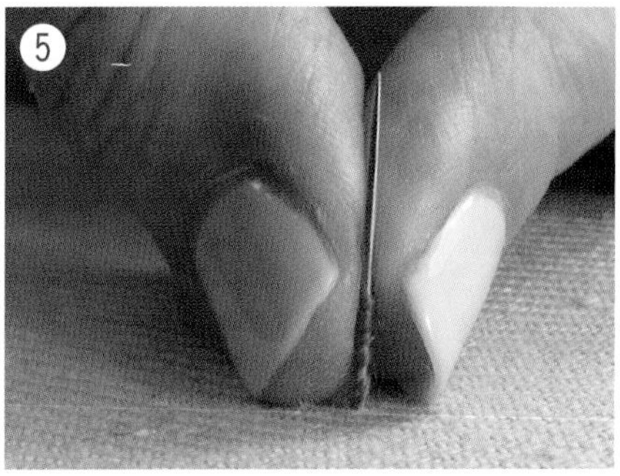

When there are sufficient wraps, pinch the needle between two fingers and gently pull it through the fabric, holding the wraps in place as you do so.

Keep pulling on the thread until the knot is formed. Pulling the thread parallel to the fabric can help to settle the stitch in place. Plunge the needle into place at the end of the stitch.

When completed, the wraps should be tight around the thread, making the knot consistent in shape. This stitch can become easily tangled, resulting in the need to cut the thread. Therefore, when working multiple stitches, it is advisable to work a couple of small stitches under the Bullion Knots to secure the knots already made.

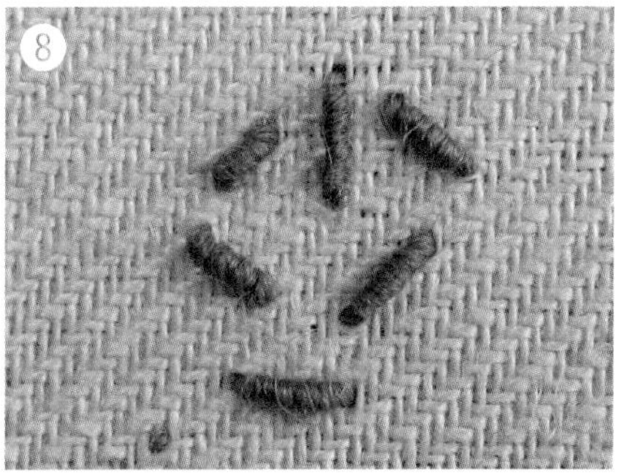

Bullion Knots can be worked in the same way as seeding with equal length stitches at random angles to one another.

Woven Wheel

Woven wheels can be worked in a variety of sizes and are often used as a way of representing berries. The weaving is worked over a foundation of spokes. For this stitch there should be an uneven number of spokes.

There needs to be enough space left within the circle to be able to see the effect of the stitch, so take care not to overcrowd the wheel with too many spokes. Larger shapes will accommodate more spokes.

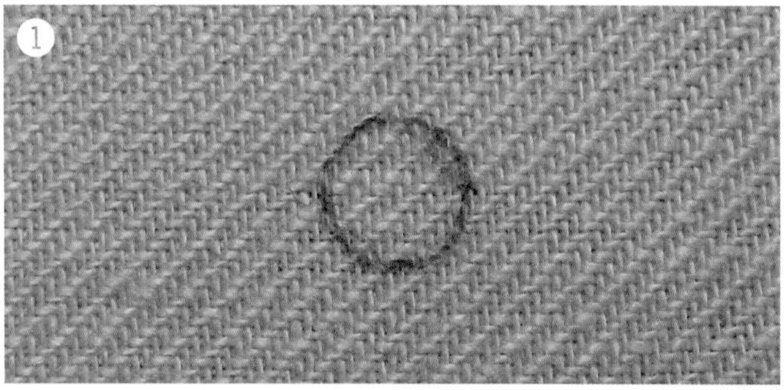

Draw a circle on the fabric. It is best to use a circle template or small circular object to draw around.

Work a Fly Stitch within the shape, taking the stitches to just outside of the paintlines to ensure that they are covered.

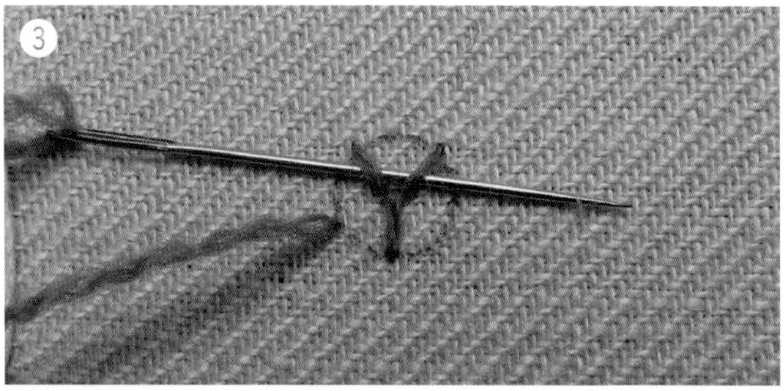

Bring the needle up on one side of the circle. Slide the needle under the Fly Stitch and plunge on the opposite paintline. Take care when working these stitches that the shape is broken up into equal sections.

Bring the needle up in the middle of the shape and make a small catching stitch over the top of the existing stitches to stabilize them and hold them in place.

Cast on a new thread and bring it up in the middle of the wheel. At this point switch to a tapestry needle. Take the thread over the first spoke then slide the needle under the next.

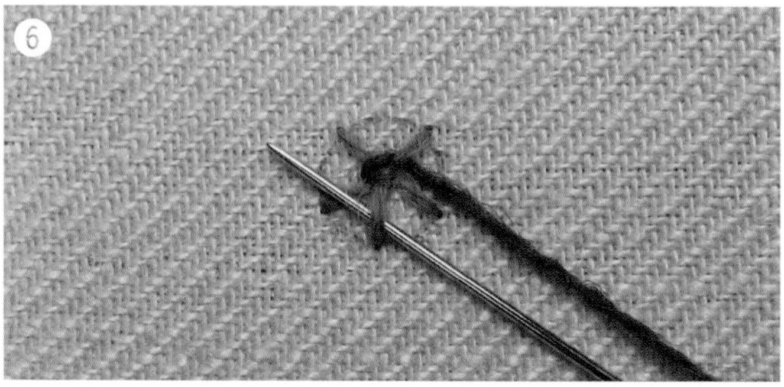

Pull all of the thread through, ensuring that it sits neatly on the fabric without distorting the spokes. Take the thread over this spoke and slide the needle under the next.

When the first row is completed, continue making the stitches in the same way. The thread should lie over the spoke that the needle has gone under in the previous row.

Keeping working around the wheel to fill the space. Pulling firmly on the thread will pack the rows in and create a raised effect. Leaving the stitches a little looser will create a slightly flatter stitch; however, the thread should not lift up off the fabric in loops.

When completed, plunge the needle under the next appropriate spoke and cast off. This example has been worked in two contrasting colours to demonstrate the stitch. The foundation spokes would usually be worked in the same colour as the top stitches.

This stitch can be worked in multiple colours. When doing so, plunge the needle under the next appropriate stitch and cast off the thread. Cast on a new thread and bring it out from underneath the same spoke on the other side. Continue working over and under the spokes until the shape is filled.

Whipped Wheel

Much like the woven wheel, a whipped wheel can be worked in a variety of sizes and can be used to represent berries. The two textures work well together to create an interesting effect. This stitch can be worked over either an even or an odd number of spokes.

There needs to be enough space left within the circle to be able to see the effect of the stitch, so take care not to overcrowd the wheel with too many spokes. Larger shapes will accommodate more spokes.

Draw a circle on the fabric. It is best to use a circle template or small circular object to draw around.

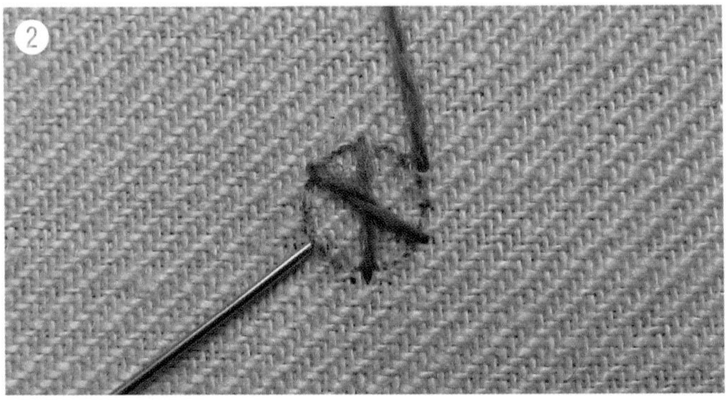

Work a series of straight stitches across the shape. Extend the stitches over the perimeter of the wheel in order to cover the paintlines.

Bring the needle up in the middle of the wheel and make a small stitch over the existing stitches to stabilize and secure the stitches.

Cast on a new thread and bring the needle up in the middle of the shape. At this point switch to a tapestry needle.

Take the needle over the spoke to the right and slide the needle to the left under this same spoke and the next spoke to the left.

Pull all of the thread through, taking care not to distort the spoke.

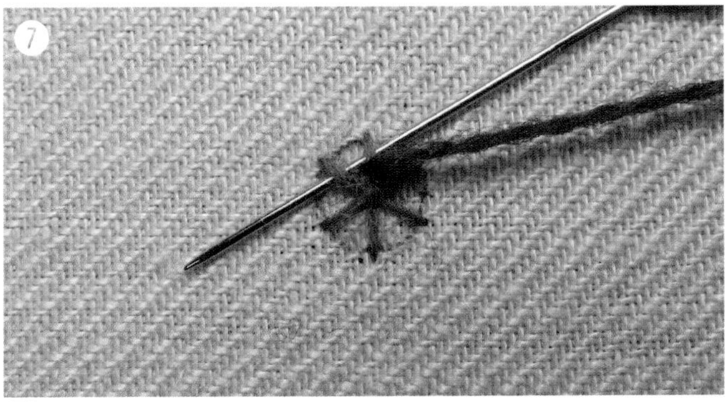

Repeat this process, taking the thread over one spoke to the right and under two spokes to the left. Pull the thread through.

Keep adding rows to fill the shape, taking care to ensure that the wraps around the spoke sit next to each other and not on top of each other.

When completed, take the thread over the last spoke, plunge the needle under it and cast off. This example has been worked in two contrasting colours to demonstrate the stitch. The foundation spokes would usually be worked in the same colour as the as the top stitches.

As with woven wheels, this stitch can be worked in multiple colours. When doing so, plunge the needle under the next appropriate spoke and cast off the thread. Cast on a new thread and bring it out from underneath the same spoke. Then take the thread over this spoke and under the next. Continue adding rows until the shape is filled.

Whipping

Whipping is worked over stitches that are regularly spaced to add an accent of colour and create a new texture. It is important that the stitches in the foundation row are consistent in size, as any variation will be emphasized by the whipping. This example is worked over a foundation row of Back Stitch

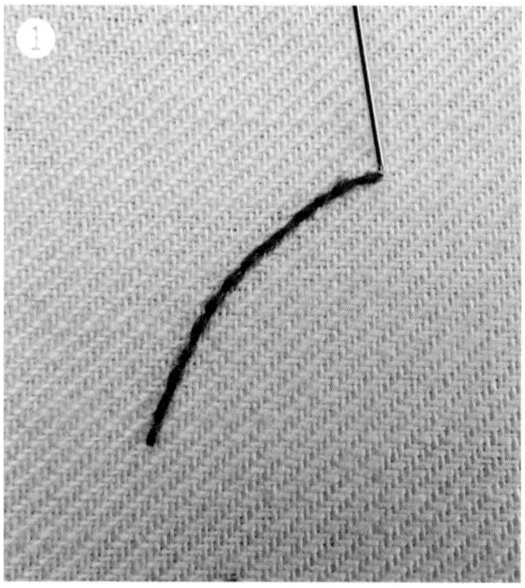

Bring the needle up on one side of the Back Stitch and switch to a tapestry needle.

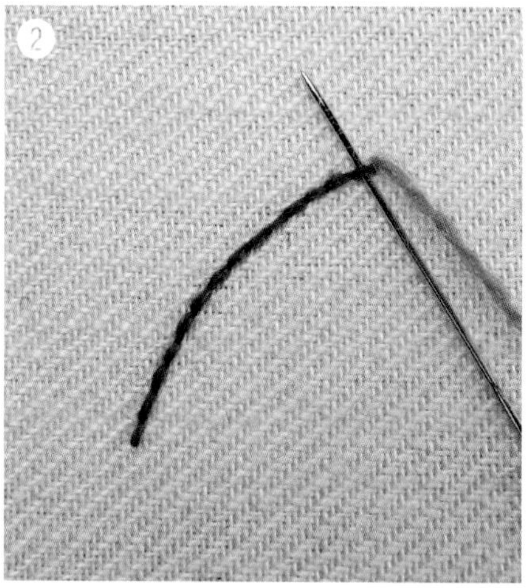

Take the needle and thread over the row of stitching and slide the needle underneath the first stitch.

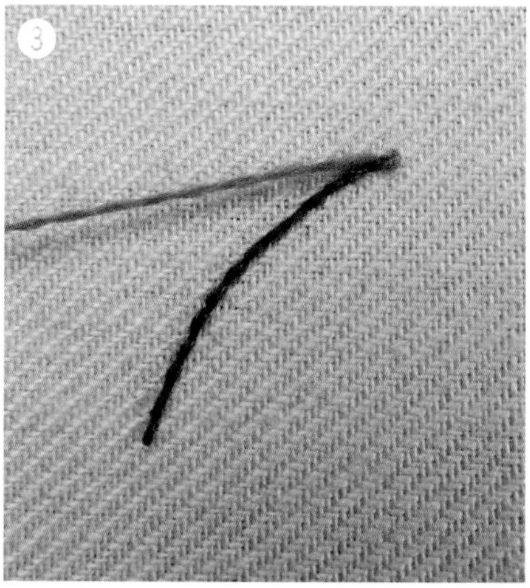

Pull all of the thread through to the other side, ensuring that the foundation stitches are not distorted.

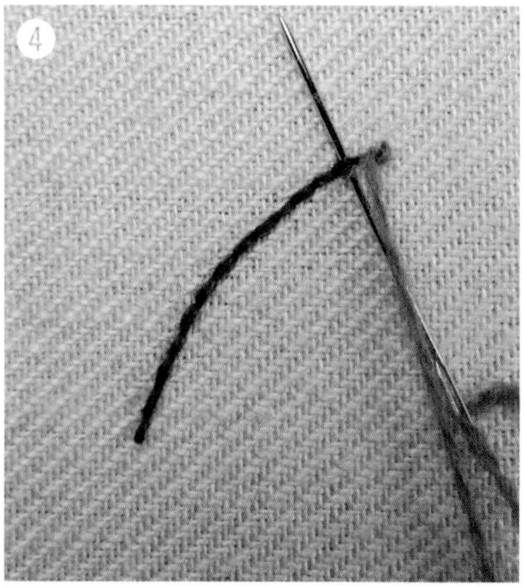

Take the thread over the row of stitching and slide the needle through to the other side.

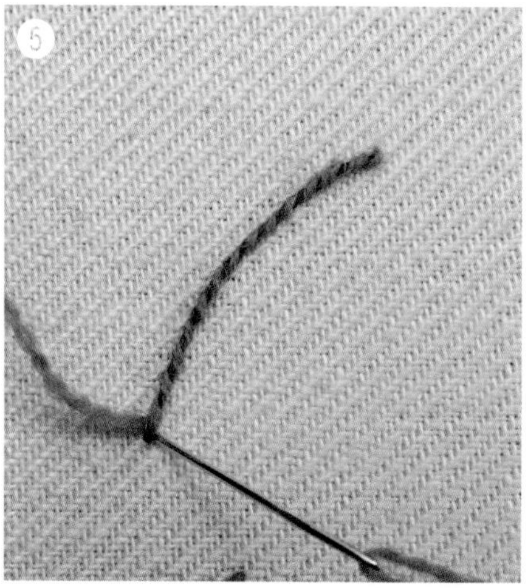

Continue working down the row. When you reach the end, take the needle over to the other side, plunge the needle through the fabric next to the foundation row and cast off.

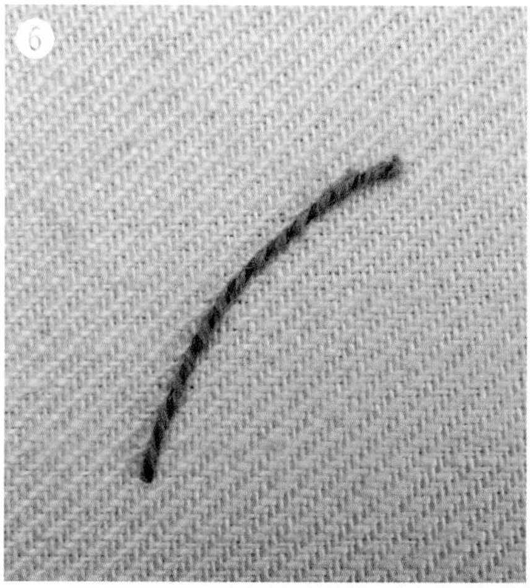

When completed, the stitch should create a diagonal stitch stripe along the foundation row. The bigger the stitch in the foundation row, the longer the stripe will be.

WEAVING

Weaving is worked over stitches that are regularly spaced and creates a frilled effect. Much like whipping, weaving can be used to add a pop of colour. This example is worked over a foundation row of Back Stitch.

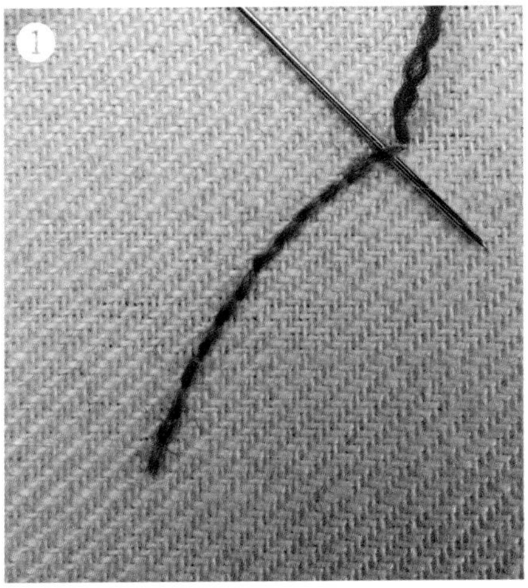

Bring the needle up on one side of the shape and switch to a tapestry needle. Slide the needle under the first stitch on the same side where the needle was brought up.

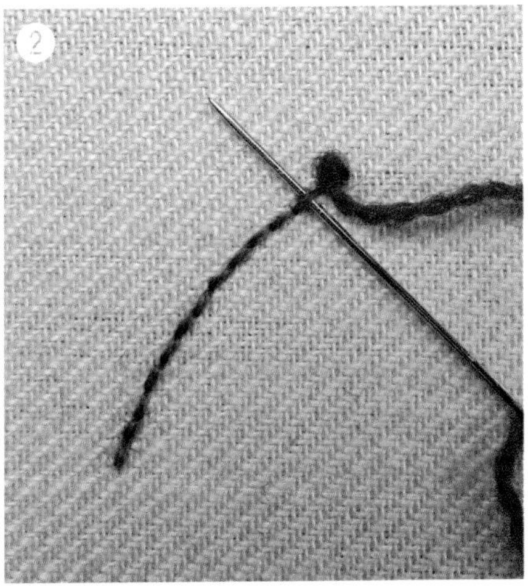

Pull the thread through, leaving a small loop, then slide the needle under the next stitch.

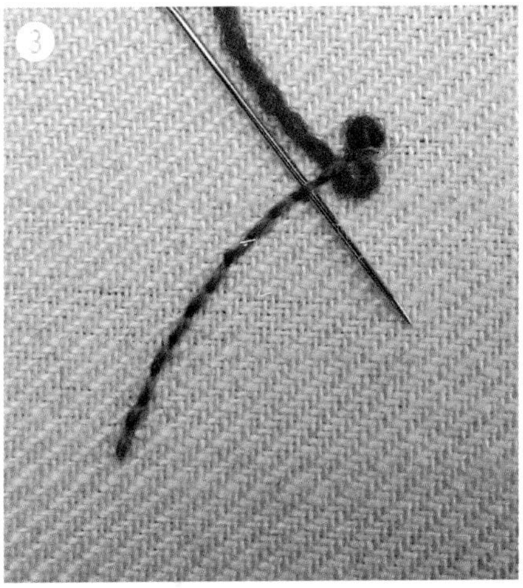

Pull most of the thread through, leaving a small loop. Continue working from side to side down the foundation row, plunging the needle through the fabric at the base of the row.

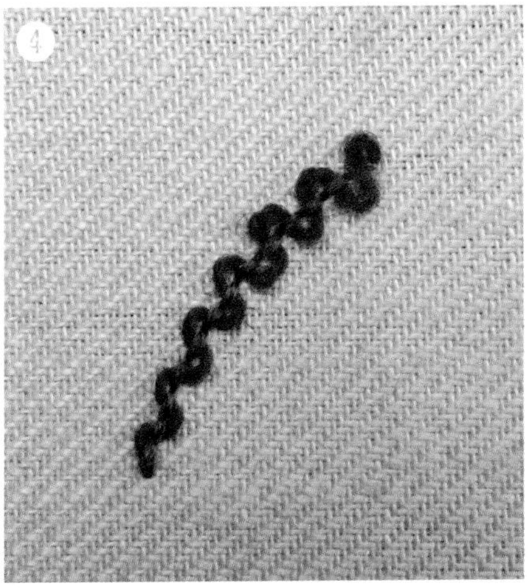

This example shows the loops or frill worked so that they diminish in size to create a sense of disappearing perspective. However, the loops can also be worked to a consistent size. Smaller loops will create a finer, more discreet effect, whilst larger loops create a bold and striking detail.

CHAPTER 9

VARIATIONS AND CREATIVE STITCHES

There are too many stitches to document in a single book, and for every stitch there are one or more variations. The following pages include a number of creative ideas to give you an idea of the broad scope of effects that can be achieved with surface stitches. The Internet can be a useful resource when looking for new stitches; there are many enthusiasts and experts who are exploring and sharing stitches through various blogs and websites. These variations can create greater interest by using new textures within a piece and may inspire the stitcher to be more creative in what they do.

One of the most exciting aspects of embroidery is taking different stitches and working them in combination with each other. For instance, what effect will be created if Open Chain Stitch was used to couch down a bundle of threads? The best way to test these ideas is with sampling; this is the term given to practising stitches and combinations. Sampling is highly recommended as a way of troubleshooting any issues before they arise when working a piece of crewelwork. If the sampled stitches don't work, the idea can be abandoned with no damage done to the main piece. The tradition of sampling started as a way for the stitcher to learn stitches and then have an example of them to refer back to. This often took the form of a long, thin strip of fabric that would be rolled up and placed in a work basket. Additional pieces of fabric could be added when necessary and new stitches included as they were learnt from books or other stitchers. The same principle can be applied today, using pieces of scrap fabric and leftover threads. It is important to annotate these experiments in order to be able to effectively recreate them in future projects.

Have a notebook and pencil to hand when stitching to keep a record of creative ideas.

When reading through this chapter, it is best to have a notepad and pencil handy to write down ideas to sample later. Consider which stitches could be combined to create a new detail.

Designed and worked by the author, this motif uses three stitches to create a simple but charming piece.

Filling Stitches

Trellis

Trellis can benefit from embellishment or simply be left plain. Traditionally, it is worked to create a grid of squares, which doesn't have to sit in line with the fabric (however novice stitchers will find this a useful way of regulating the spacing). Setting the trellis at an angle can help to draw the eye through a piece.

Tweaking the traditional format of working this stitch in a square can create some stunning results. For instance, adjusting the angle slightly can result in a diamond trellis, or even a disappearing perspective with the grid starting smaller at one end of a shape and becoming larger at the other. In the right context, a grid of rectangles could be just as striking as the traditional grid of squares.

Below are instructions for two interesting variations of trellis that can create depth and detail within a piece.

Battlement Couching

This form of trellis can be used to fill an area without additional embellishment. Using a single range of colours will create depth and draw the eye through the piece.

Work the first two layers of trellis. It should be quite large to accommodate multiple layers. Do not catch the threads down.

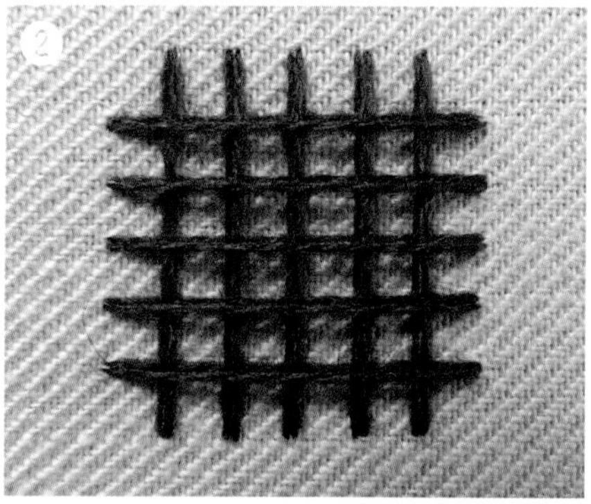

Work another full trellis over the top, taking care to bring the needle up next to the original stitches so that the first grid can be seen. Take care to place the new stitches on the same side of the original stitches each time.

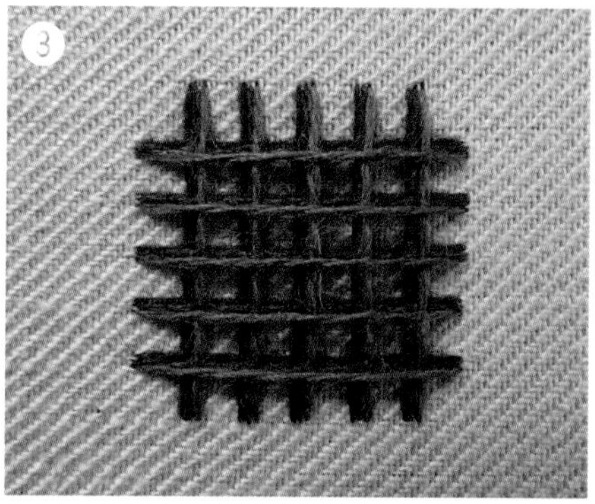

Work a third layer in the same way. Three is the minimum number of layers needed to create the effect, but it is preferable to work more layers than this. Keep in mind that multiple layers require a bigger starting trellis.

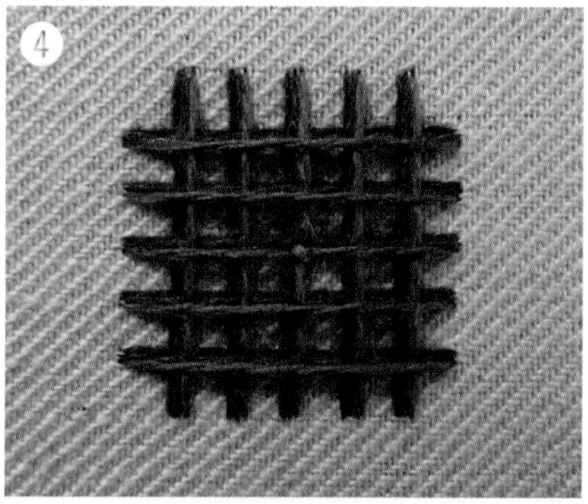

Cast on a new thread and bring the needle up in the middle of the trellis. Make a securing stitch over the top layer of the trellis only. This will pull down the layers and stabilize all of them.

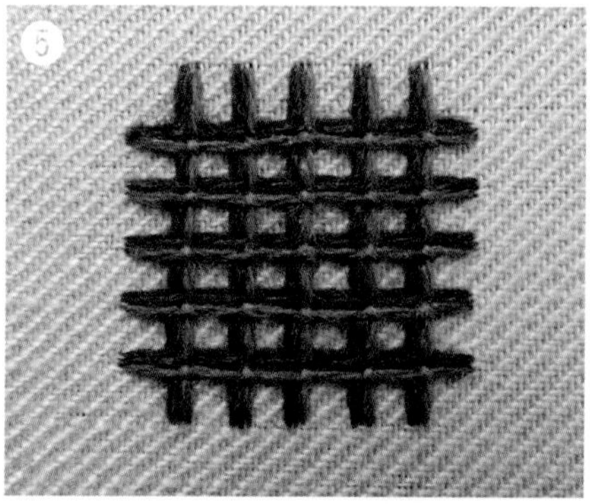

When completed, battlement couching should have the same properties as a regular trellis; the shapes should be even and the threads straight. Consider using more than one colour to secure the trellis, so that the stitches transition from dark to light.

Double Woven Trellis

This unusual filling pattern stands alone to create a pretty effect; additional embellishments are unnecessary.

Work a basic trellis. There is no need to work a securing stitch. Working a slightly larger trellis is preferable.

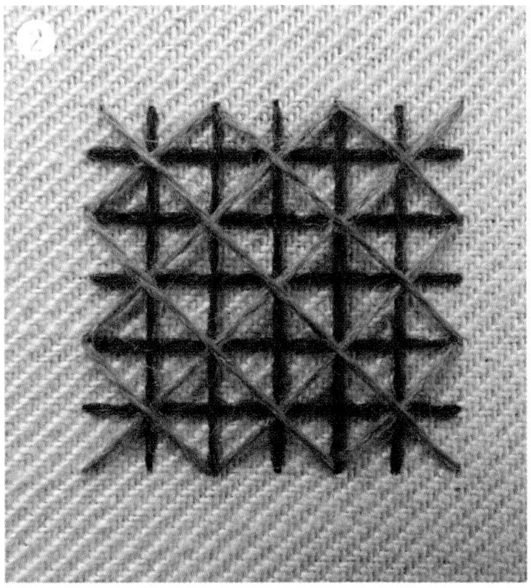

Work another layer of trellis at a 45-degree angle to the first layer. In this example the top trellis is slightly larger than the layer below.

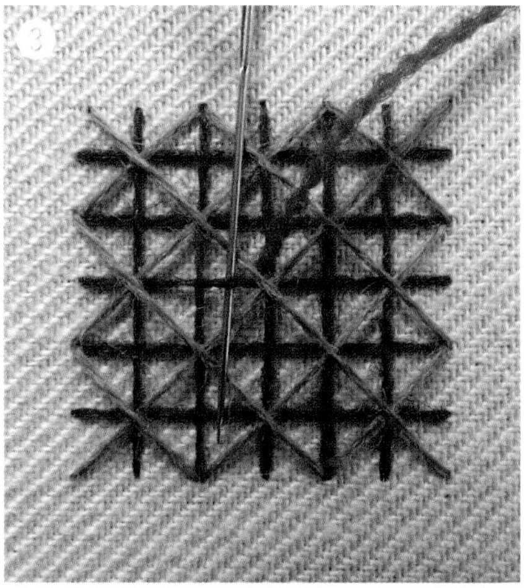

Cast on a new thread and bring the needle up in the middle of the shape where the two layers of trellis intersect. Weave the thread over the top layer and slide the needle under the bottom layer of trellis. This will draw the top layer down to hold the two trellises together.

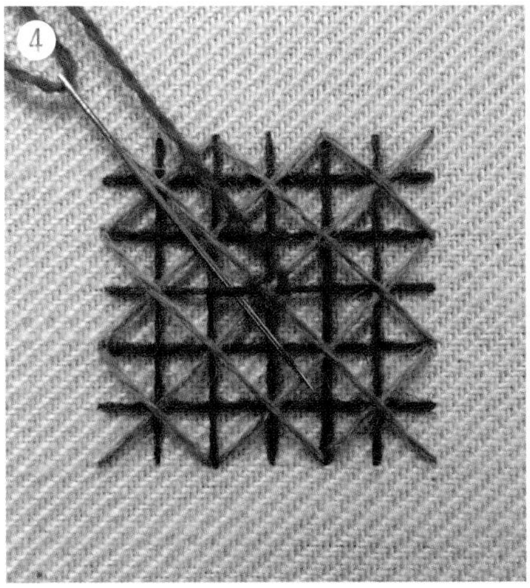

Work around the intersection twice, ensuring that the needle always slides under the lower layer of trellis.

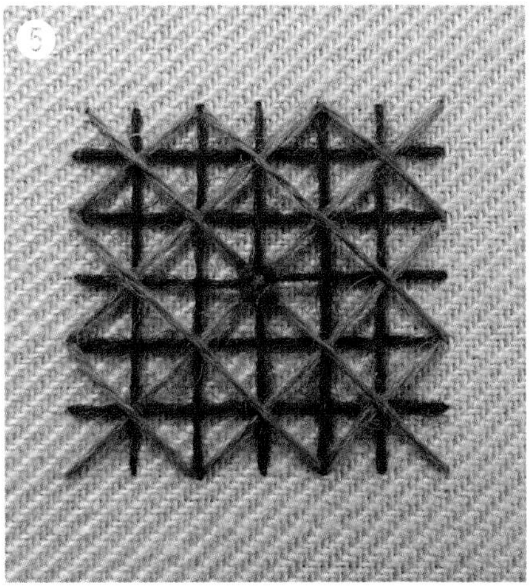

After completing the two rows, plunge the needle through the fabric. Angle the needle slightly under the woven circle to keep the round shape. Bring the needle up at the next intersection of the two layers of trellis.

Repeat this process across the shape, working in a logical fashion either horizontally or vertically. As with other types of embellishment, taking the weaving out to the edges will ensure continuity in the pattern and that no gaps are left at the edges that will draw the eye.

Long Armed Feather Stitch

This variation of Feather Stitch creates a lovely texture that can be used to fill small shapes. The stitch is made up of a series of offset 'V' shapes; however, in this stitch one arm of the 'V' is longer than the other. It helps to have a central guideline when working this stitch. When drawing this line on, take care to do so lightly as there is a possibility that any marks could be seen once the stitch is worked.

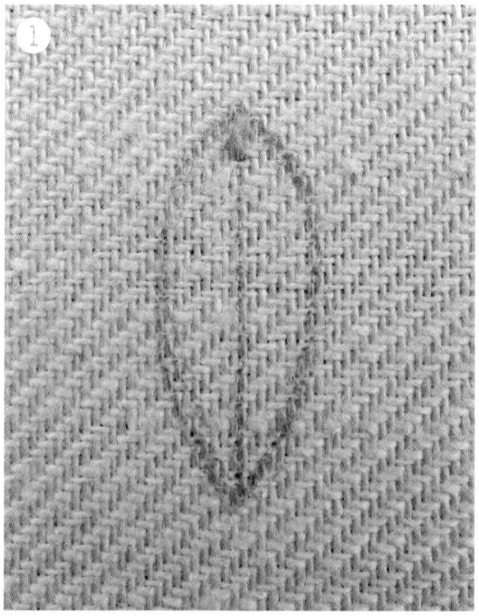

Bring the needle up on the top paintline in the middle of the shape. Make a straight stitch down the middle along the central guide line.

Bring the needle back up on one side of the straight stitch and plunge on the other. Do not pull all of the thread through; instead, leave a loop on top. Bring the needle up at the base of the straight stitch and through the loop.

Pull all of the thread through until the stitch lies flat against the fabric. Plunge the needle on the right-hand paintline a short distance away from the last stitch.

Do not pull all of the thread through; instead, leave a loop on top. Bring the needle up on the guideline and through the loop a short distance away from the last stitch.

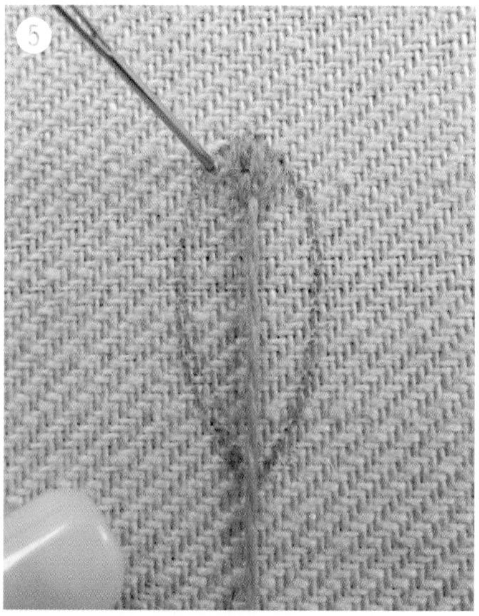

Pull all of the thread through until the stitch lies flat on the fabric. Plunge the needle on the left-hand paintline.

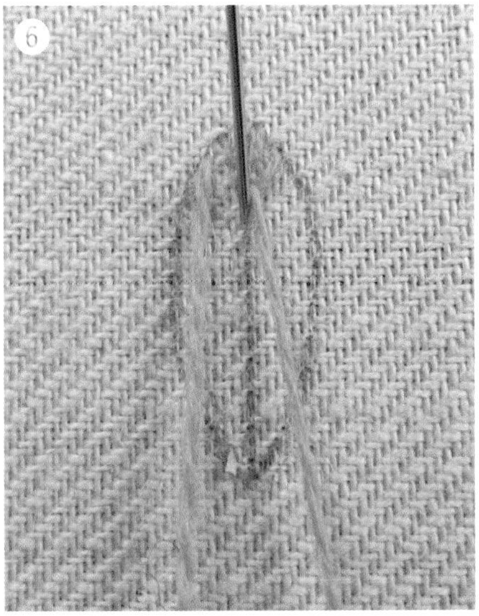

Bring the needle up on the guideline and through the loop. Pull all of the thread through until the stitch lies flat on the fabric.

Continue making stitches in this way, alternating between plunging the needle on the left and right. Try to keep the spacing between stitches consistent.

Once the shape is full, take the needle down over the last stitch on the bottom paintline just under where it was brought out. Cast off the thread.

As with Feather Stitch, this variation usually requires an Outline Stitch, but it can also be worked with multiple stitches on each side rather than simply alternating left and right.

If worked closely enough, this stitch may not need an Outline Stitch. It is always important to check whether paintlines are visible once the stitch is completed.

Whipped Band

As with the raised band stitches, this stitch works well in long, narrow spaces. It creates a similar texture to a whipped wheel.

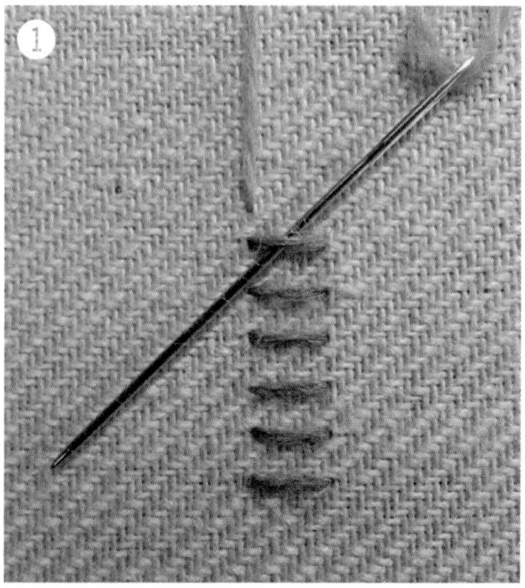

Work a foundation row of straight stitches; these should start just below the top of the shape. Bring the needle up at the top of the shape, then slide it under the first straight stitch from top to bottom.

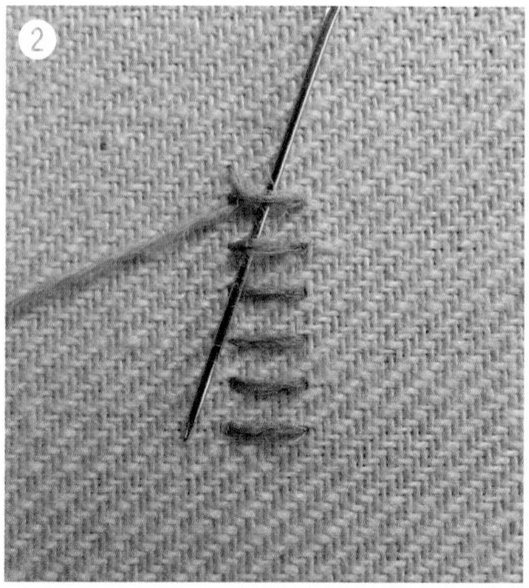

Pull all of the thread through, take the needle and thread back over the first stitch and slide the needle under that stitch and the next straight stitch. Pull all of the thread through, taking care not to distort the foundation row.

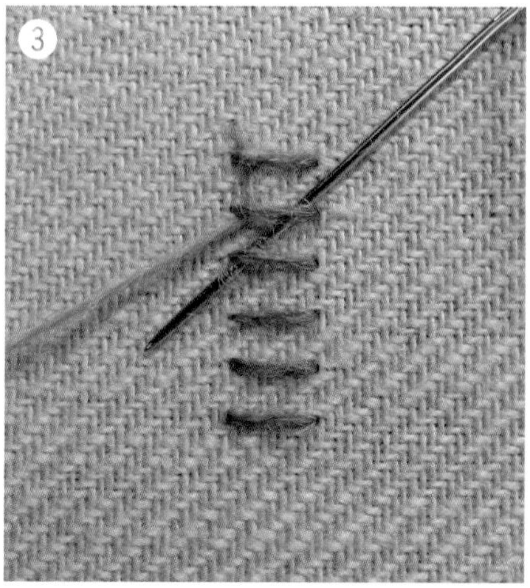

Take the needle up and over the previous straight stitch, slide it under that stitch and the next stitch, then pull all of the thread through.

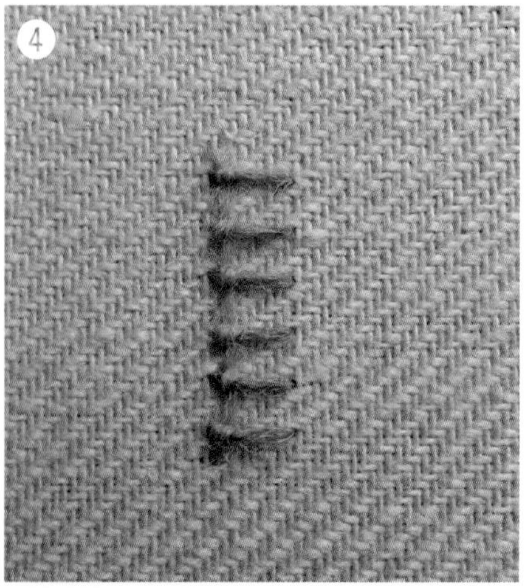

Continue working down the shape in the same way and plunge the needle neatly on the bottom paintline.

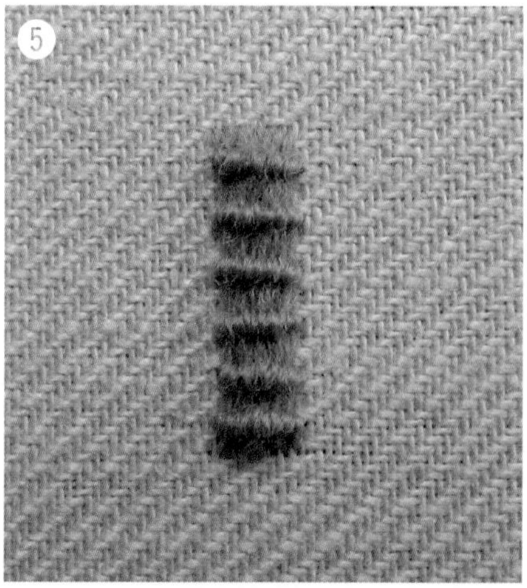

Add rows in the same way until the shape is filled, taking care to ensure that the foundation rows are not distorted. If working this stitch around a curve, remember to space the foundation row accordingly.

Woven Band

Consider working a woven band in a similar way to a woven wheel.

Fishbone Stitch

A variation of Herringbone Stitch, Fishbone Stitch can be used to fill areas to create a dense effect. Due to the length of the stitch, Fishbone Stitch is not as padded as Herringbone Stitch; however, it works well around steep curves, where Herringbone Stitch will not.

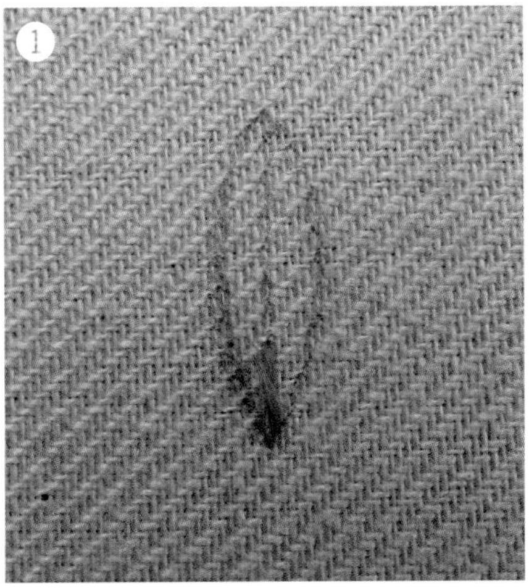

When working this stitch, it is best to use a central guideline; this can be added with a pencil. Bring the needle up at one end of the shape and make a straight stitch along the pencil line.

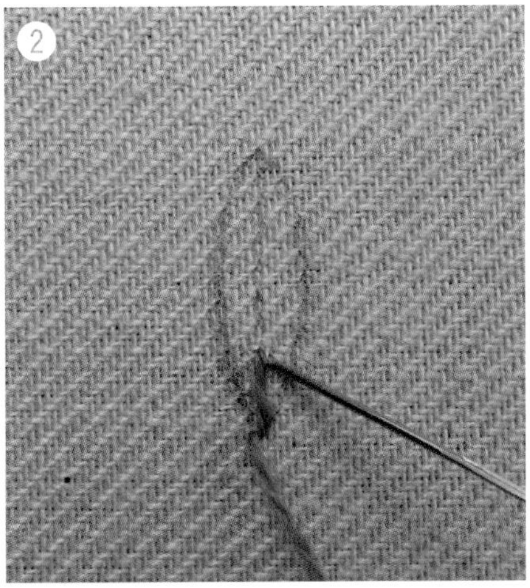

Bring the needle up close to the first stitch on the left-hand side paintline. Plunge the needle, level with the base of the initial stitch, on the right-hand side of the pencil line. Pull all of the thread through.

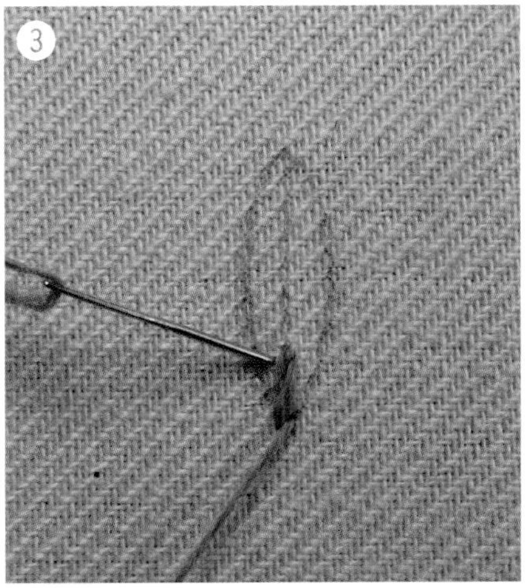

Bring the needle up close to the first stitch, level with the base of the first stitch, but on the left-hand side of the pencil line. Pull all of the thread through.

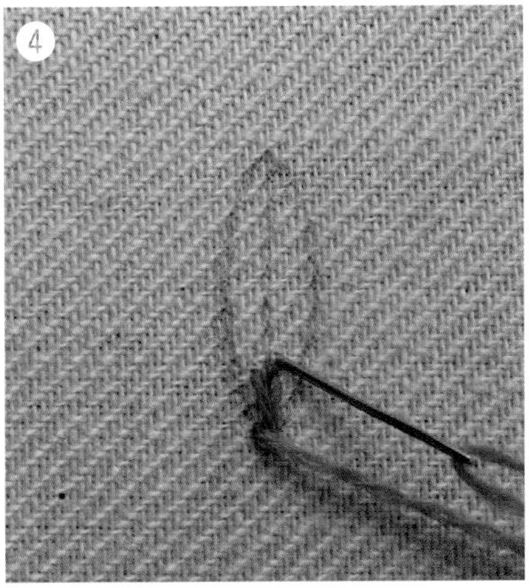

Bring the needle back up on the left-hand paintline close to the second stitch. Plunge the needle on the right-hand side of the pencil line just below the third stitch.

Keep working down the shape, making stitches alternatively on each side of the shape until it is full, then cast off the thread.

Outlining Stitches

When worked in multiple adjoining rows, outlining stitches can be used to fill areas. This can be a useful technique to use when working with stitches such as raised stem band and Stem Stitch. They both have a similar texture but a difference in height; as a result, one will sit lower than the other. This can help to create a sense of perspective.

The examples below show the effect when Chain Stitch, Stem Stitch and Coral Knot Stitch are worked in rows to fill a shape. Consider using other stitches, such as couching, Scroll Stitch or Portuguese Knotted Stem, in the same way. Buttonhole Stitch works particularly well in a scalloped shape, worked either open or closed.

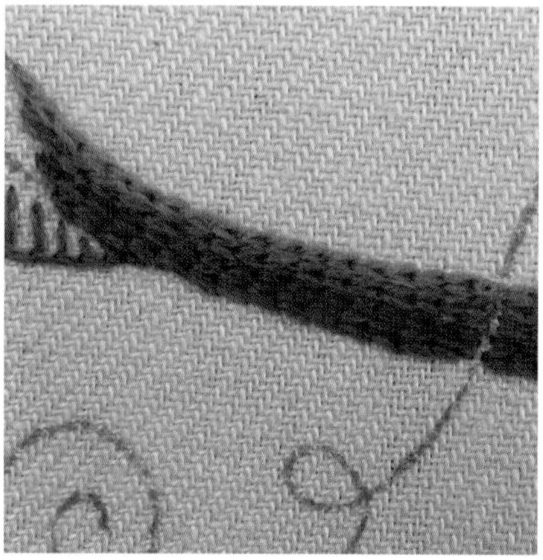

Chain stitch used to fill an area creates a rough texture that is ideal for trees or bark.

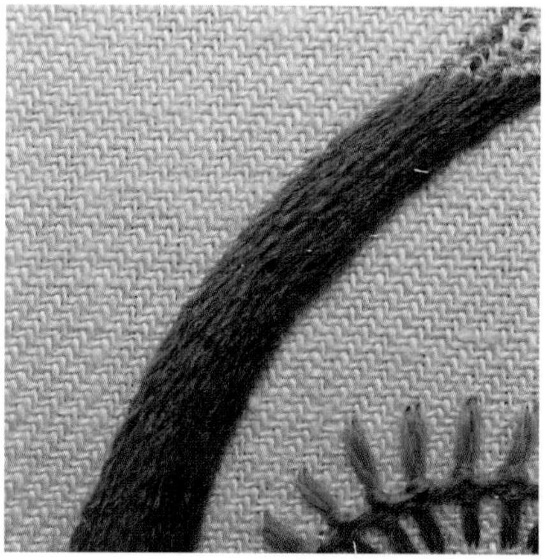

Stem Stitch creates a slightly smoother texture, and can be worked in rows as Stem Stitch or Outline Stitch. Consider working alternating rows of both.

Coral Knot Stitch is worked in offset rows. Knots are placed level with the bars on the previous row.

THORN STITCH

This is a form of couching that can create a decorative touch or be used to fill small shapes.

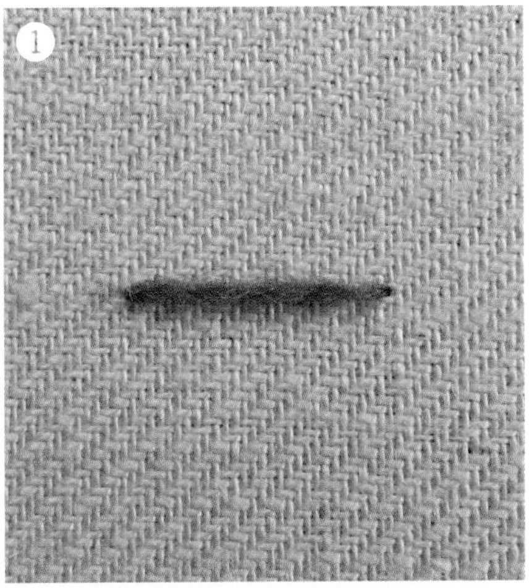

Make a straight stitch on the fabric.

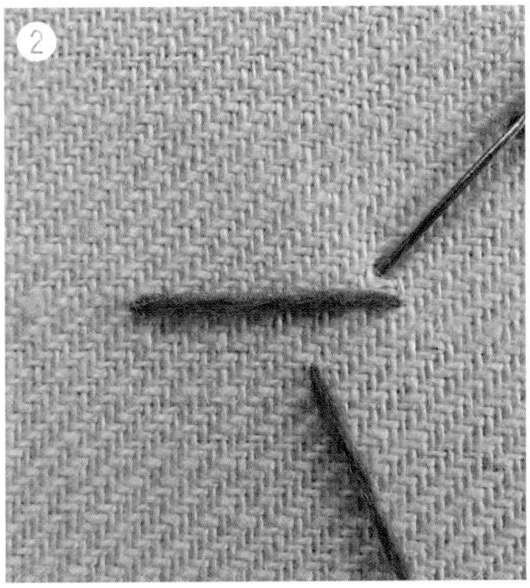

Bring the needle up away from the first stitch and plunge over and away from it. A diagonal stitch should be created.

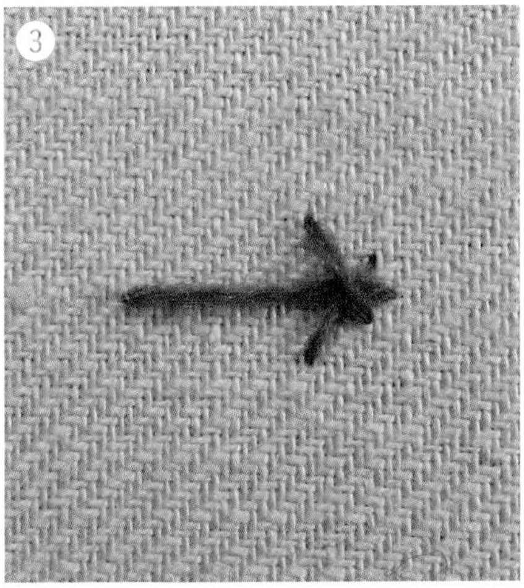

Come up on the other side and repeat the process, plunging to create a diagonal stitch. This should mirror the other side.

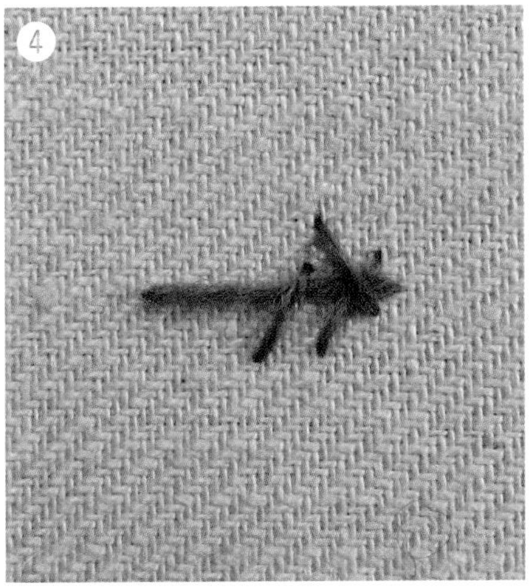

Work additional stitches along the straight stitch. Consider where the needle is brought up to create a slightly oval shape.

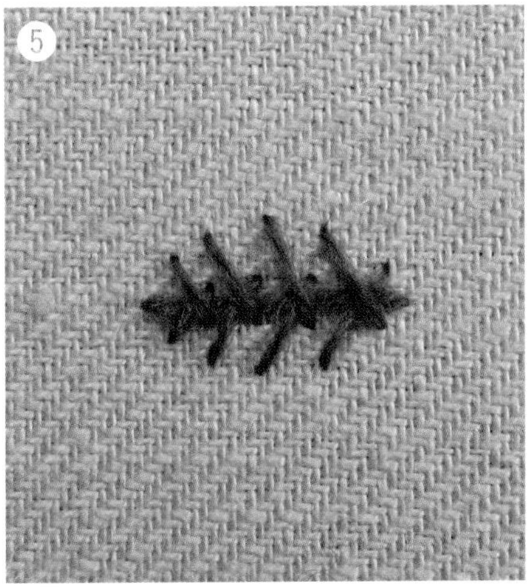

If working to a paintline, you will need to work an Outline Stitch.

Puffy Couching

This is a variation of couching that creates an unusual outline and works well for most shapes.

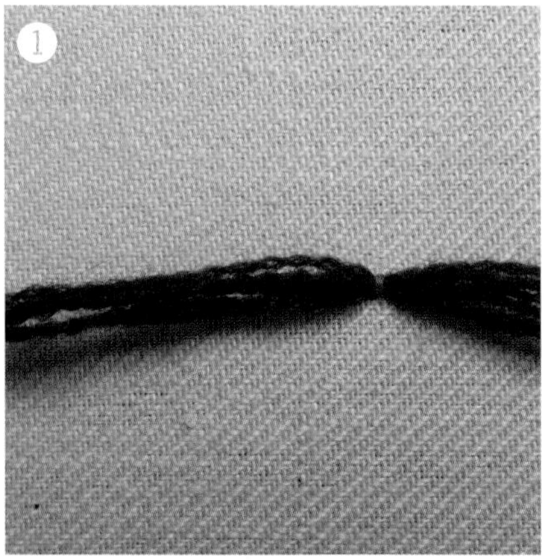

Lay a bundle of threads on the fabric; in this example six threads have been used. Bring the needle up on one side of the threads and plunge on the other. Make the Couching Stitch quite small in order to 'pinch' the threads together; this will exaggerate the puffs.

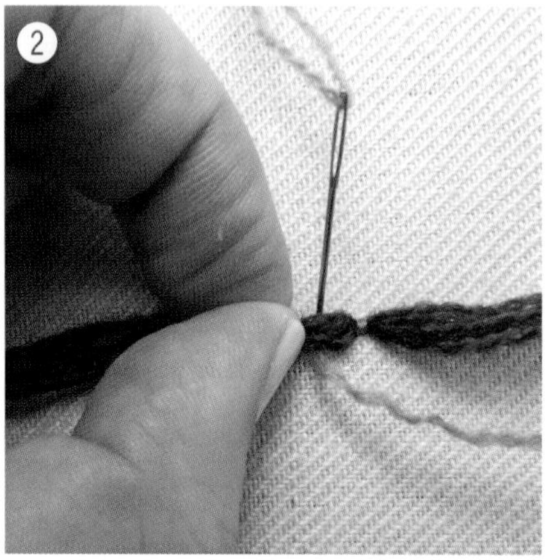

Bring the needle back up a little further along the shape. Pinch the couching threads and push them back slightly towards the last stitch; this will increase the amount of thread between the two stitches. Plunge the needle down over the couched threads to catch them in place.

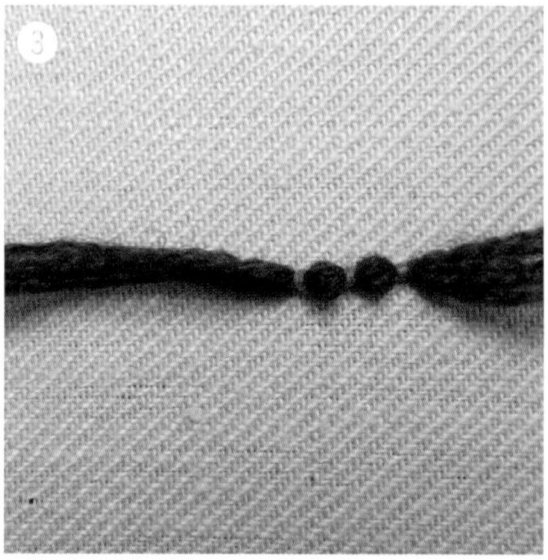

Bring the needle back up further along the shape. Take care to make the distances between the stitches consistent to create a better finish. Repeat the process of pinching and pushing back the couched threads and make the stitch.

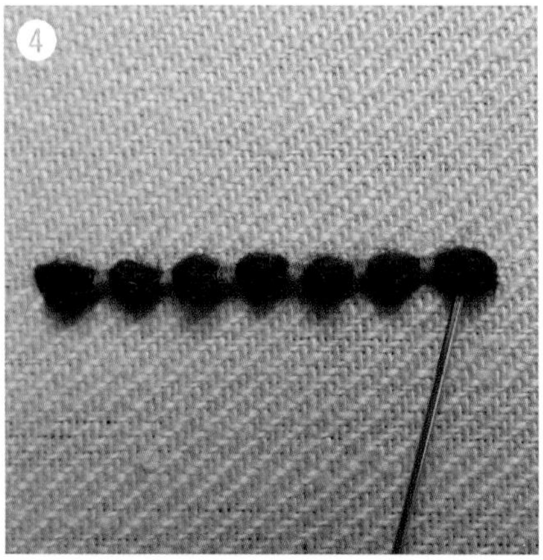

Continue working along the shape. When you are finished, cast off the couching thread and, if necessary, use the eye of the needle to adjust the puffs. When finished, thread the couched threads onto a needle and plunge through neatly to the back. These ends can be woven through the stitching on the back.

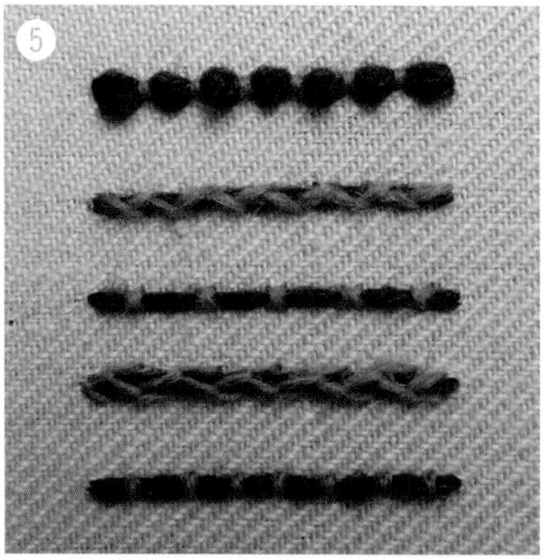

Try experimenting with different stitches to catch down couching. This example shows, from top to bottom: puffy couching, Herringbone Stitch, Cross Stitch, Feather Stitch and Pistol Stitch. Other stitches that could be used are Bullion Knots, Coral Knot Stitch worked in a zigzag fashion, Buttonhole Stitch or Open Chain Stitch.

Open Chain Stitch

Open Chain Stitch is worked in the same way as Chain Stitch. It can be tricky to cover paintlines with this stitch due to its open nature.

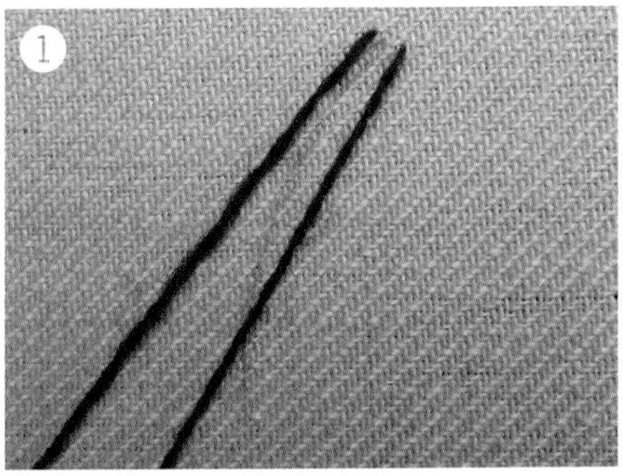

Bring the needle up on the left and plunge down on the right, leaving a gap between these points. Do not pull all of the thread through; instead, leave a loop on top.

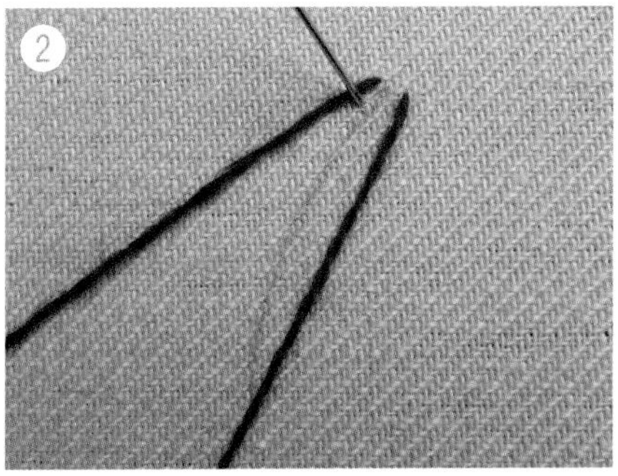

Bring the needle up a short distance below on the left and through the loop. Pull the thread and settle the stitch into place.

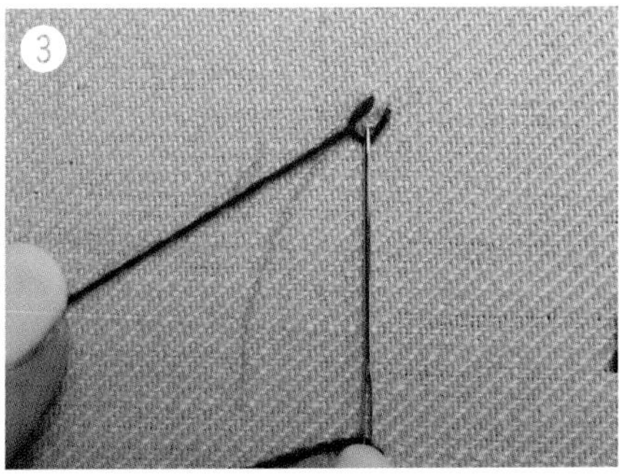

Plunge the needle within the loop on the right-hand side; there should be a gap of fabric between these two points. This should create a 'U' shape. Do not pull all of the thread through; instead, leave a loop on top.

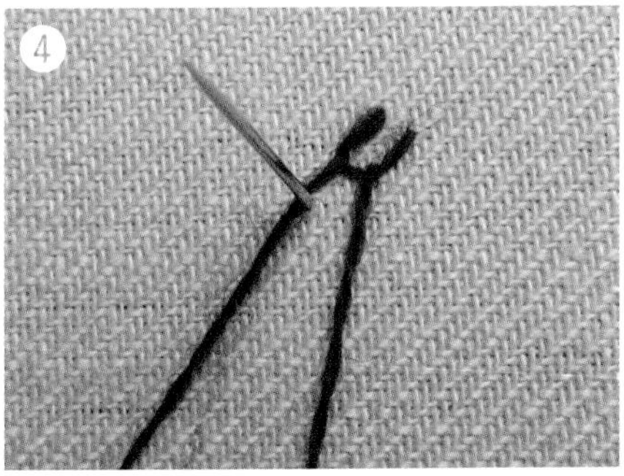

Bring the needle up on the left and through the loop. Pull the thread to tighten the stitch and settle it into place.

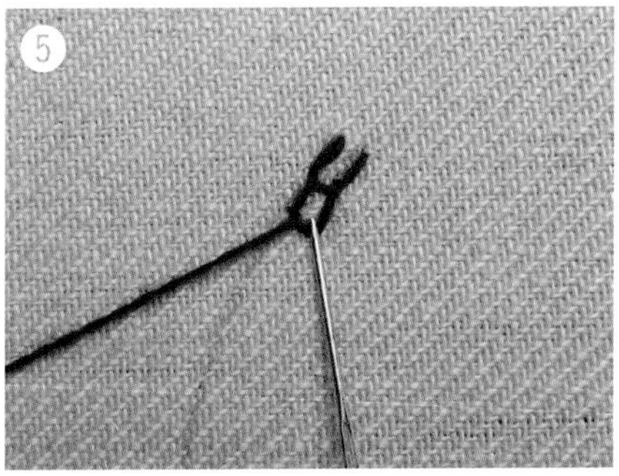

Plunge the needle through the loop on the right-hand side leaving a gap between where the needle was brought up and plunged down.

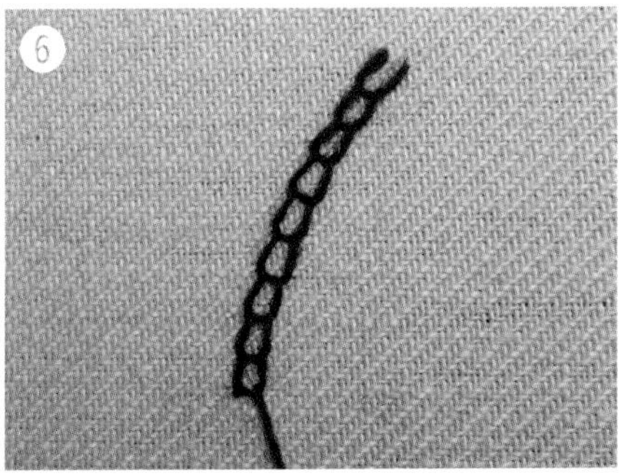

Continue working the stitch in this way. To finish, take the needle over the last loop, on the left-hand side, to secure it in place. Bring the needle up through the loop on the right-hand side and pass the needle over the edge of the last stitch to secure the right-hand side in place. Cast off the thread.

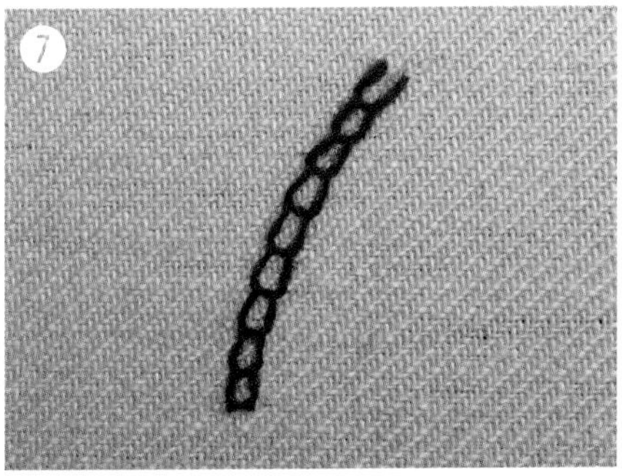

When completed, the stitch creates a ladder-like effect.

Heavy Chain Stitch

This stitch creates a heavier outline with an interesting feather-like texture. Take care not to catch other stitches when working it.

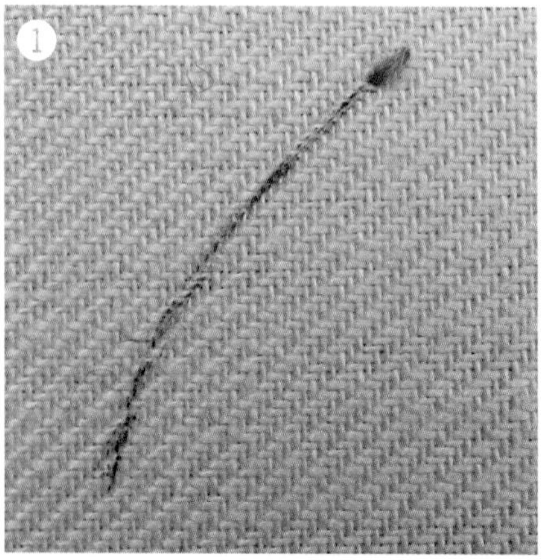

Bring the needle up at the start of the paintline and make a small straight stitch.

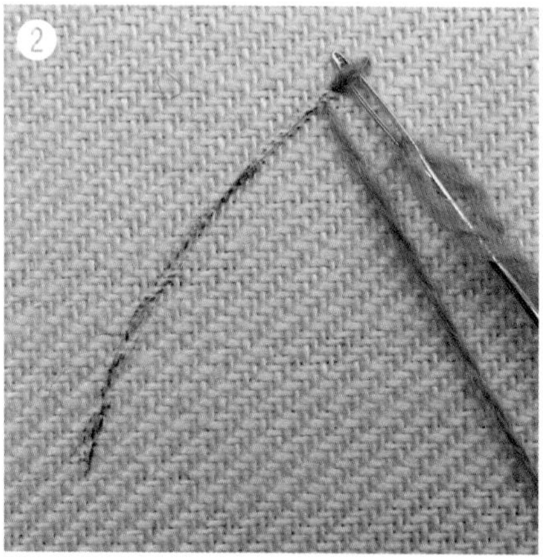

Bring the needle up on the paintline, below the first stitch. Slide the needle under the straight stitch. Consider using the eye of the needle to do this to prevent splitting the thread.

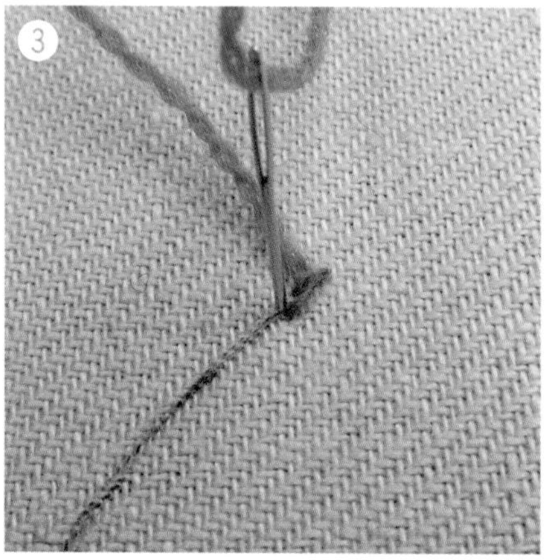

Pull all of the thread through and plunge the needle down where it was just brought out. Then pull all of the thread through to the back. This creates the first Chain Stitch.

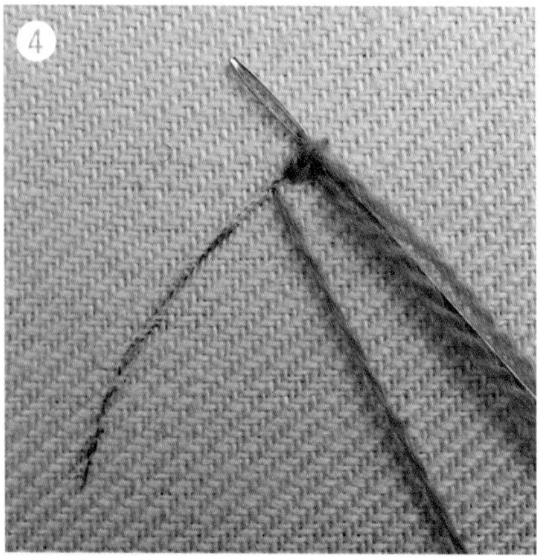

Bring the needle up on the paintline just below the last stitch. Slide the needle under the straight stitch. Pull all of the thread through and plunge where the needle was just brought out. This creates the second Chain Stitch.

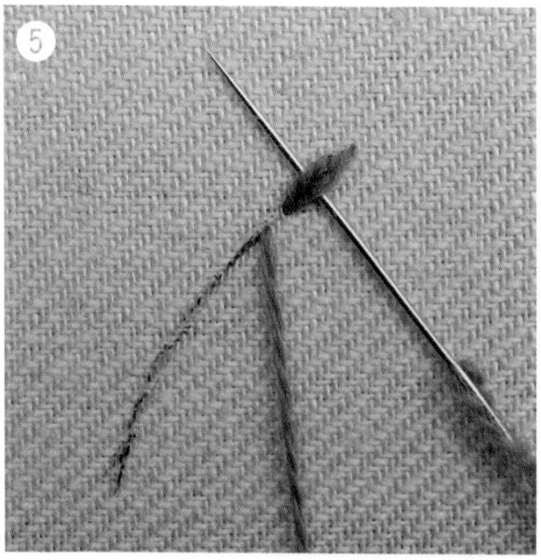

Bring the needle up on the paintline and slide the needle under the first Chain Stitch (the next-but-one stitch from the needle) and plunge where it was just brought out.

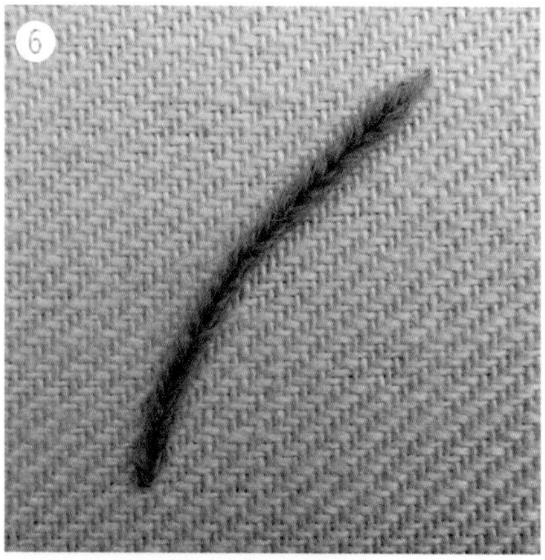

Continue working along the paintline in this manner, always taking the needle underneath the next-but-one stitch from the needle. When completed, the stitch should look like a denser form of Chain Stitch.

Hungarian Braided Chain Stitch

This stitch is very similar to Heavy Chain Stitch but has a braided texture. It creates a heavier outline than Chain Stitch.

Work a straight stitch along the paintline. Bring the needle up just below the stitch and slide the needle under it. Plunge the needle where it was just brought out. Make another stitch in the same way; do not pull it tight.

Bring the needle up a short distance below the previous stitch. Gently ease the thread of the previous stitch out of the way and slide the needle under the stitch below; the new stitch should sit on top of the previous one. Pull the last stitch tight and pull the thread through. Plunge the needle where it was just brought out.

Leaving the previous stitch slightly loose, slide the needle under the stitch underneath it. Pull the previous stitch tight, pull the needle and thread through, and plunge the needle where it was just brought out.

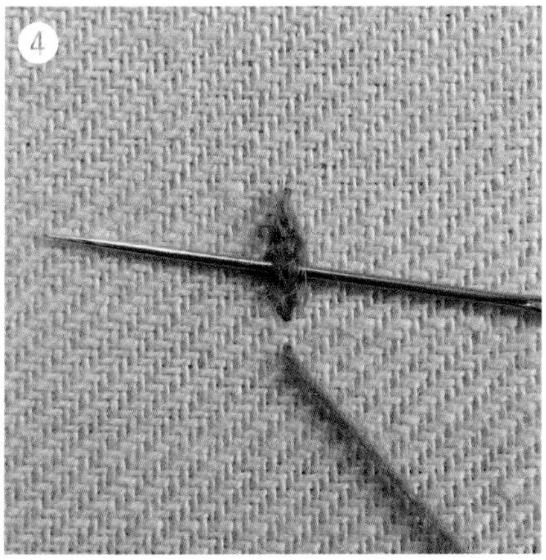

Continue working down the paintline making stitches in this way.

Make one last small stitch, then cast off the thread.

Long Armed Chain Stitch

This is worked as a Detached Chain Stitch with a long holding stitch. It works well to create fine detail or scattered as a form of seeding.

Bring the needle through the fabric and plunge in the same place. Do not pull all of the thread through; instead, leave a loop on top. Bring the needle back up through the loop a short distance below where it was plunged.

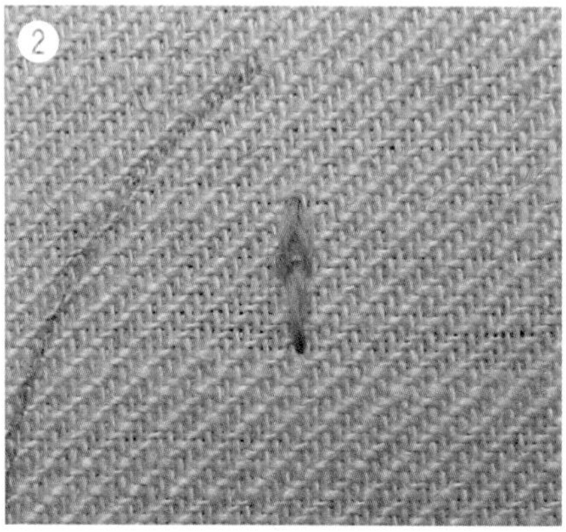

Pull all the thread through to tighten the stitch and settle it into place.

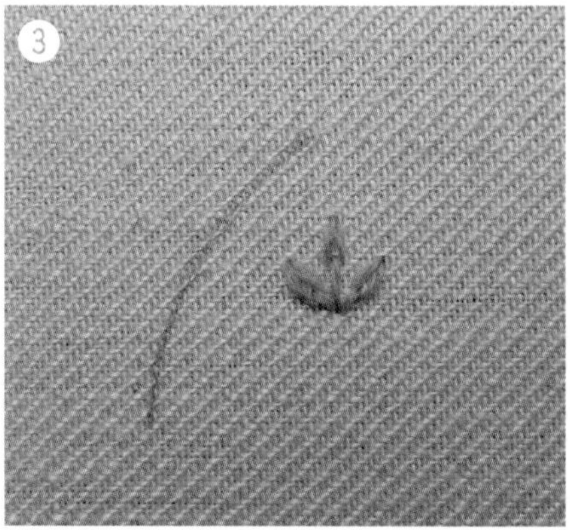

This stitch creates a small bud-like shape. Due to the fine nature of the stitch, it could be challenging to use it to cover paintlines. When worked along a paintline it is referred to as Feathered Chain Stitch.

Feathered Chain Stitch

This stitch creates a delicate vine-like effect that would work well as a wandering tendril. However, it would be difficult to work around a steep curve, or for covering paintlines due to its open nature.

Bring the needle up at start of the line and make a Long Armed Chain Stitch.

Bring the needle up to the left of the first stitch and work another Long Armed Chain Stitch, ensuring the needle is brought up at the bottom of the previous stitch.

Plunge the needle down on the paintline to secure the chain in place. Take care to ensure the long arm is worked at a shallow angle in comparison to the chain. If the angle of the long arm is too steep, the chain will not sit well.

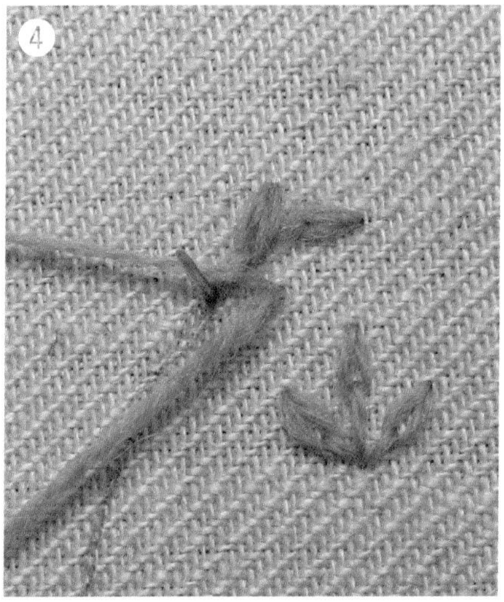

Bring the needle up on the other side of the line to create the next Long Armed Chain Stitch. Continue making stitches in this manner, ending each Chain Stitch at the base of the previous long arm.

When completed, the stitches should look like a small branch of leaves or flower buds. They could be further embellished with other stitches such as detached Fly Stitch or French Knots.

Up and Down Buttonhole Stitch

This two-pronged variation of Buttonhole Stitch works well as an Outline Stitch, filling stitch or wandering tendril. It could be further embellished with Detached Chain Stitch, Long Armed Chain Stitch, French Knots or Pistol Stitch.

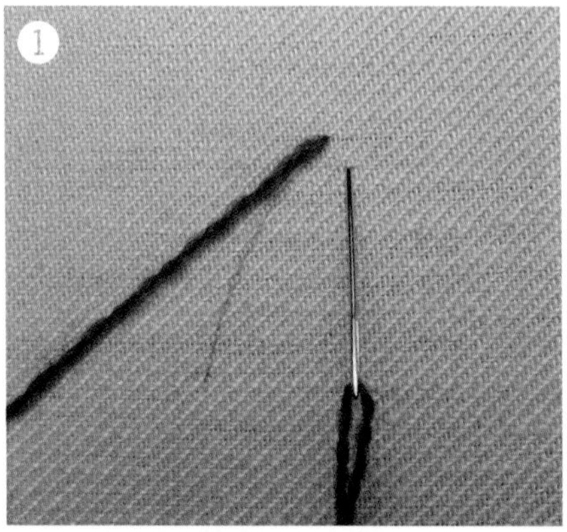

Bring the needle up at one end of the paintline and plunge away from it to one side. Do not pull all of the thread through; instead, leave a loop on top.

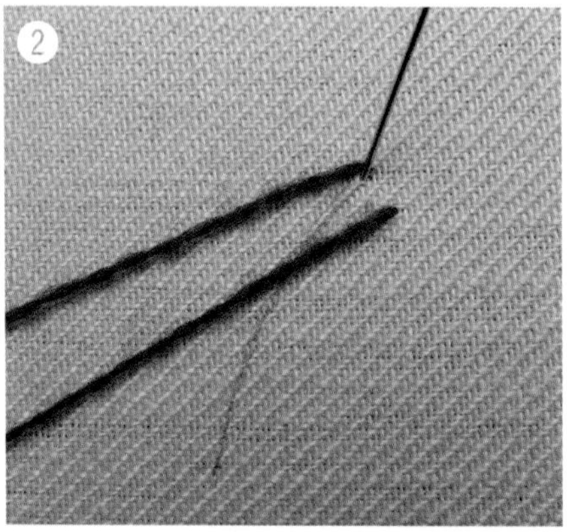

Bring the needle up on the paintline a short distance away from where it was first brought out and through the loop. Pull all of the thread through; this should create an 'L' shape.

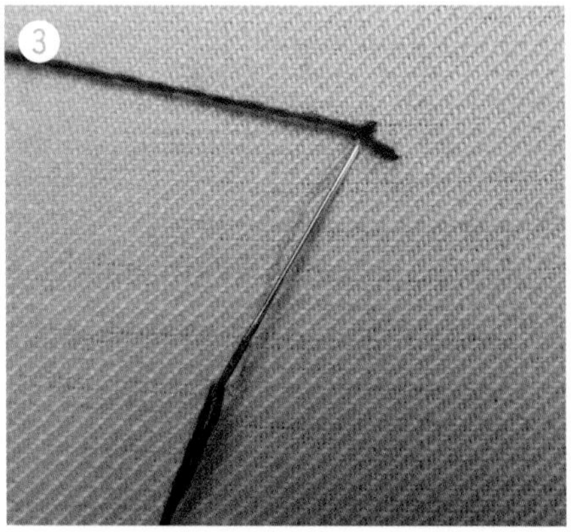

Plunge the needle down on the paintline over the top of the last stitch. Do not pull all of the thread through; instead, leave a loop on top.

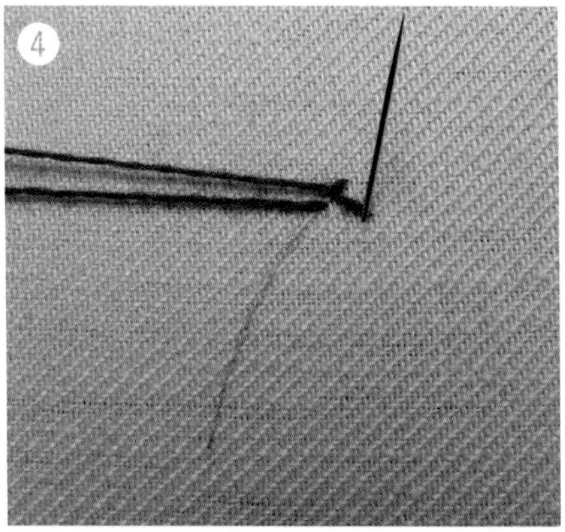

Bring the needle up away from the paintline level with the top of the first stitch. Do not pull the thread through.

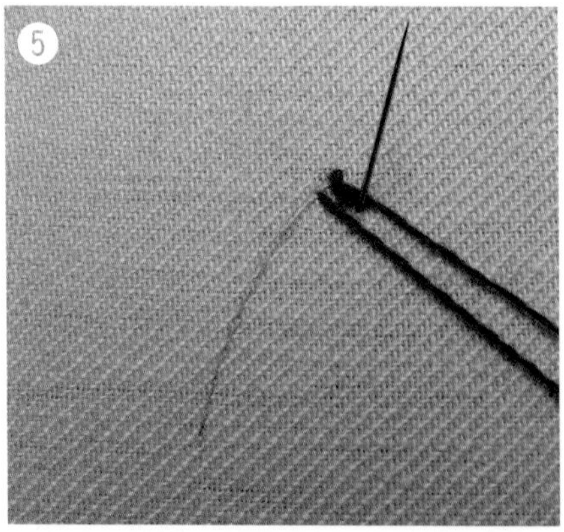

Take the loop over the top of the needle.

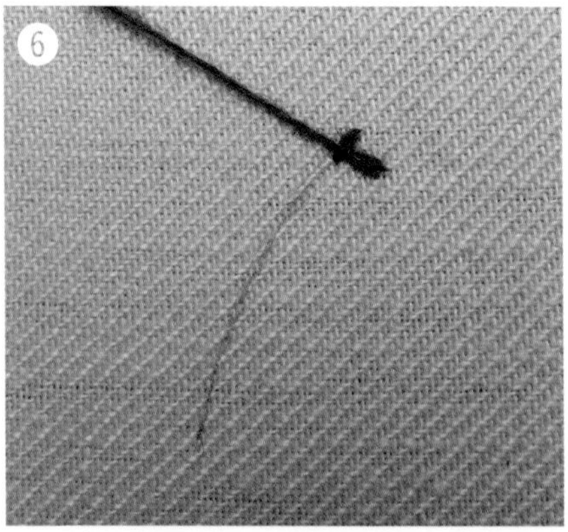

Pull the stitch tight, guiding the thread and stitch back towards the paintline.

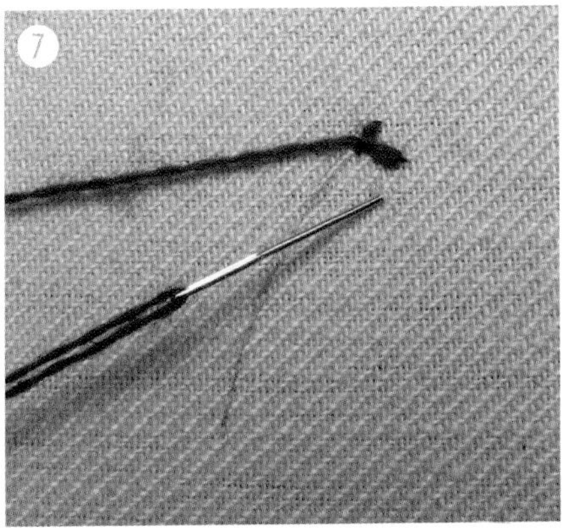

Plunge the needle away from the paintline level with the previous stitch with a small gap between the two. Do not pull all of the thread through; instead, leave a loop on top.

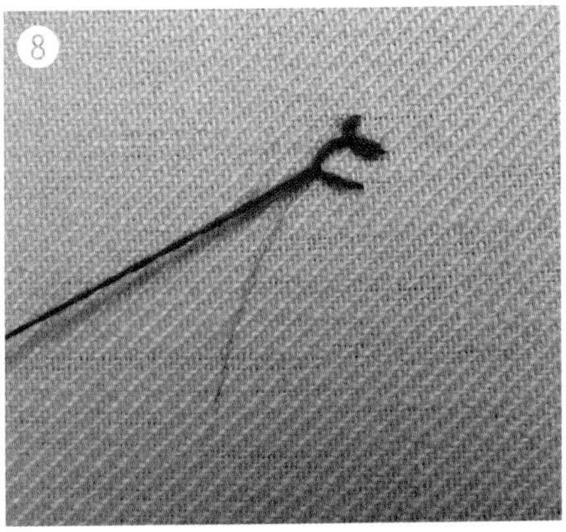

Bring the needle back up through the loop, on the paintline, a short distance away from the base of the previous stitch. Pull all of the thread through to create an 'L' shape.

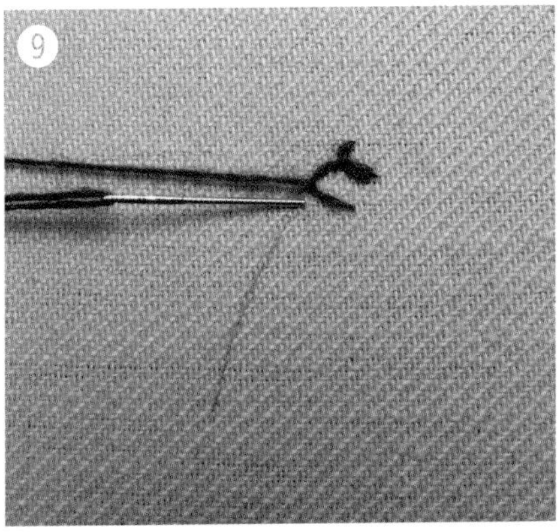

Plunge the needle over the edge of the stitch. Do not pull all of the thread through; instead, leave a loop on top.

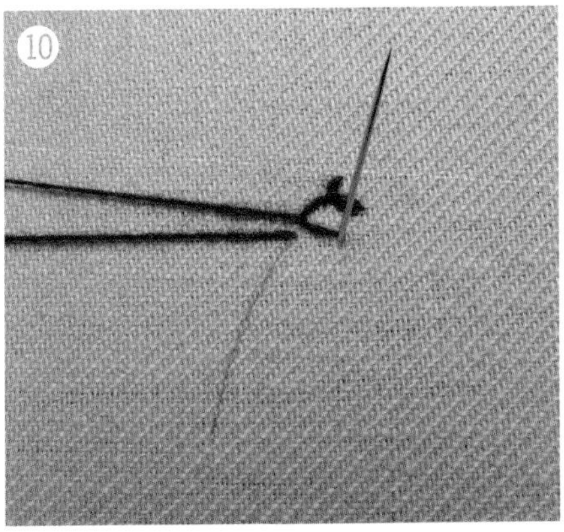

Bring the needle up away from the paintline level with the previous stitch. Do not pull the needle through.

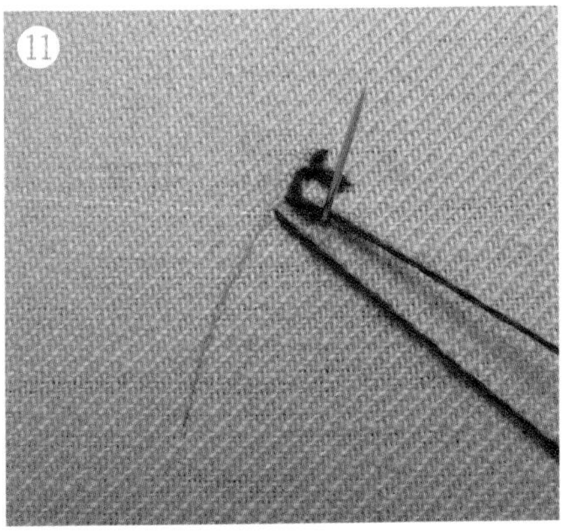

Take the loop over the needle.

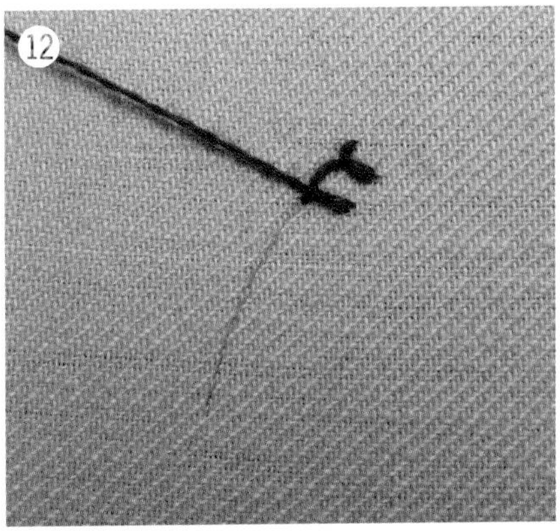

Pull the stitch tight, guiding the thread and stitch back towards the paintline.

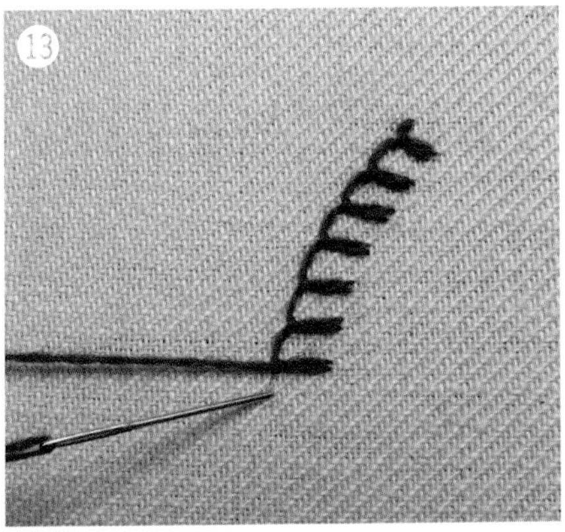

Continue working stitches in this way until the line is complete. To finish the stitch, take the needle over the last stitch and plunge through the fabric.

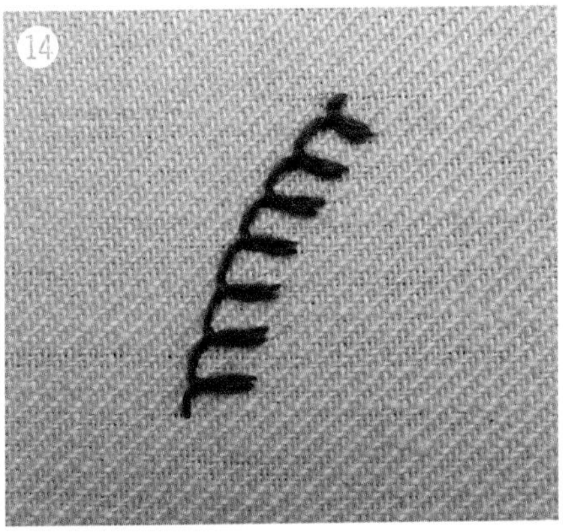

When completed, the stitch will create a slightly scalloped effect. Consider working the stitches at different lengths, or so that the bars are at angles to one another.

Cable Chain Stitch

This is an exciting variation of the traditional Chain Stitch that will create a delicate texture within the embroidery.

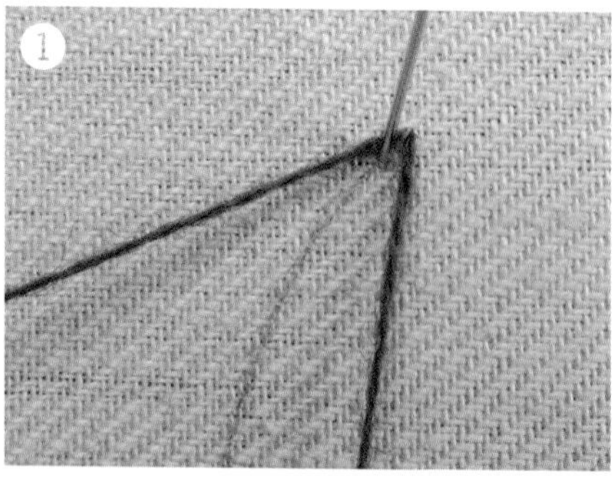

Bring the needle up at the start of the paint-line, then plunge the needle in the same place. Do not pull all of the thread through; instead, leave a loop on top.

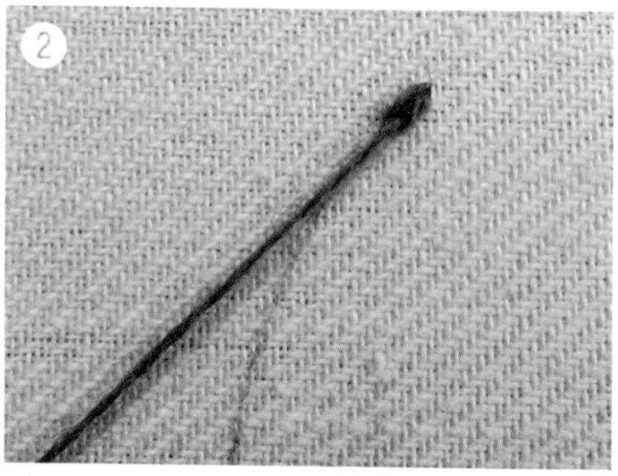

Bring the needle up through the loop a short distance away from where it was last plunged. Pull all of the thread through and settle the stitch in place.

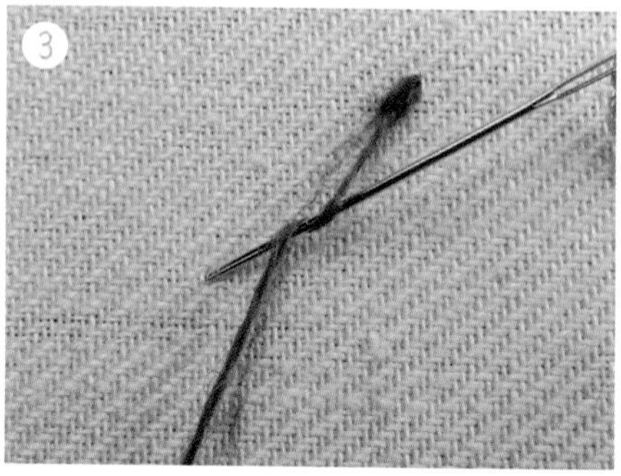

Wrap the thread once around the needle.

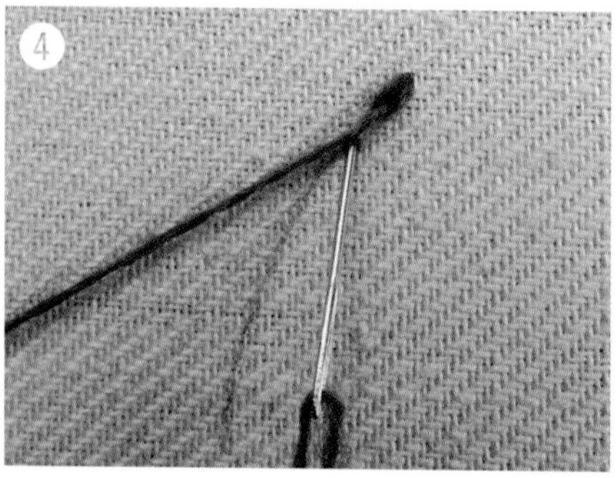

Plunge the needle a short distance away from the last stitch, pull the thread tight around the needle and start to pull the thread through the fabric, leaving a loop on top.

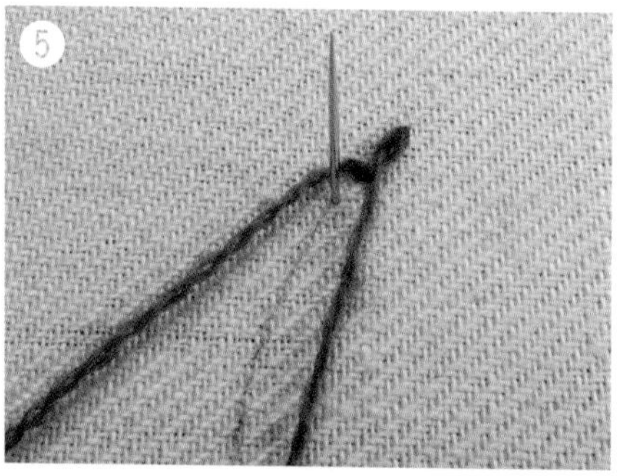

Bring the needle back up through the fabric a short distance away from where it was last plunged. Pull the thread through and settle the stitch into place. Take care to keep the chains and bars consistent in length.

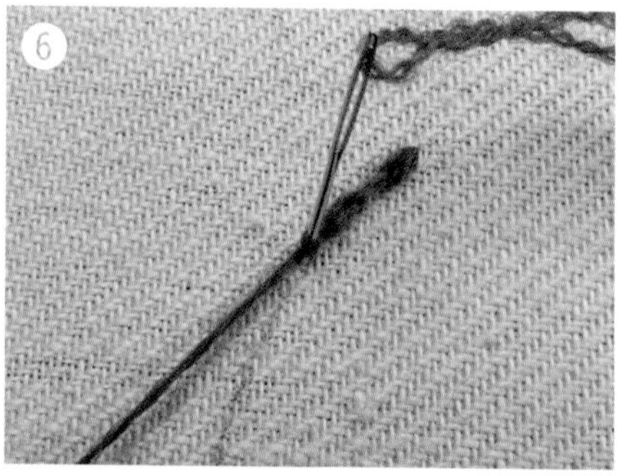

Wrap the thread once around the needle and plunge on the paintline. Do not pull all of the thread through; instead, leave a loop on top.

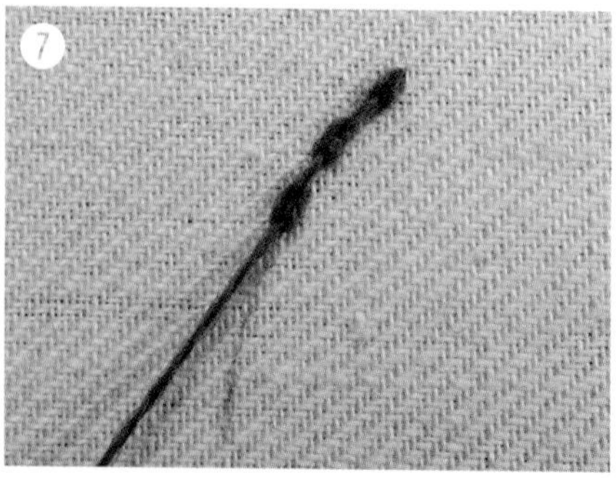

Bring the needle up in the loop and pull the thread through to settle the stitch in place.

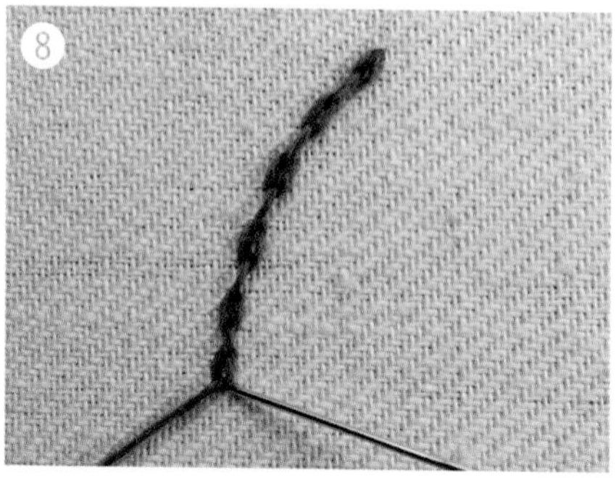

Continue working along the paintline in this manner. At the bottom of the line take the needle over the edge of the last chain and plunge it through the fabric. Cast off the thread.

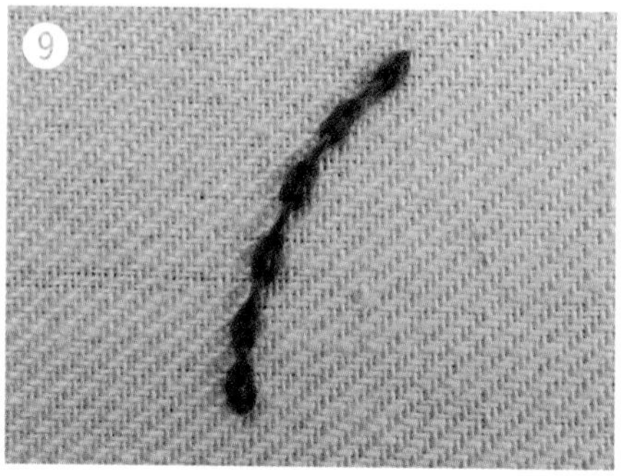

When completed, the stitches should be consistent in length to create a neat finish. Take care as it could be tricky to cover particularly thick lines with this stitch.

Pekinese Stitch

Pekinese Stitch works well as a decorative outlining stitch and is based on a combination of Back Stitch and weaving. There are two elements to it, which means it can be worked in different colours.

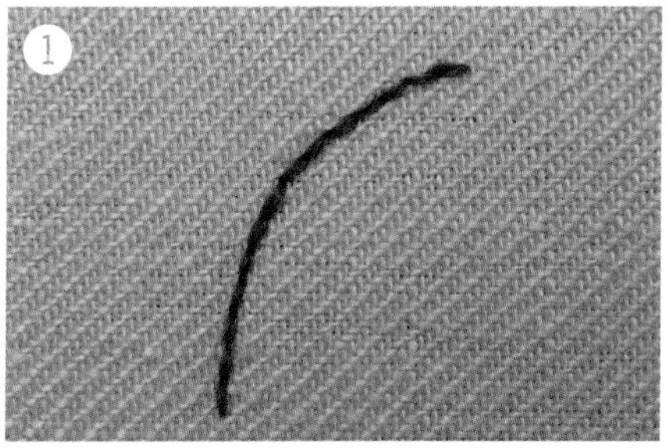

Start by working a row of Back Stitch along the paintline. These should be between 3–4mm/⅛in in length in order to accommodate the additional thread needed for this stitch.

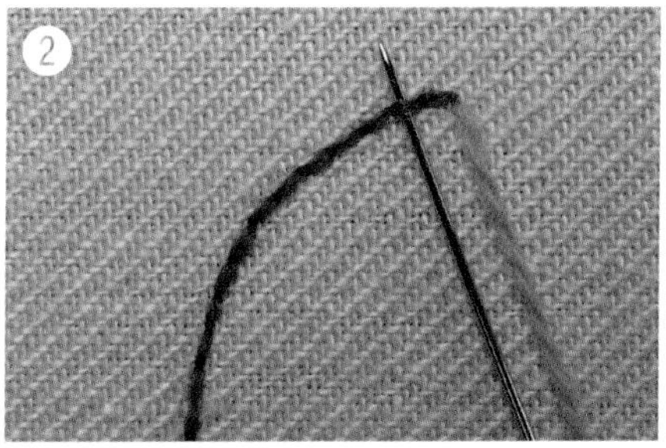

Cast on a new thread and bring it up at the start of the Back Stitch. At this stage it is advisable to switch to a tapestry needle, as the remaining stitches will be worked on the surface of the fabric. Slide the needle under the second stitch in the row and pull all of the thread through gently.

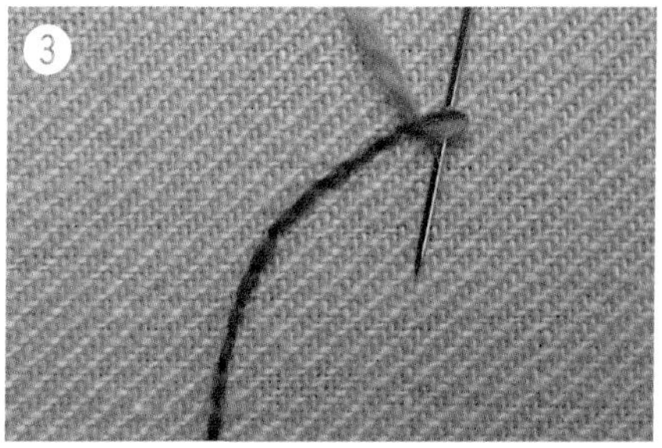

Working back towards the start point, slide the needle under the first stitch and pull all of the thread through gently. This will create a loop where the first and second Back Stitch meet.

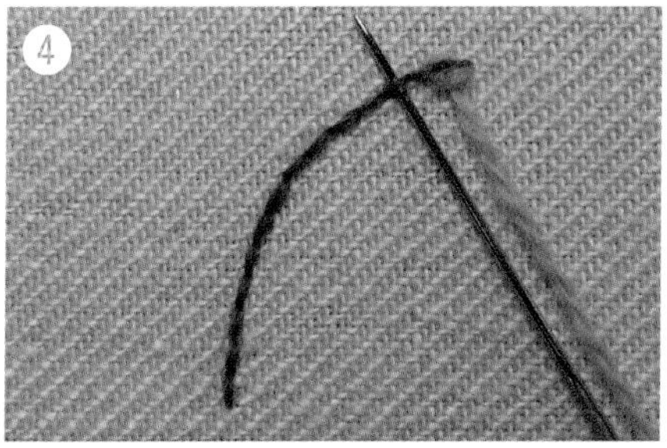

Slide the needle under the third stitch in the row and pull all of the thread through gently.

Working towards the start point, slide the needle under the second stitch (and new thread) and pull the thread through gently. This will create a loop around where the second and third stitch meet.

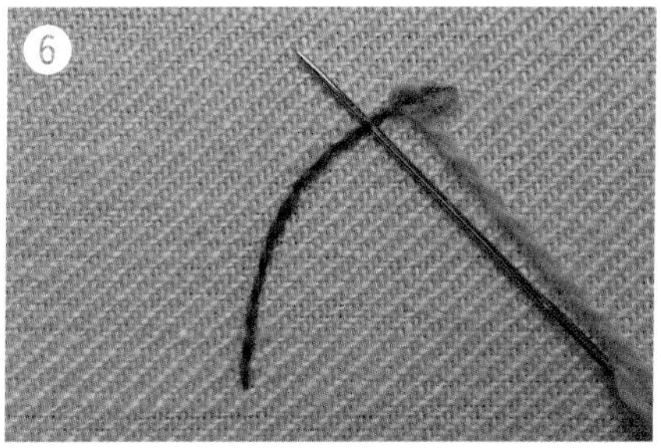

Continue working along the row by sliding the needle under the fourth thread.

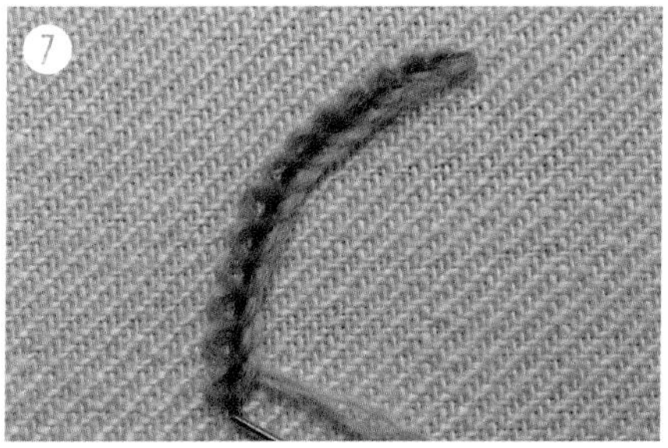

To finish the thread, make the last loop and plunge the needle at the end of the Back Stitch.

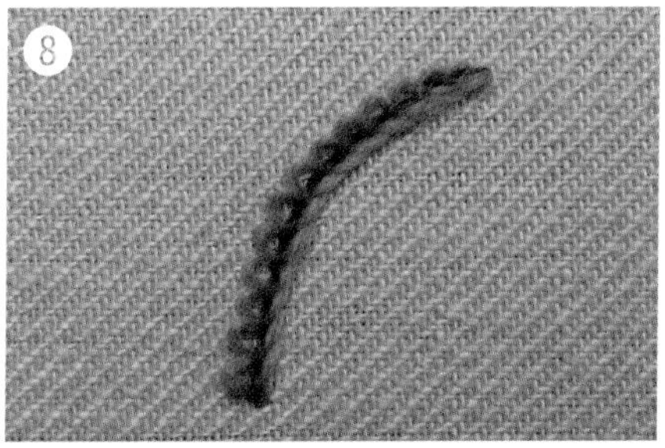

The loops can be kept quite small to create a discreet effect or left slightly bigger to emphasize the loop. Take care not to make the loops too big as they will be unstable. Try gradually increasing or decreasing the size of the loop.

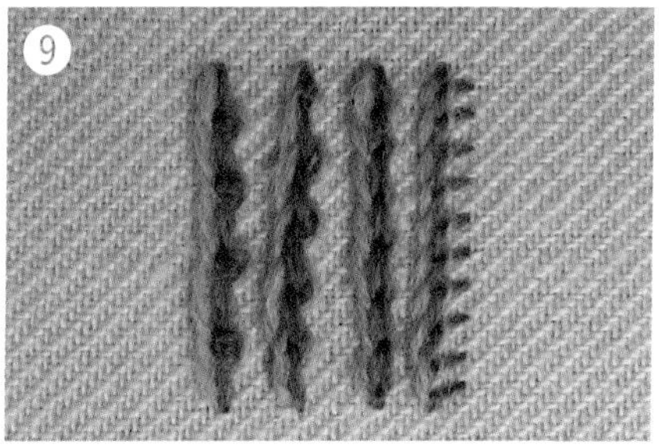

This type of weaving is not limited to use with Back Stitch. This example shows stitches that could be used as an alternative. From left to right: Coral Knot Stitch, Scroll Stitch, Chain Stitch and Buttonhole Stitch.

Whipping and Weaving Ideas

Whipping and weaving do not have to be limited to Back Stitch. Wonderful effects can be achieved by working these stitches over other outlining stitches. The stitches described below are not the only stitches suitable to be worked with these techniques. It's worth sampling additional stitches to see what effects can be created.

These are not the only stitches suitable to be worked with these techniques; it's worth sampling additional stitches to see what effects can be created. For instance, weaving could be worked twice through a stitch, or a whipped stitch could then be woven with another colour.

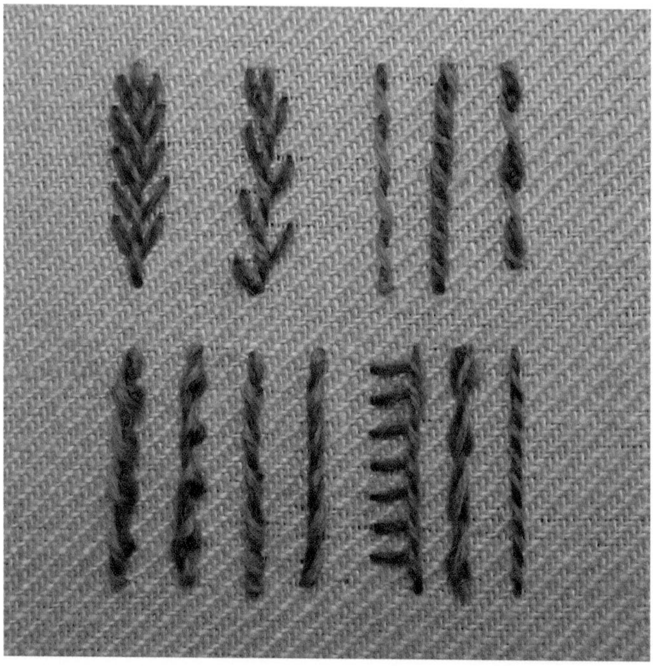

The example shows a number of stitches that are suitable for whipping. Top row from left to right: Fly Stitch, Feather Stitch, Running Stitch, Chain Stitch, Detached Chain Stitch. Second row from left to right: Portuguese Knotted Stem Stitch, Scroll Stitch, Coral Knot Stitch, Stem Stitch, Buttonhole Stitch, Cable Chain Stitch, Running Stitch where the gaps have been filled in (known as Double Running Stitch) with a different colour and then whipped.

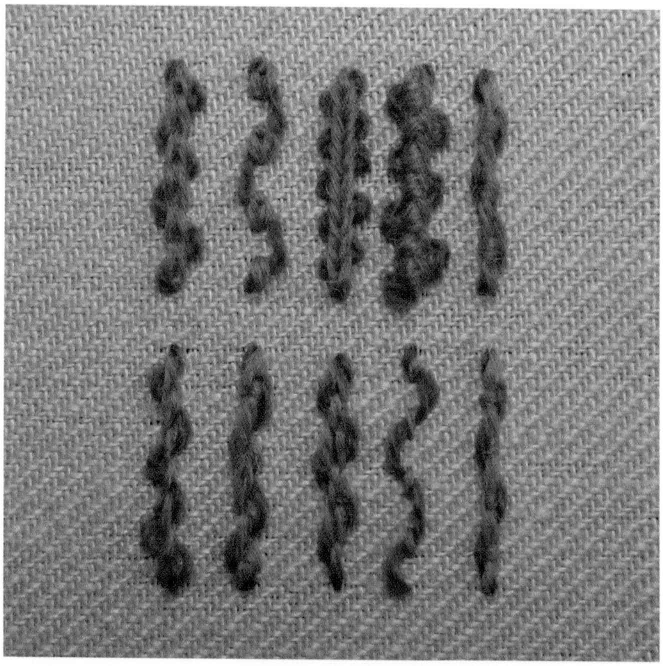

The example shows a number of stitches that are suitable for weaving. Top row from left to right: Chain Stitch, Detached Chain Stitch, Heavy Chain Stitch, Portuguese Knotted Stem Stitch, Coral Knot Stitch. Second row from left to right: Stem Stitch, Scroll Stitch, Cable Chain Stitch, Running Stitch, couching.

Whipped and Woven Wheel Variations

Whipped and woven wheels can add lovely detail and do not necessarily have to be worked separately. Both techniques can be worked together in a slightly larger circle, over an odd number of spokes.

This combination of a woven centre and whipped perimeter creates an unusual texture that can be used to create flower heads.

Similarly, both types of wheel do not have to be worked whole; they could have a void in the middle.

Draw two circles, one inside the other and work bars from just outside the bigger circle to just inside the smaller circle.

Work the desired wheel; the example shows a whipped wheel. The void could be left empty or filled with French Knots. Alternatively, Pistol Stitches could be worked from the void over the flat areas.

Wheels also do not have to be worked only in circles; they can be worked in other shapes and asymmetrically.

Work the foundation bars across the shape, taking the stitches just outside the paintlines. Place the bars so that they intersect slightly off-centre. Work a securing stitch over the top to stabilize the stitches.

Cast on a new thread, bring the needle up in the centre of the shape and work the desired wheel; this example shows a whipped wheel. Keep working around the wheel until the first of the bars are filled. When there is no more space for wraps, plunge the needle under the next bar.

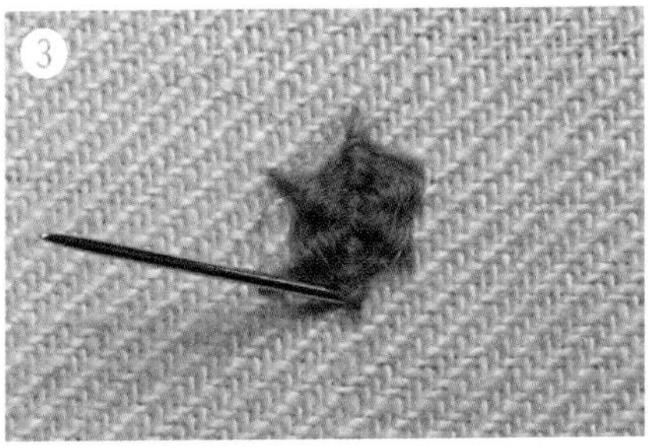

Bring the needle up from underneath the next bar to be whipped, taking care not to pierce it.

Continue working the wheel as before.

When the bars are full, cast off the thread.

Pistol Stitch

This is worked in a similar way to French Knots and can be used to embellish other stitches such as trellis, or to create fine detail such as antennae on insects.

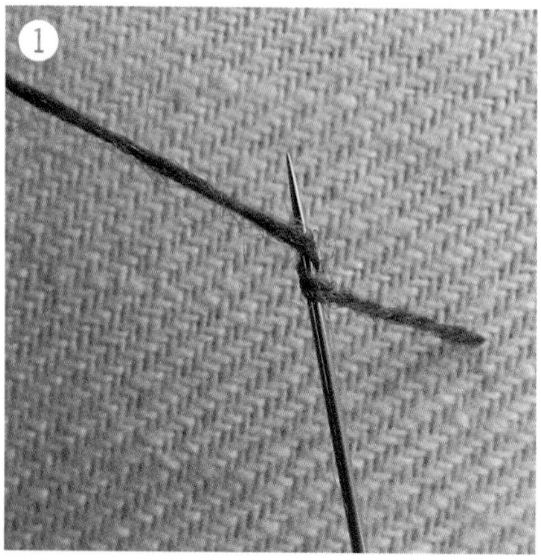

Bring the needle up in the fabric and wrap the thread around the needle once.

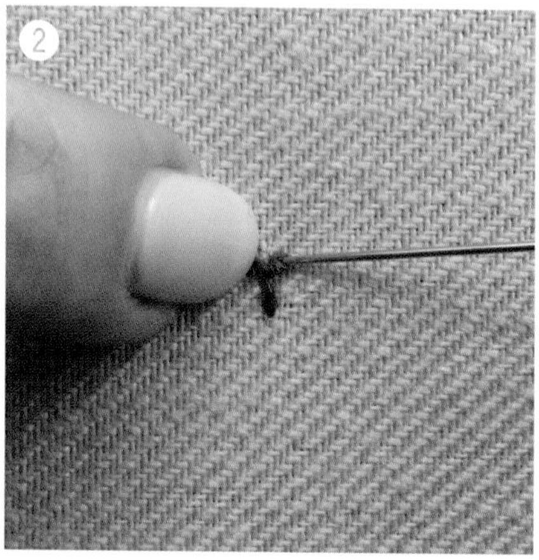

Plunge the needle a short distance away from where it came out. Pull the wrap tight against the needle and place a fingernail on the thread next to the needle to hold the tension.

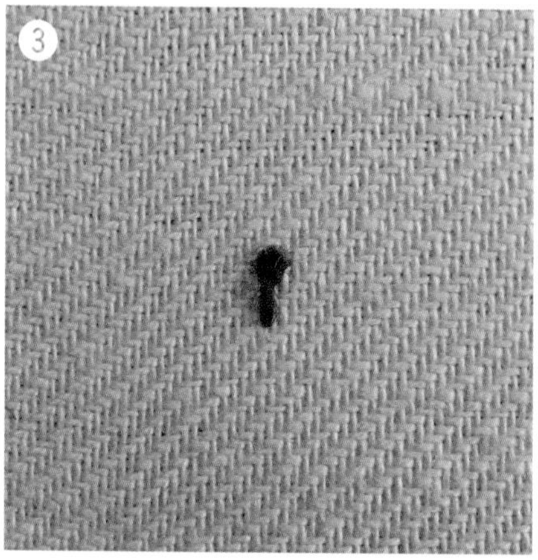

Pull the thread through, keeping the fingernail in place until the knot is formed. When completed, the stitch should look like a French Knot on a stalk.

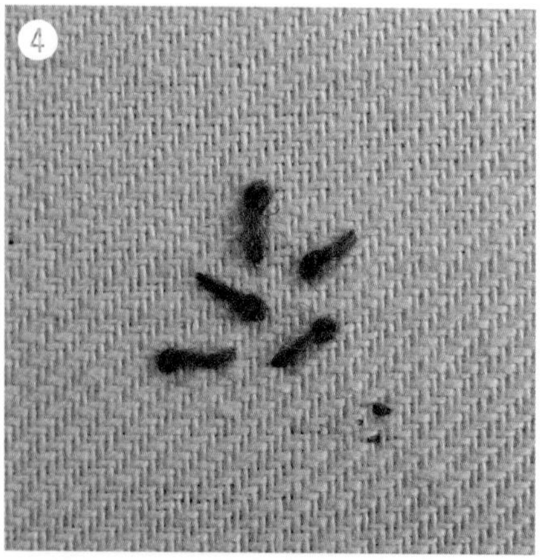

Worked at various angles, Pistol Stitch can be used in place of seeding.

Oak Leaf Stitch

Oak Leaf Stitch is a series of straight stitches that make up a small motif that looks similar to the veining on a leaf. It can be used in shapes that are too small for stitches like Feather Stitch or Fly Stitch, or as a form of seeding.

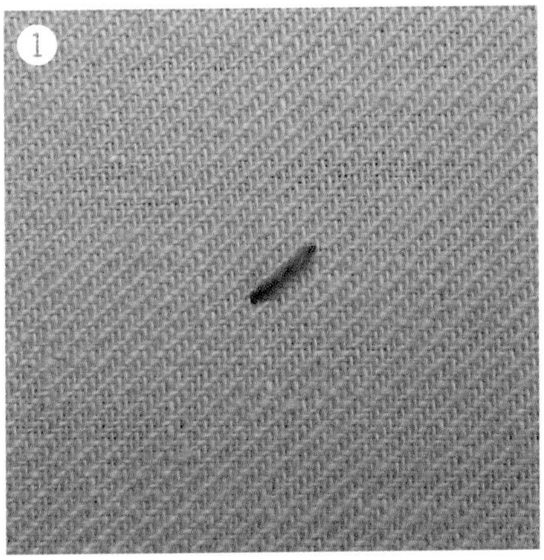

Make a straight stitch in the fabric.

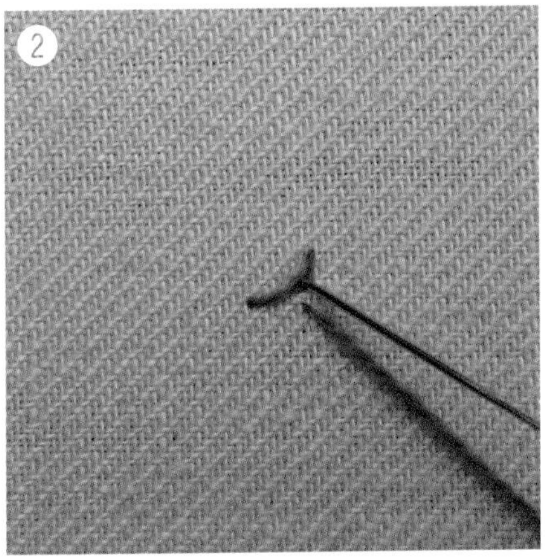

Bring the needle up a short distance away from the first stitch. Use the needle to draw the stitch to one side to create a curve and plunge the needle through the thread to secure it in place.

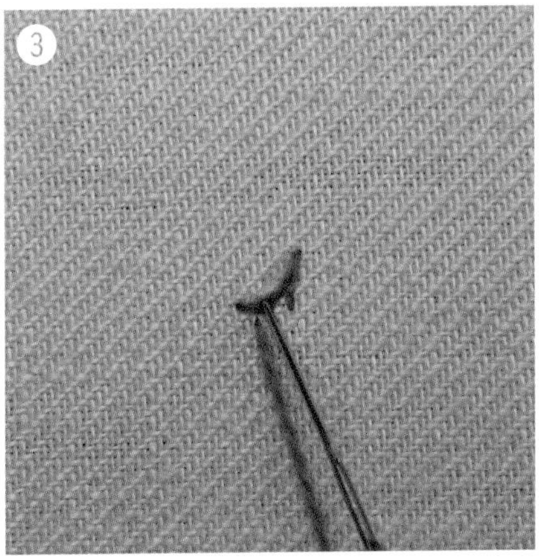

Bring the needle back up away from the first stitch and above the second stitch. Plunge the needle through the thread.

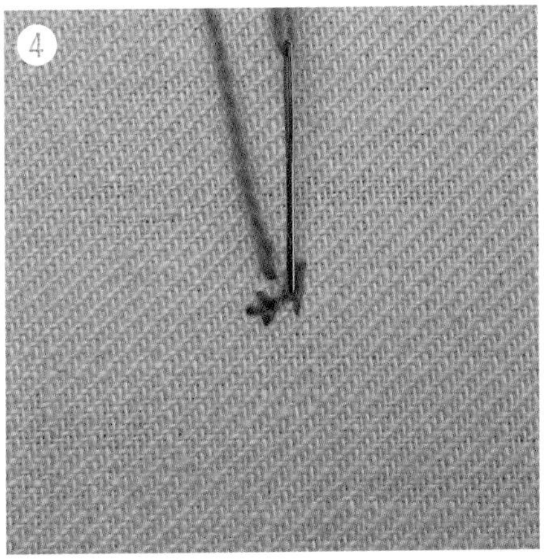

Repeat this process on the other side, making two stitches level with the other side. Plunge the needle in the same place, splitting the first stitch.

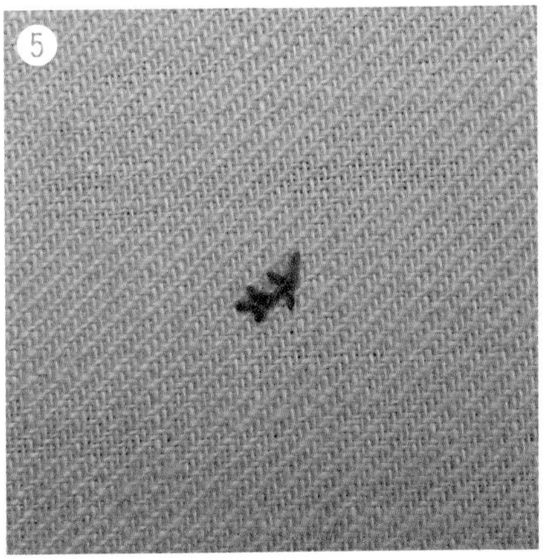

This stitch is better worked on a small scale to add fine detail.

Combining Stitches

The easiest combinations are those that have that have similar properties. However, once you understand the mechanics of a stitch it is possible to combine very different stitches; this can result in some unique combinations. You may find during these experiments that you stumble across a combination that looks similar to or is already an existing stitch; this doesn't matter. Experimenting in this manner will only enhance your skill, and improve your understanding of how stitches work and the limitations of the technique.

Portugese Knotted Stem/ Stem Stitch

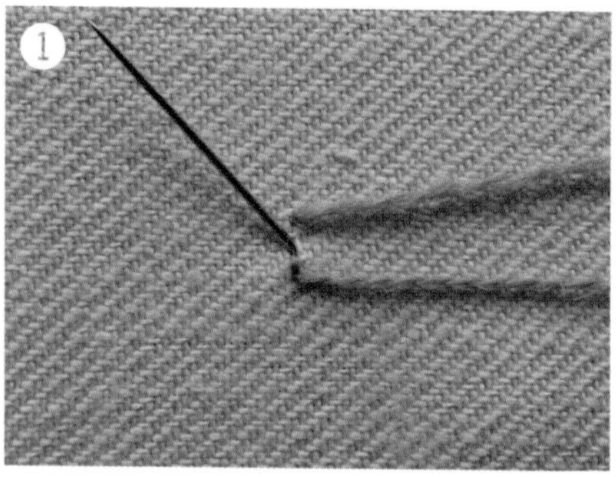

Make a short straight stitch at the start of the paintline, bring the needle back up at the start and make a stitch that is twice the length of the first. Do not pull all of the thread through; instead leave a loop to one side, and bring the needle up in the middle of the stitch being made.

Pull all of the thread through. Take the needle over and slide under the stitch twice, working back towards the start point. This will create a knot-like effect. Plunge the needle on the paintline, ensuring that the stitch length is the same as the previous stitch. Work steps 1 and 2 twice.

With two knots in place, plunge the needle on the paintline, again ensuring that the stitch length is consistent. Bring the needle up in the middle of the stitch being made and pull the thread through. Work two more stitches in this way.

Take the needle over and slide under the stitch twice, working back towards the start point. Make another stitch in the same fashion.

Continue working stitches in this manner, alternating between Portuguese Knotted Stem and Stem Stitch.

Fly/Chain Stitch

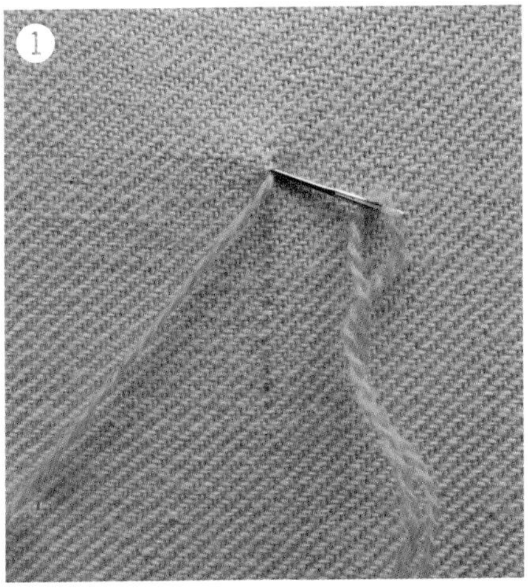

This stitch is a combination of Fly and Chain Stitches. Bring the needle up and take it back down at the end of the paintline. Do not pull all of thread through.

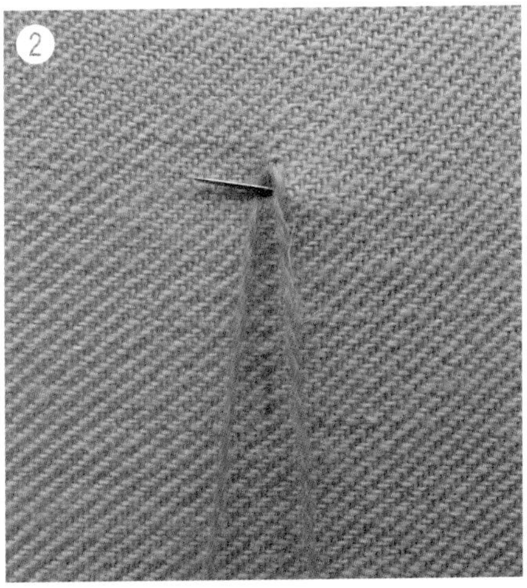

Bring the needle up on the paintline approximately 3mm away from the start and through the loop. Pull all of the thread through and settle the stitch into place, creating a Chain Stitch.

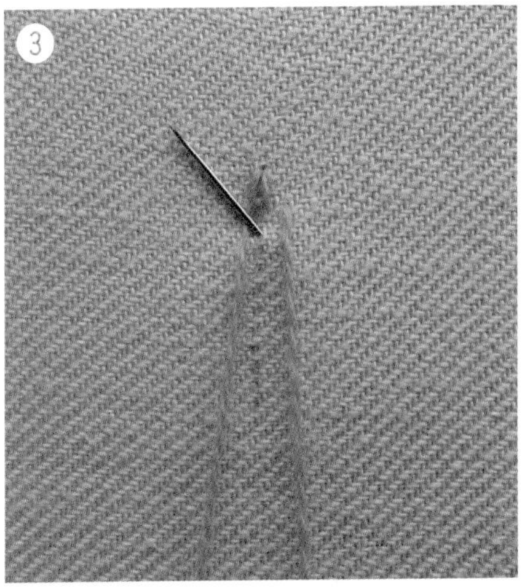

Plunge the needle to the right, outside of the chain. Don't pull all of the thread through; instead bring the needle up on the line and through the loop to form a V shape, creating a Fly Stitch.

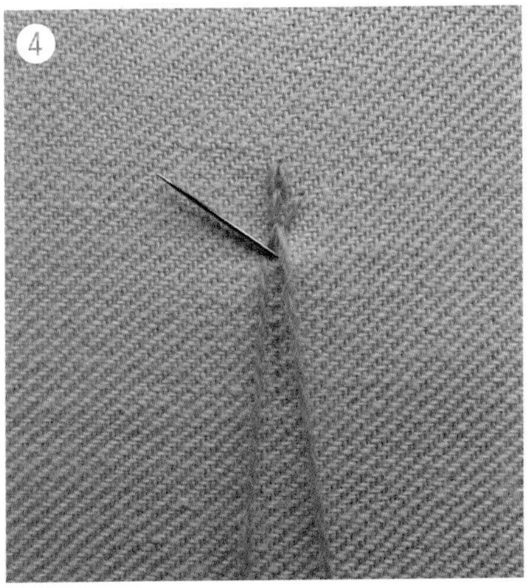

Plunge the needle in the same place as where it was just brought out, creating a loop. Bring the needle up on the paintline and within the loop, creating another Chain Stitch.

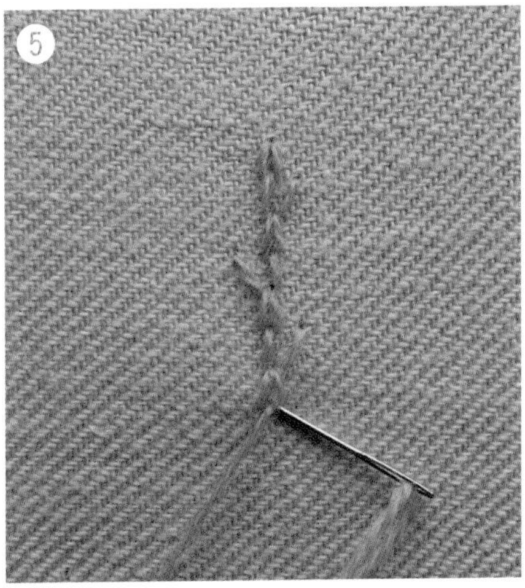

Continue working stitches in this way, alternating between chain and Fly Stitch. Consider make the two stitches different sizes or in a zig zag pattern to create a different effect.

Van Dyke/Fly Stitch

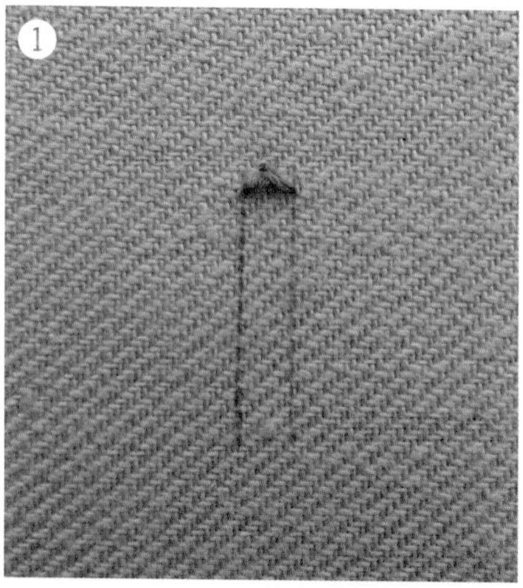

Work the first stage of Van Dyke Stitch by making two stitches that cross over in the centre of the shape.

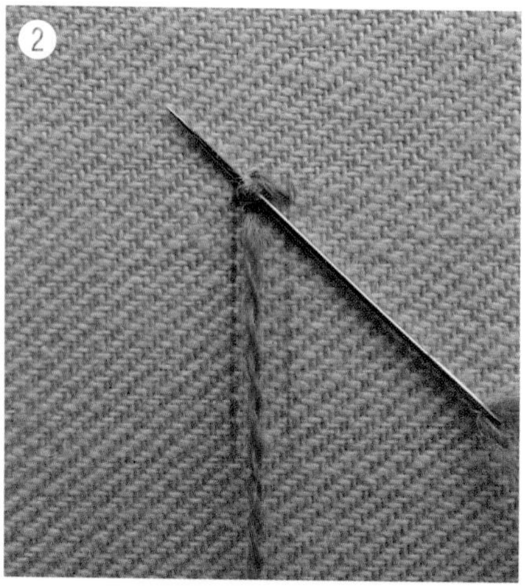

Bring the needle up underneath these stitches, just inside the edge of the left-hand side of the shape. Slide the needle under the first row on the left hand side.

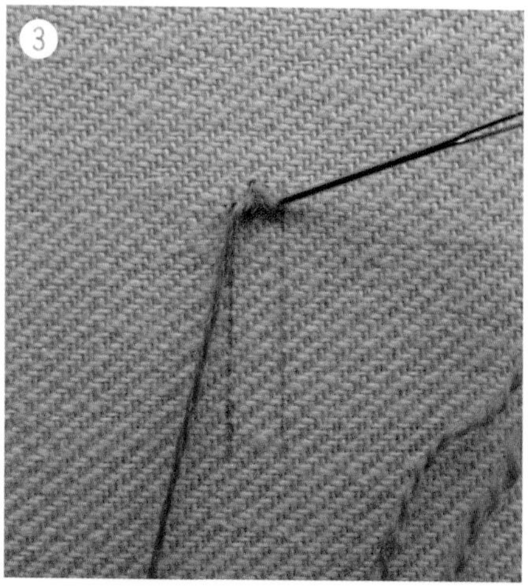

Use the tip of the needle to draw down the right hand stitch and plunge the needle level with where it was just brought out. Do not pull all of the thread through.

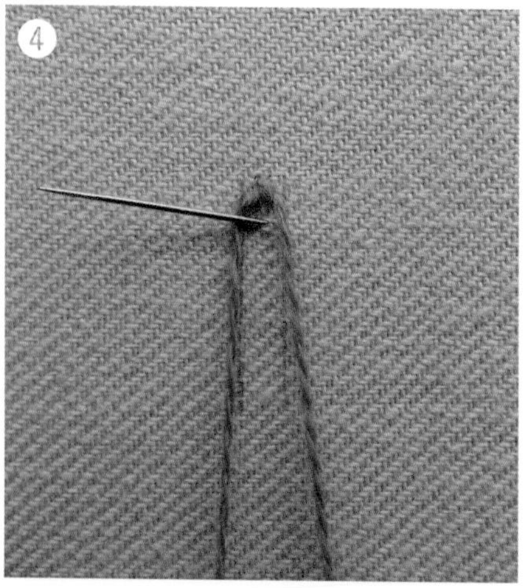

Bring the needle up in the middle of the shape and through the loop to create a V shape (Fly Stitch). Plunge the needle over the thread to catch the V in place.

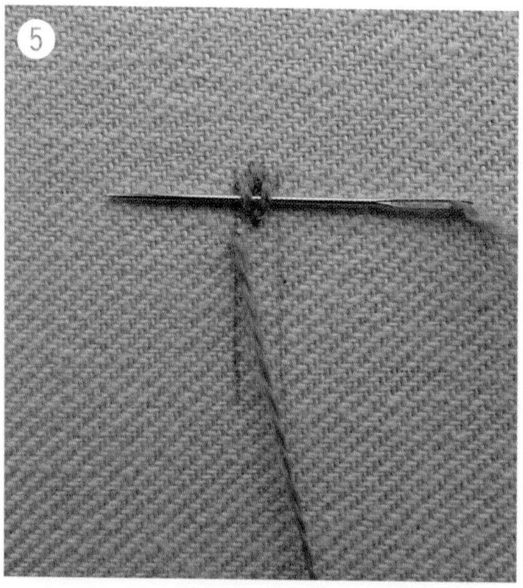

Bring the needle up on the left hand side of the shape, take it across to the right-hand side and slide it underneath the Fly Stitch. Plunge the needle on the right-hand side of the shape, level with where it was brought up on the left.

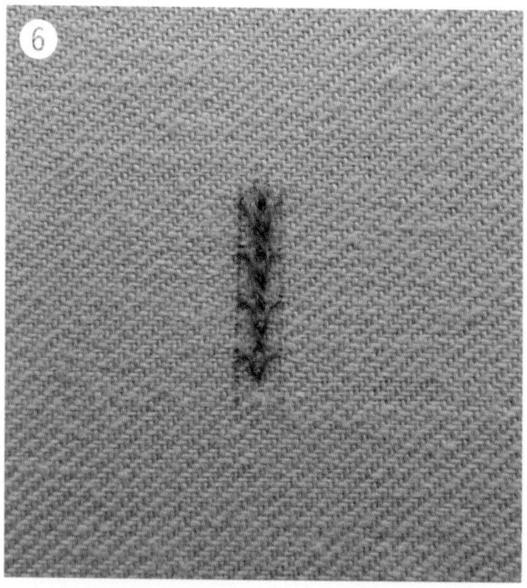

Work additional stitches alternating between the two stitches. The stitch can be ended on either a Fly or Van Dyke Stitch.

Herringbone With A Knot

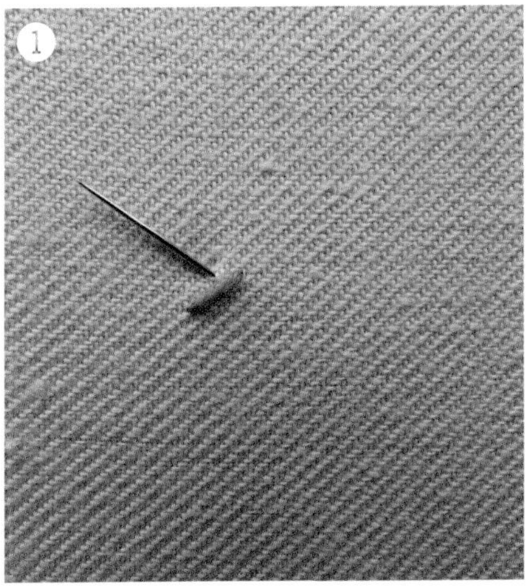

Bring the needle up and work a diagonal stitch. Bring the needle up behind the first stitch level with the last plunge point.

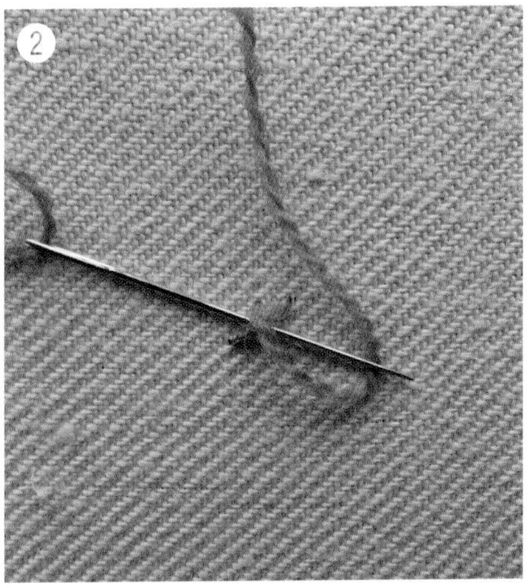

Lay the thread across the stitch, then take the needle round anti-clockwise behind where the thread was just brought out. Slide the needle under the stitch and bring it up through the loop.

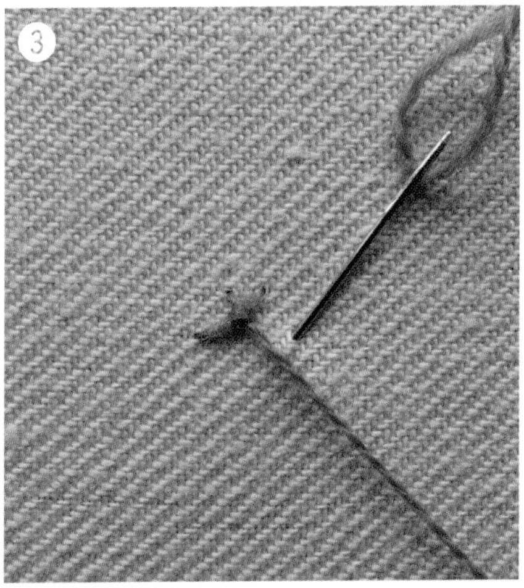

Pull the thread tight to create the knot. Plunge the needle down level with the bottom of the previous stitch.

Bring the needle out behind and level with the last plunge point level. Lay the thread across the previous stitch, bring the thread round clockwise behind where it was just brought out. Slide the needle under the stitch and up through the loop to tie the knot.

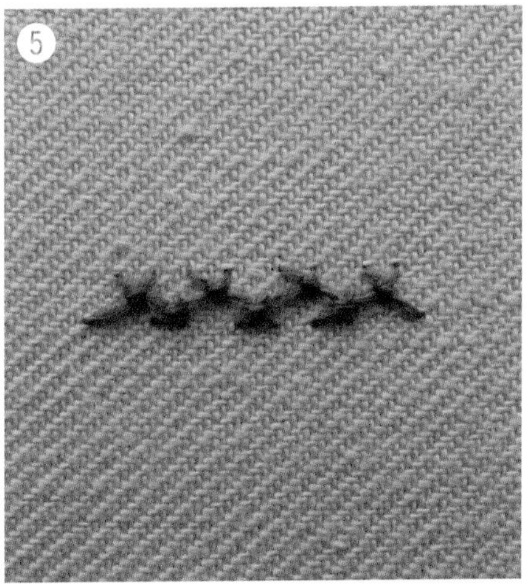

Continue working stitches in this manner until the line or shape is complete. This type of textured stitch can be further embellished to create a vine or tendril.

CHAPTER 10

MOUNTING

Once a piece is finished, presenting and preserving it is the last step. This chapter sets out the process for hard mounting, that is placing the piece on a board in preparation for framing.

Hard mounting is not the only way to present a piece of work; traditionally crewelwork was used on household items. Large wall hangings were used to insulate draughty rooms and, due to the hard-wearing nature of the materials, crewelwork was often used to upholster furniture. These days cushions, needle books or pencil cases are a good alternative for smaller pieces.

Mounting is a complex process and the method detailed in the following pages is designed to preserve the piece for as long as possible. Again, it is important to invest in good-quality materials for mounting, and to use conservation grade if possible (although these are specialist materials that can be difficult to source). It is important to read through the following pages in their entirety, to fully understand the different stages, before embarking on mounting a piece. It is also advisable to have the book nearby when working through the stages.

Hard mounting is a good way to preserve a piece of work once it is completed.

Designed and worked by the author, this piece uses common stitches in a traditional motif.

Cutting the Board

If the frame for the piece has already been chosen, it is best to cut the board 2–3mm/⅛in smaller than the interior dimensions of the frame. This will allow for the thickness of the fabric that will be wrapped over the edges of the board. If the frame has not been chosen, the dimensions can be calculated to suit the piece being mounted and the frame made to accommodate these.

When using a slate frame, it is best to decide on the dimensions of the board before it comes off the frame. If using a hoop, it is often better to take the piece out of the hoop and lay it on a flat surface before making this decision. However, the same process can be applied in both circumstances.

For this process you will need the following:

- Mountboard
- Ruler
- Set square
- Craft knife
- Pencil
- Cutting mat
- Four sheets of white A4 paper

> **Hints and tips**
>
> When using 2mm-thick mountboard, remember to cut two identical pieces. These should be glued together and left overnight to dry.

Lay four pieces of white paper on the four sides of the piece. These are used to imitate how the piece will look when framed. There should be enough space around the piece so that it does not look cramped, and consideration should also be given to whether additional picture mounts will be added on top. Generally speaking, leaving a rebate of between 3–5cm/1 3/8in of fabric around a piece is sufficient. Move the paper around the piece until the layout is satisfactory. At this point measure the window the paper has created; these measurements are the dimensions of the board.

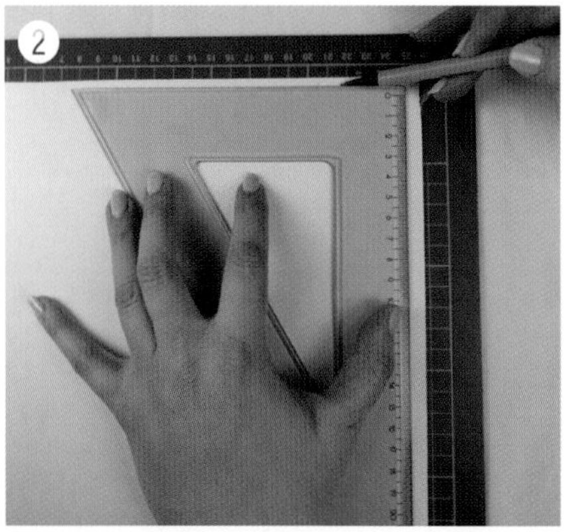

The corners and sides of the piece of mountboard need to be perfectly straight; therefore, it is best to check the sides of a fresh piece of mountboard for any dents or scrapes. If there are portions of the mountboard that have been used, it is best to draw a fresh corner to use as a starting point. This can be done with a set square.

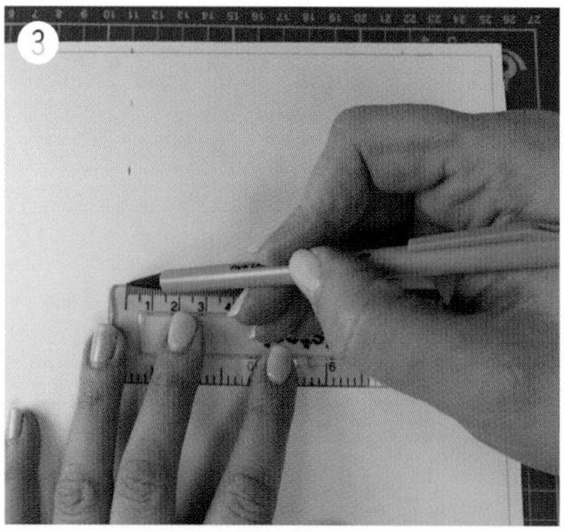

Using the pencil line or edges as a starting point, mark out the dimensions of the mountboard. It is best to make multiple marks along each side – between three and five depending on the size. Lining up the ruler with multiple points will help to ensure you draw a straight line. When the dimensions have been drawn on, check the corners with the set square. They should all be 90 degrees.

Cut the mountboard using a sharp, sturdy craft knife and a ruler. Take care when cutting to keep the blade at right angles to the mountboard to ensure that the sides of the board are cut straight and are not chamfered. Place a hand on the ruler to keep it in place when cutting. Do not try to cut through the mountboard in one stroke; instead, make multiple cuts to get through the mountboard. To keep the cut line straight, try not to move the ruler between cuts.

Covering the Mountboard

When working the next stage, a sheet of tissue paper or clean cloth should be laid under the piece to prevent it getting dirty. This has been omitted for clarity in the illustrations.

It is important to get the calico covering the mountboard as tight as possible across the mountboard. If the calico isn't taut, the piece of embroidery will never stay taut on the front. This will cause bubbles and ripples to appear in the fabric, which will detract from the piece when displayed.

For this process you will need the following:

- Glue
- Pins
- Calico or cotton
- Scissors

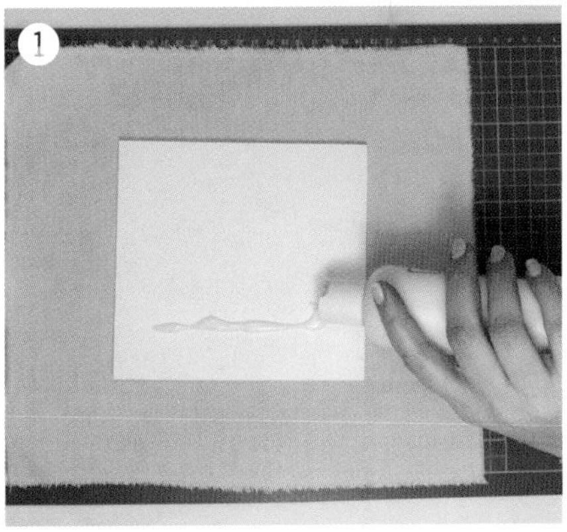

Cut a piece of neutral-coloured calico that is no more than 10cm/4in bigger than the mountboard on all four sides. Run a line of glue along one of the edges of the mount-board, approximately 5cm/2in in from the edge to leave a margin of unglued fabric. This margin is important as it is the area that will be stitched into later.

Fold the calico over the edges of the mountboard and smooth onto the line of glue, towards the centre of the mountboard.

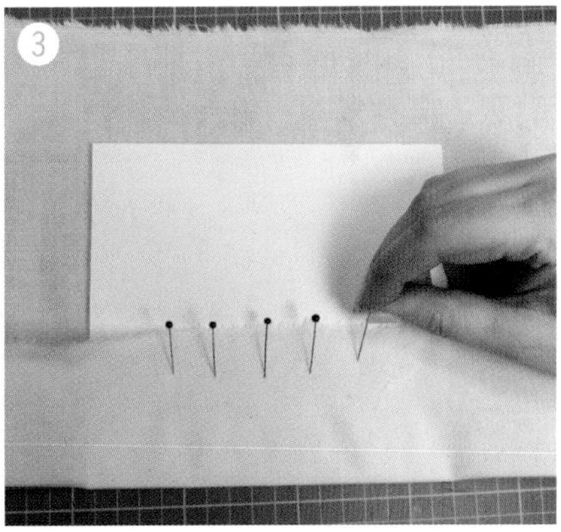

Add pins to the calico above the glue line. Insert the pin into the calico with the glass head towards the edge of the mountboard, then pull the pin backwards towards the centre of the mountboard; this will help to stretch the calico. This will secure the calico so that you can work the other side. Alternatively, leave the mountboard until the glue is completely dry.

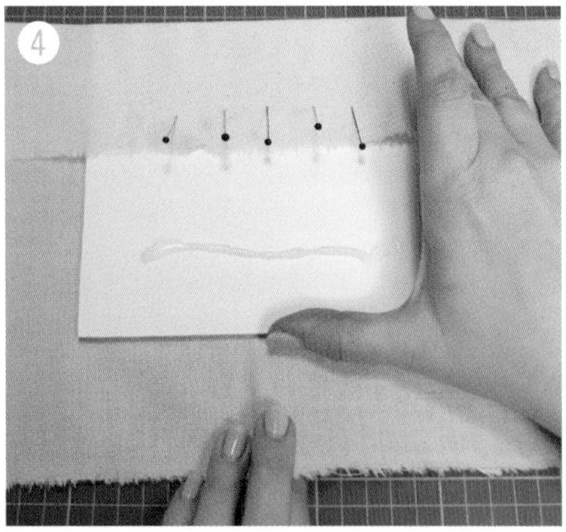

On the opposite side add another line of glue to the mountboard, again approximately 5cm/2in in from the edge. Push the mountboard back against the glued/pinned side and fold the calico over the edge of the mountboard; add pins as before. Smooth the calico onto the line of glue towards the centre of the mountboard. Leave the mountboard to dry completely.

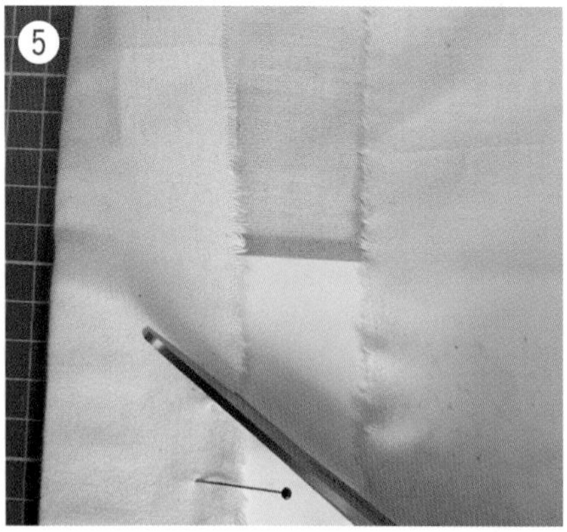

The excess fabric should be cut away at the corners to create a neater finish. Using the edges of the mountboard as a guide, cut the calico from the centre of the mountboard on a roughly 45-degree angle. A small amount of fabric should be left overlapping at the corner.

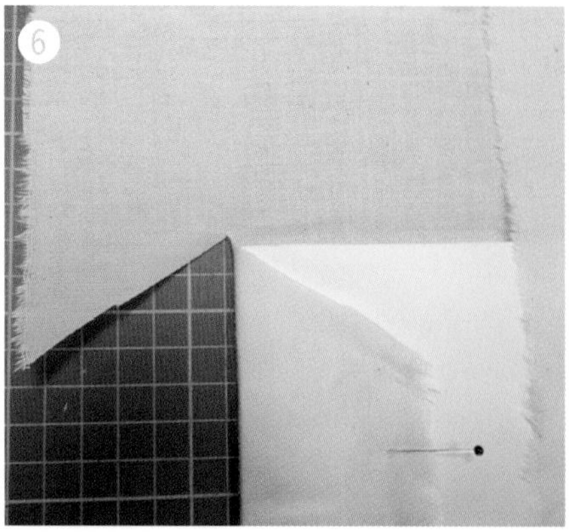

Lay the cut section of calico flat on the table in preparation for the next cut.

Working from the corner of the mountboard, cut the remaining calico away, remembering to leave a small section of overlapping calico at the corners.

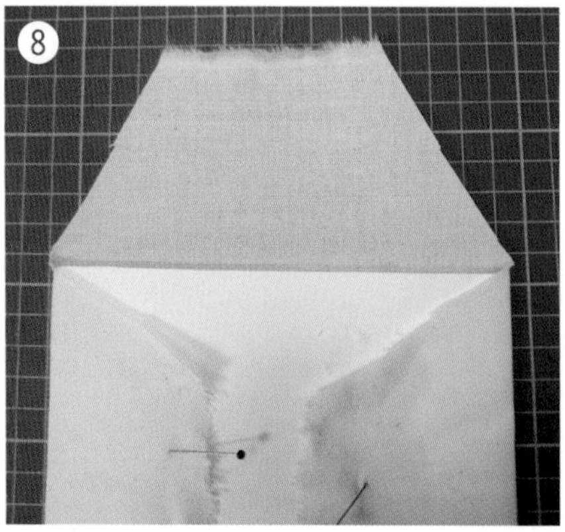

Work the other corner in the same way. When completed, it should look similar to the top flap of an envelope. Then work the opposite side in the same way.

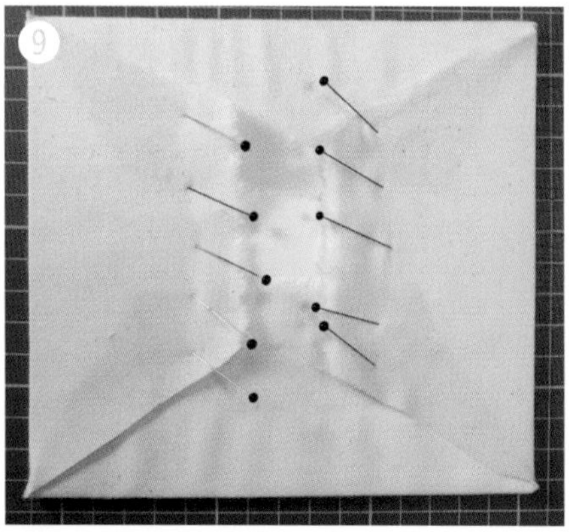

Add the glue to the remaining sides of the mountboard as described above. When folding the calico over and pinning into place, remember to pull slightly on the fabric; this is particularly important on the final side. The calico should be tight. To check this, run a finger along the front of the mountboard. If a bubble of fabric appears, it is not tight enough. Leave the mountboard to dry overnight.

Pinning On

The piece should be kept central on the board. To do this, start by measuring and marking the centre of each edge by pushing a pin into the edge of the board on each side. To mark the centre of each side of the piece, measure the most extreme points of the motif and add a pin to the centre of the fabric, taking care not to position the pin through the embroidery or too far into the stitched area.

For this process you will need the following:

- The embroidery
- Pins
- Measuring tape
- Calico-covered mountboard

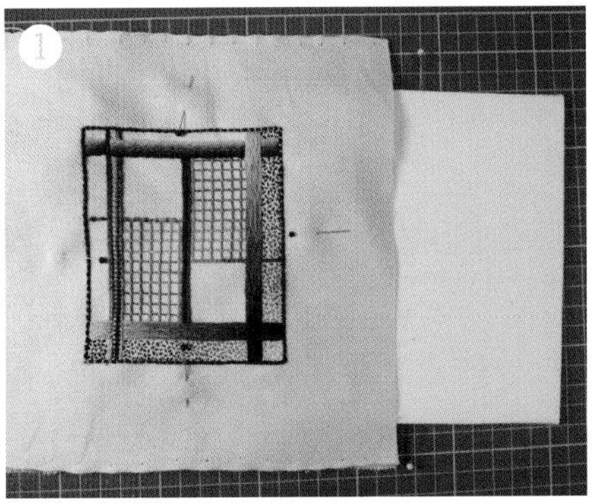

To centre the piece on the board, match the pins in the fabric to the pins in the board. Remove the pins from the board and push the pin in the fabric into the side of the board to secure the fabric in place.

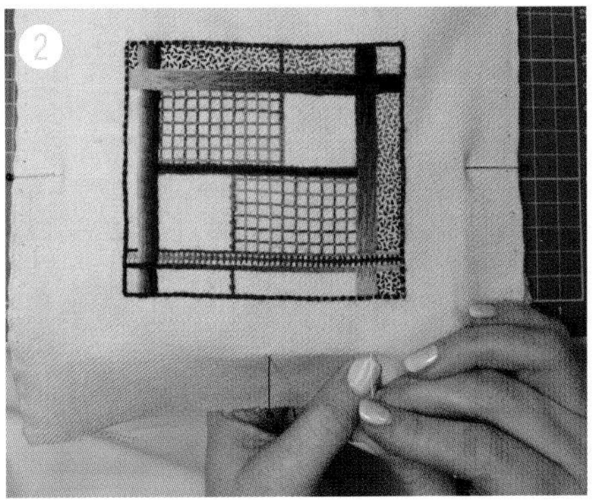

With all four pins in place, measure the rebate on all four sides to ensure the piece is central. If it is only 2–3mm/⅛in off-centre, continue to the next step. if the disparity is larger than this, the piece needs to be unpinned and repositioned.

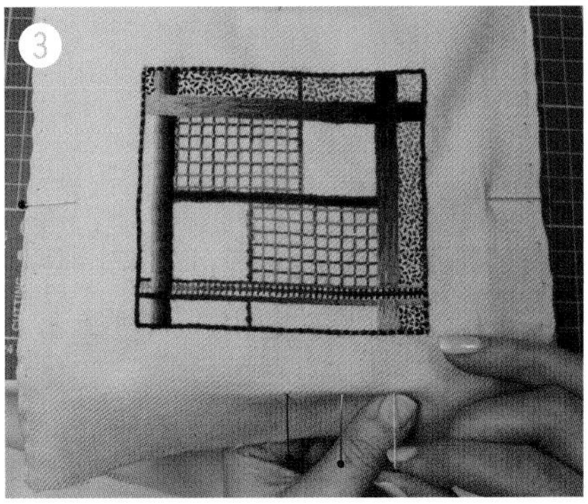

Working from the middle out on one edge, add extra pins into the side of the board, spaced approximately 2.5cm/1in apart. As the pins are added, the fabric should be pulled only enough so that the grain of the fabric runs parallel to the edge of the board. Turn the board 90 degrees and repeat the process so that one corner is pinned.

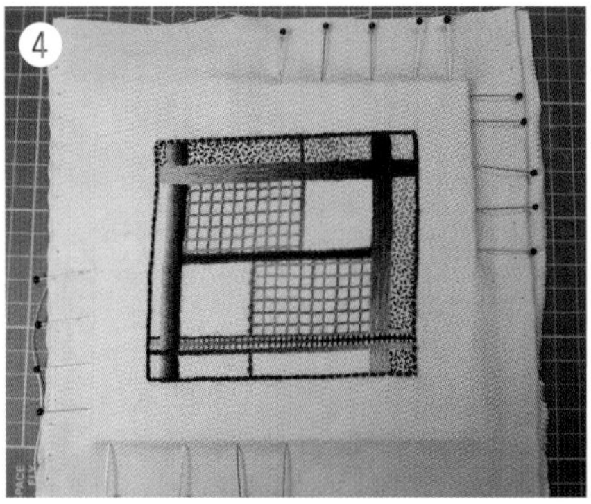

Work the opposite corner in the same way, ensuring that the grain of the fabric is straight to the board. Again, take a moment to measure the rebates in the pinned corners to ensure they are equal.

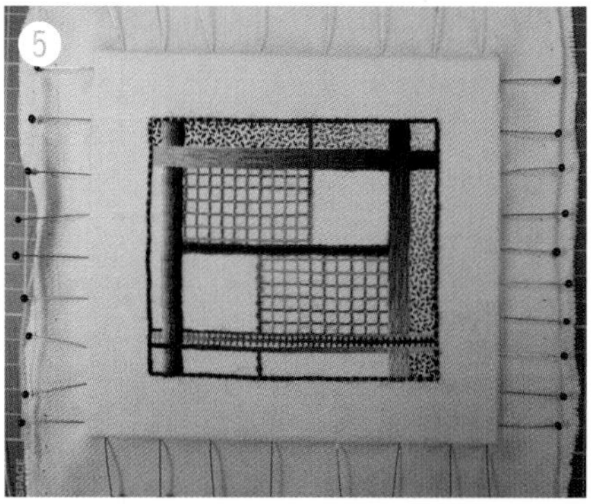

Work the two remaining corners in the same way, ensuring the grainline is consistently parallel along each edge of the board. Measure the rebate along each edge to ensure it is consistent.

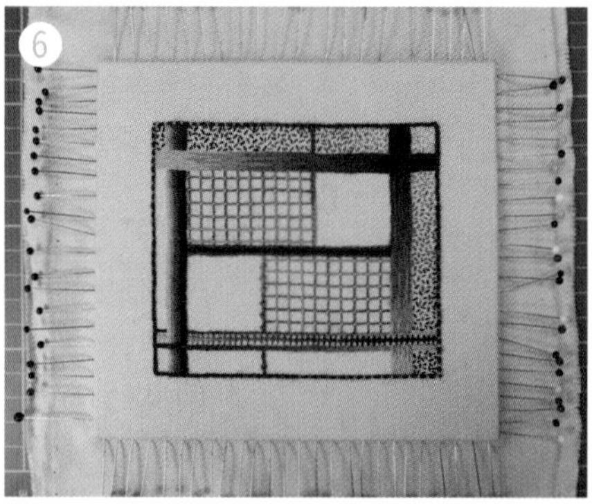

At this point move the piece so that the edge of the board sits on the edge of the table and the fabric hangs off; this makes pulling on the fabric easier. Working from the middle of the board, remove each pin, pull the fabric and replace the pin; in order to keep the increased tension on the fabric, the pins should be placed closer together, so you will need to use more. Try to keep the grainline consistent along the edge of the board, particularly at the corners. When one half is complete, return to the middle and work in the opposite direction. Work around the board in this manner. Repeat until the fabric is tight across the board. When completed, check the fabric grainline is parallel to the edge of the board and the rebate is even on each side.

The black line in this illustration shows how the grain (weave) of the fabric is not in line with the board; it lifts up from the bottom left. This can lead to the motif looking off-balance or off-centre, which can detract from the overall effect once framed.

Hints and tips

At this stage the piece can be left for a few days before moving on. The fabric may relax in this time, which will cause bubbles or ripples to appear in the fabric. If this happens, simply repeat the last step to retension the fabric.

Stitching On

The piece is now ready to be stitched to the calico to secure it in place. Before starting, double-check there are no ripples or bubbles in the fabric on the front.

For this process you will need the following:

- Pins
- Curved needle
- Button thread
- Scissors
- Large tapestry needle

The corners of the piece should be mitred to create a neater, flatter finish. They can be pinned before starting or in turn as the piece is worked.

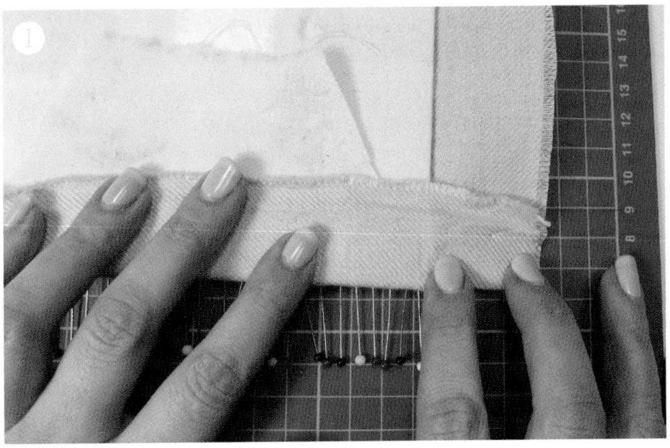

To mitre the corner, fold one edge of the fabric over the board and press a crease into it. Unfold the fabric and repeat on the adjoining side.

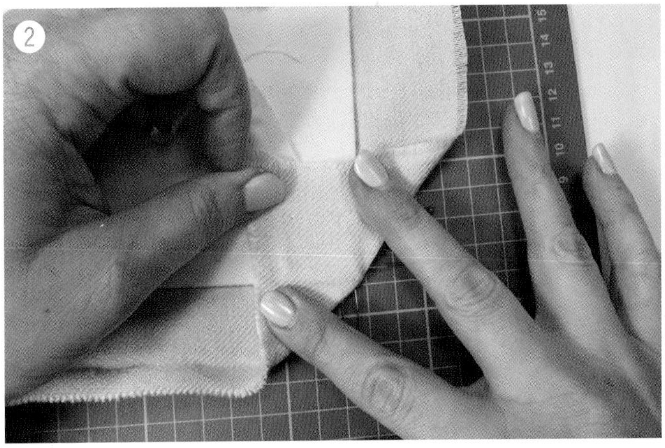

Lay the fabric flat on the surface and fold the corner back onto the board. Line the creases up with the edges of the board; this will ensure a more accurate mitre.

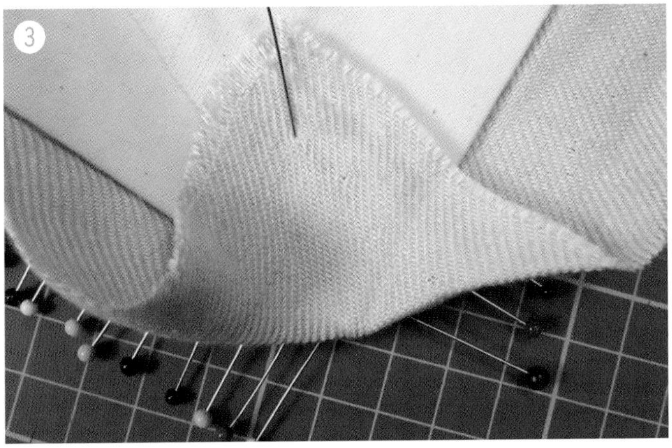

Use a pin to hold the fabric in place whilst the rest of the corner is folded in. Smooth the fabric across the corner so that it lies flat.

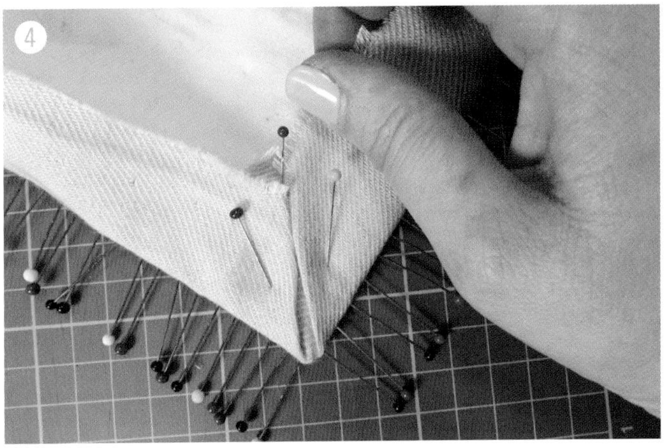

Fold the two edges in; they should meet in the middle and line up with the corner. Pin the folds into place and repeat on the remaining corners.

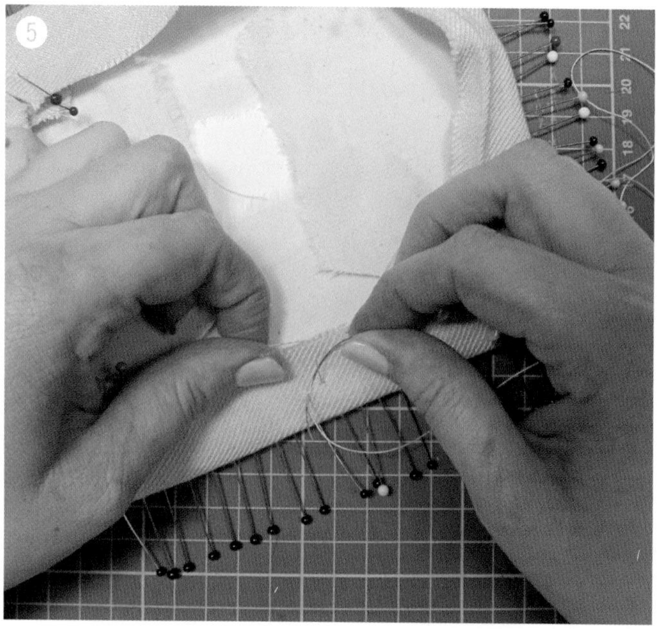

Thread a curved needle with a length of button thread. Fold the fabric over the edge of the board and cast on the thread in the middle of one side. Cut the knot off, as, if left, it can create an unsightly lump when the piece is complete.

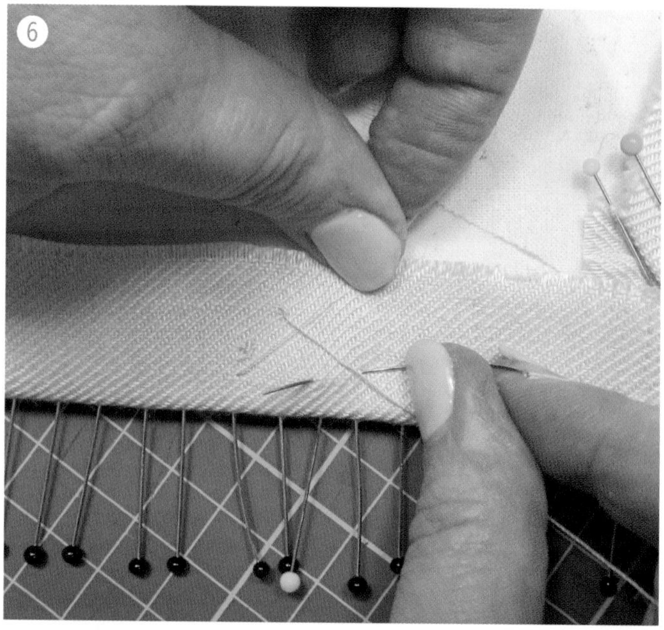

Pull firmly on the fabric and work a Herringbone Stitch to secure the two layers together, checking periodically that both layers of fabric are being caught with the stitching. Do not take the stitching right to the edge of the board; instead, leave a rebate. This is where the sateen fabric will sit.

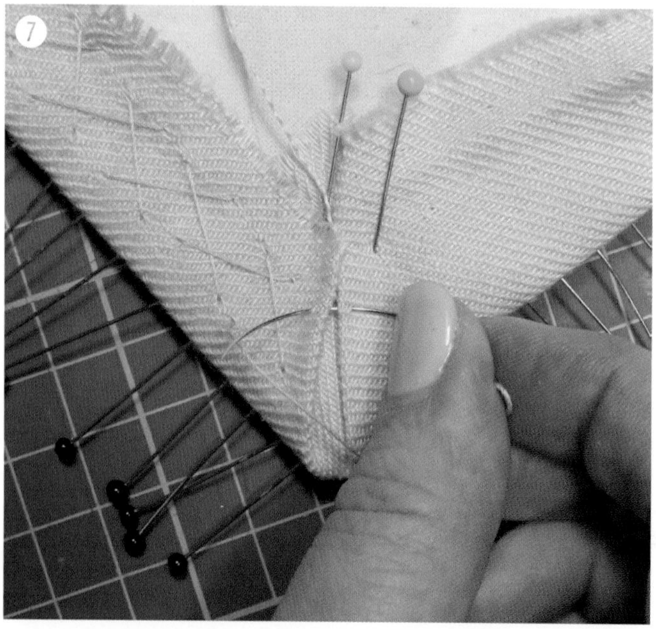

Before working the corner, use a large tapestry needle to pull up the stitches to remove any slack. The fabric may pucker slightly on the back; however, as long as it remains smooth and tight on the front, this won't be a problem. Take the needle across the corner, level with the last Herringbone Stitch, and make a straight stitch drawing both folds of the fabric together.

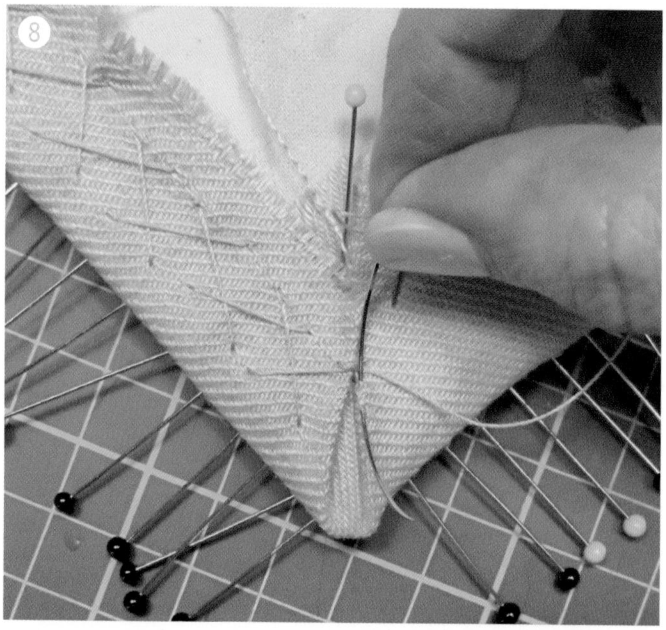

Slide the needle into the fold of one side of the mitre and make a short stitch. It is important to ensure the needle goes in and comes out of the fold of fabric.

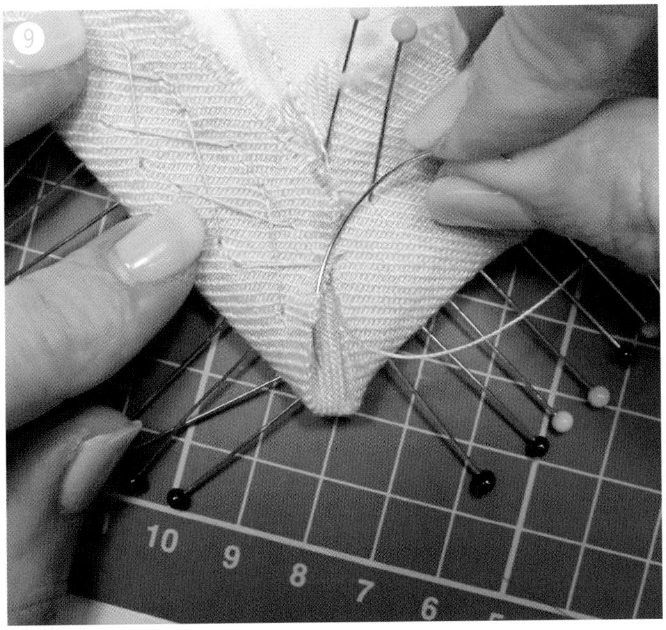

Lay the thread across the corner at right angles to the fold. Then insert the needle into the opposite fold behind where the thread lies and make a small stitch. As the thread is pulled through, the two edges should pull together. This stitch is known as slip stitch.

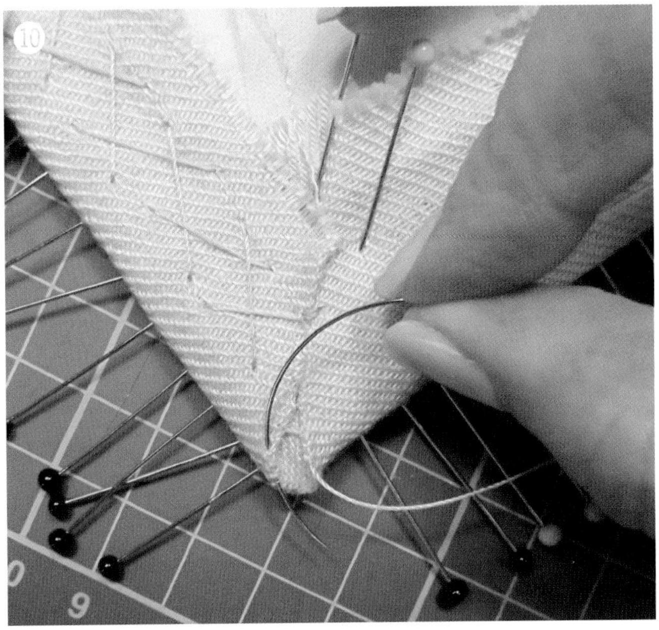

Continue working stitches right into the point of the corner.

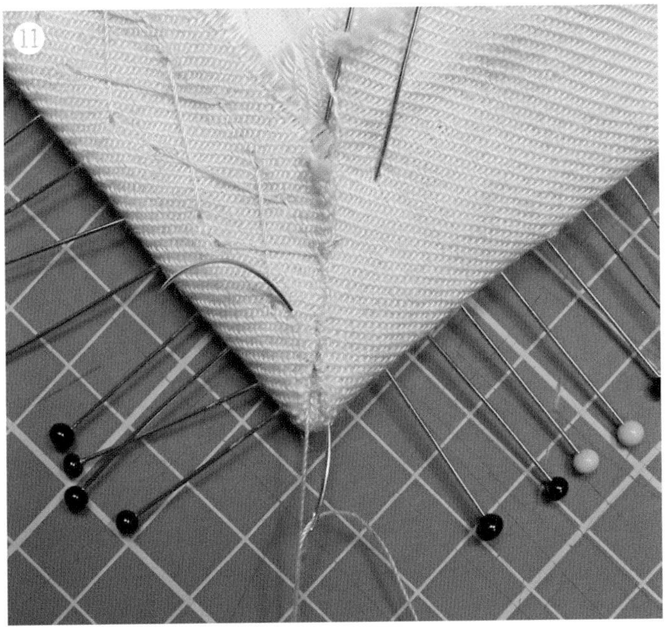

Take the needle in on the opposite fold and bring it up on the side that has been secured. Gently pull all the thread through. The fabric should pull together and around the corner.

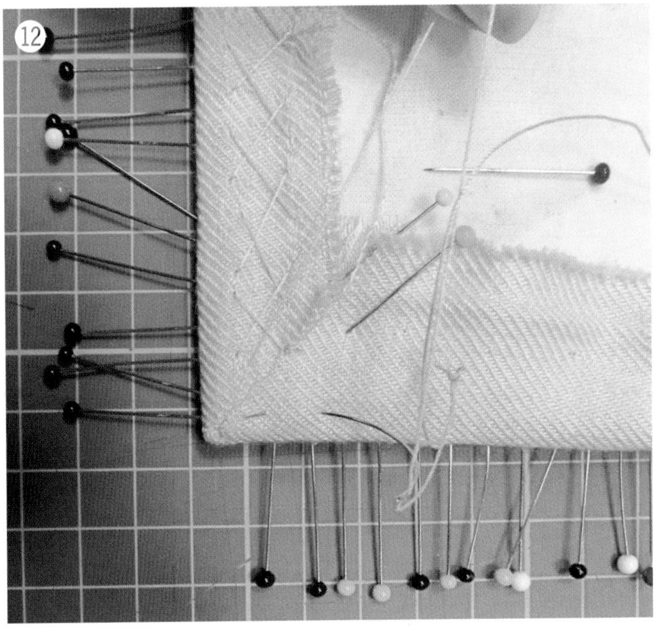

Take the needle across the corner and restart the Herringbone Stitch, remembering to pull firmly on the fabric as the stitches are worked.

Applying the Backing

A good-quality cotton or sateen fabric can be used to back the piece. It is important that it is clean and ironed before it is applied. When applying the fabric, take care to ensure that it is as tight as possible.

For this process you will need the following:

- Pins
- Sateen or cotton
- Curved needle
- Button thread
- Scissors

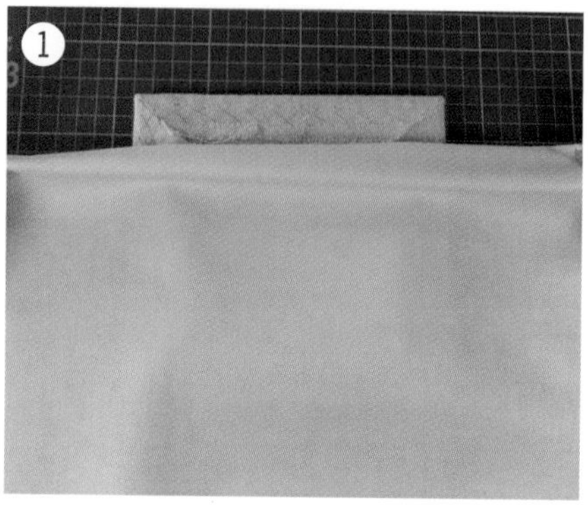

Cut a piece of fabric (in this example sateen) approximately 10cm/4in bigger on all four sides than the piece of embroidery. Fold under one edge of the sateen and lay it along the edge of the mounted piece. There should be no Herringbone Stitch showing and a small rebate of fabric. This rebate should be consistent in depth across all four sides.

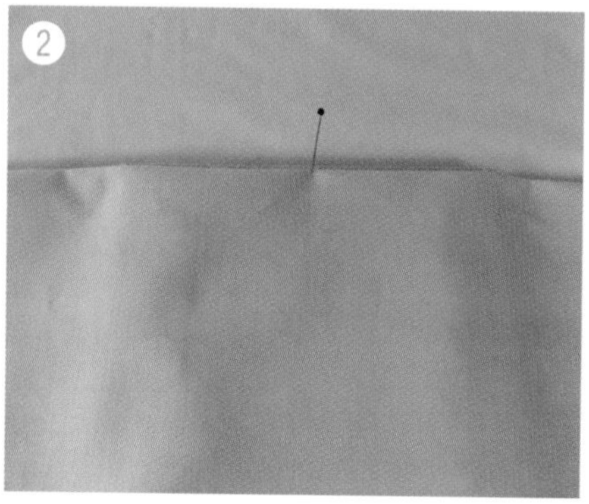

Use a pin to secure the fabric in place and, as before, work from the middle out.

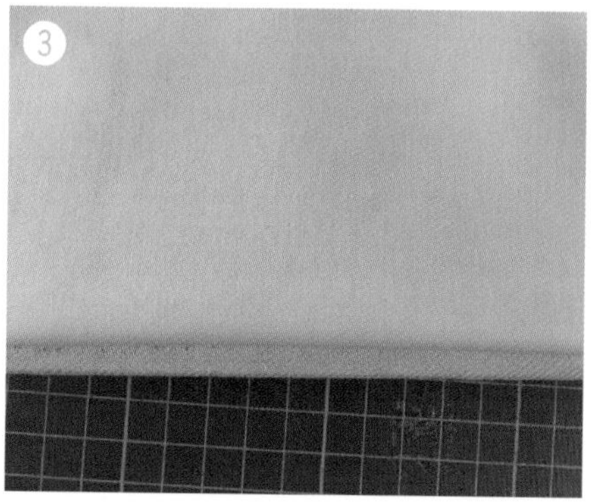

Fold under the opposite side and lay the fabric on the board. This time the rebate should be slightly larger.

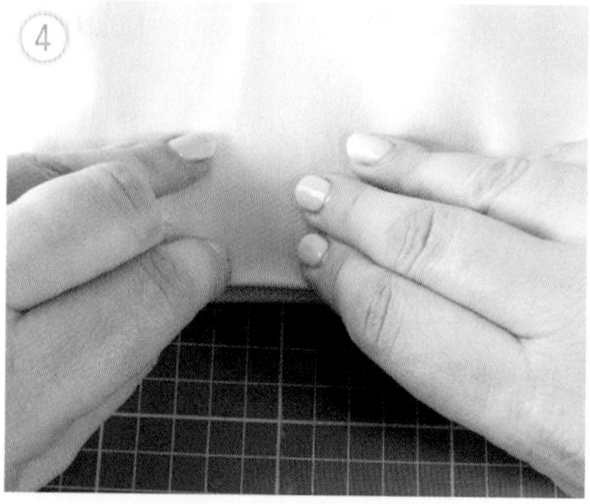

Pull the sateen across the board and pin it into place. Try to make the rebate the same size as on the opposite side. Work the two remaining sides in the same way. If the piece is quite large, add more pins approximately 2.5cm/1in apart.

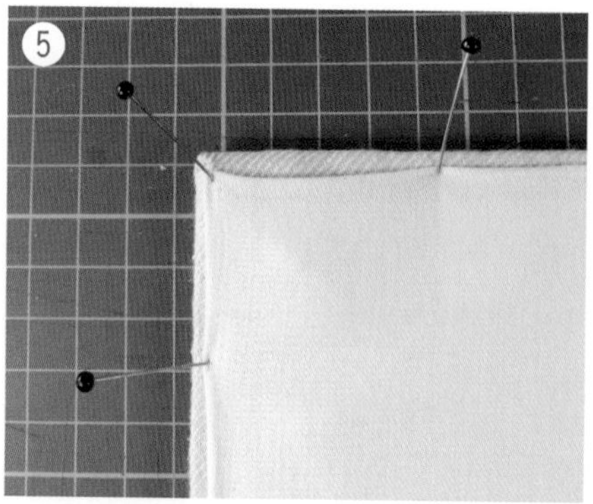

Pull the fabric into the corners and add another pin. If the fabric sags a lot between pins, extra pins can be added to straighten it. When working with sateen in particular, take care not to add too many pins as this fabric marks easily. To check the tension of the fabric, run a fingertip across the sateen, both horizontally and vertically. If a bubble of fabric appears, the sateen is not tight enough.

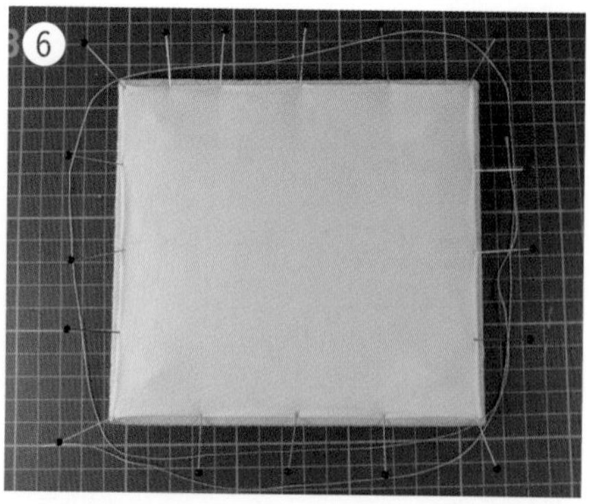

The sateen should be stitched on with a continuous length of button thread. To ensure enough thread is cut, lay it around the piece, leaving a 5–10cm/2–4in length at either end, before cutting.

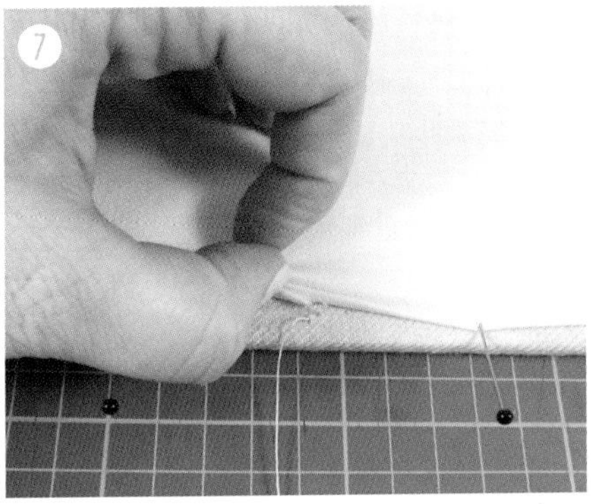

Thread a curved needle with the length of button thread. Remove the middle pin from one side of the piece, cast on underneath the sateen and cut off the knot.

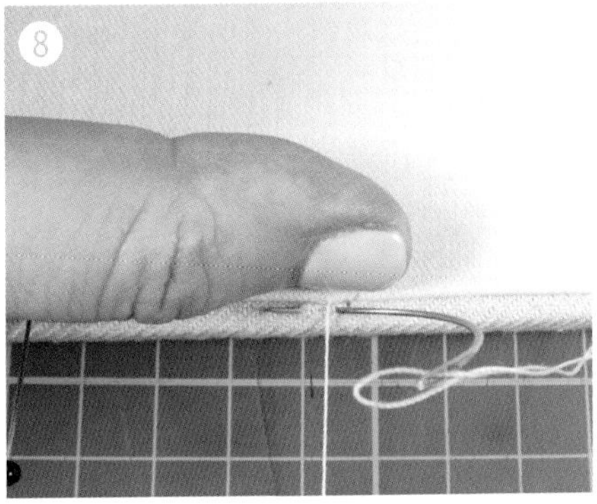

Bring the needle out in the fabric level with where the sateen is to be secured. Make a small straight stitch into the fabric and pull all of the thread through.

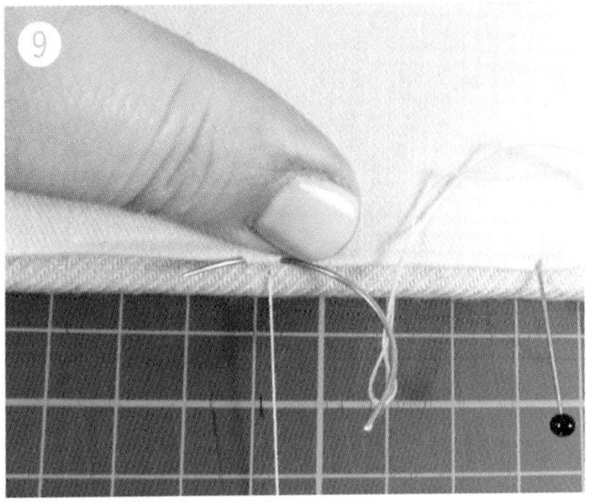

Lay the button thread at right angles to the board. Insert the needle into the fold of the sateen, behind where the button thread lies. This will create a slightly diagonal stitch, which helps the thread to disappear when it is pulled tightly. This is the same stitch (slip stitch) that is used to work the corners of the embroidery.

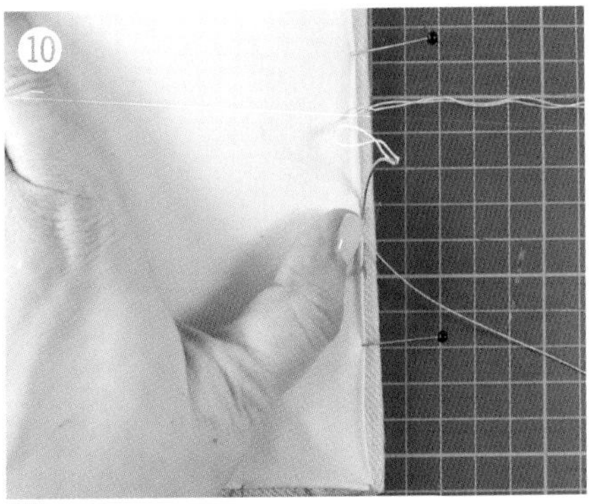

Continue working slip stitches in this manner, alternating between the embroidery and the sateen, pulling the stitches tight so that the thread disappears. As you work, it can be beneficial to turn the piece so that it sits at right angles to you. This way, if the rebate starts to become uneven, you will notice it sooner. Placing a thumb on the edge of the sateen is a good way of supporting the fabric as the stitches are worked.

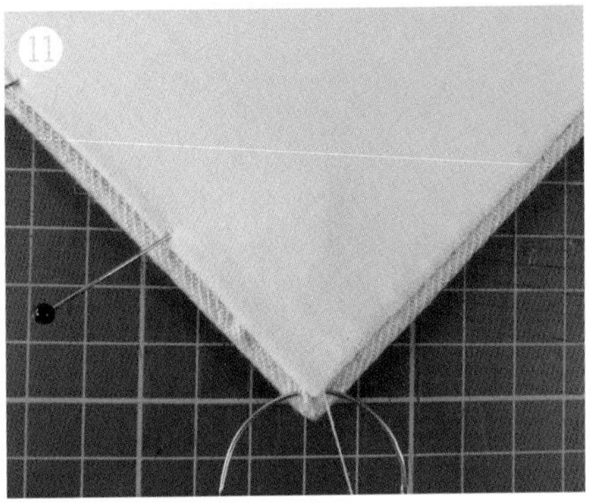

Work the slip stitches almost to the point of the corner. Then slide the needle through the very tip of the sateen and recommence the slip stitch on the next side. Taking the needle right into the point of the fabric can cause the corner to become rounded when the thread is pulled tight.

When completed, the sateen should be clean and taut. The corners should be sharp, but also lying flat and smooth. This final stage is an important one; by keeping the backing fabric taut, this will help to support the piece of work. Over time the glue used to secure the calico will fail and release the tension on the embroidery on the front. When this happens, the backing fabric should hold the tension. However, if the backing is loose, the embroidery will also become loose. As the embroidery loses tension, bubbles and puckers will slowly appear.

CHAPTER 11

MOVING ON WITH CREWELWORK

Creativity can strike at any time, which is why it is important to have a notebook and pencil nearby when stitching. This becomes an important reference point for including new and exciting ideas into future projects.

As discussed in Chapter 9, when looking to develop crewelwork, sampling becomes a very important exercise. Practising stitches and exploring the effects they can create is a rewarding pursuit. Selecting a stitch, such as Herringbone Stitch, and experimenting with it can vastly improve not only the stitcher's accuracy but also their knowledge.

The stitches outlined in this book can be worked in any fibre and within most other techniques. Working a greater variety of techniques not only increases knowledge of materials, techniques and their limitations, but also accuracy of stitching. It is worthwhile looking at the other books in this series and incorporating those techniques within crewelwork: stumpwork, appliqué and ribbonwork are all techniques that can incorporate or be incorporated into crewelwork quite easily. It is less usual to combine goldwork and crewelwork; however, the contrast between the materials can create a beautiful and striking effect.

If this seems a little intimidating, the simplest way to move on is to combine other thread types in a piece. The combination of the sheen of stranded cotton or coton perlé against the matte texture of wool can create a beautiful contrast. Consider also the scale the piece is being worked at; using finer threads mean a smaller scale is achievable. Once a small piece is worked, there are many different ways to mount and present it – as brooch or a pendant, for example.

Adding new materials such as stranded cotton, imitation gemstones, beads or sequins can add a new dimension to a technique. Consider exploring other embroidery techniques to combine with crewelwork.

Designed and worked by Shelley Cox, this design is reminiscent of the Jacobean period. The piece is worked in wool and cotton with beaded accents.

Designed and worked by the author, this piece measures just 3.4cm/1 ⅜in in diameter and is worked in a fine two-ply worsted wool using Long and Short Stitch Oak Leaf Stitch, French Knots and couching. Even on a small scale a surprising amount of depth can be created.

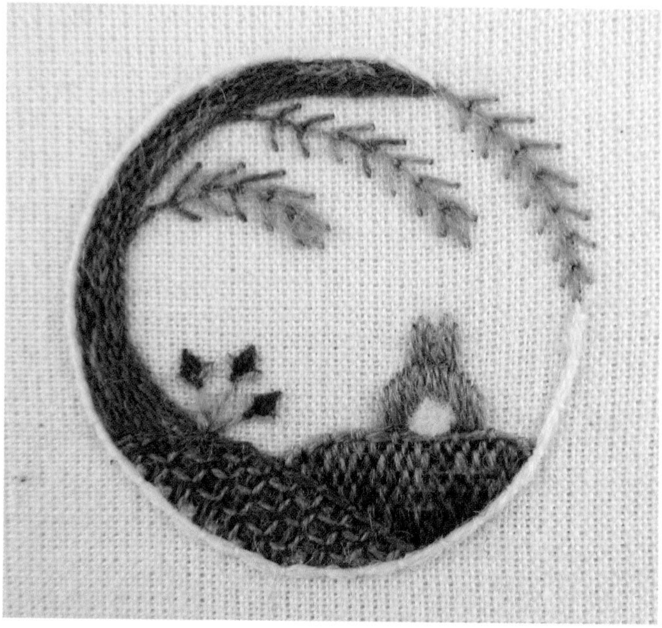

Designed and worked by the author, this piece measures just 3.4cm/1 ⅜in in diameter and is worked in a fine two-ply worsted wool. The motif is inspired by the Jacobean style and in worked in Split Stitch, Fly Stitch, Burden Stitch, battlement couching, Satin Stitch, Turkey Rug Stitch, Detached Chain Stitch and couching.

One of the most exciting things about surface stitches is how easily they can be combined with other techniques; for instance, Long and Short Stitch is commonly worked in goldwork, although usually in silk rather than wool. Surface stitches can be combined with most techniques; some of the easiest are appliqué, goldwork or stumpwork.

- Appliqué is the term used to refer to the application of fabrics. It is usually found in medium to large shapes. Surface stitches can be used to add fine detail to sit in contrast to patterned fabrics.
- Goldwork refers to metal threads that are worked in various ways. They are most commonly gold in colour; however, the threads are now available in a much wider variety of colours.
- Stumpwork is a form of raised embroidery, often used for figures. Crewelwork stitches can be used to add detail to the background or on one of the raised elements.

There are many other techniques that are also suitable. When exploring other techniques and fibres, the texture of wool becomes much more important. As a matte, rough fibre, it can sit in contrast to a great many other materials, which should be taken into consideration when placing it within a design.

Designed and worked by Shelley Cox, this piece uses a very traditional Jacobean motif and is worked in wool, stranded cotton and coton perlé. The stitches are a mixture of traditional stitches such as double woven trellis, laidwork and Coral Knot Stitch, along with creative elements such as Buttonhole Stitch over rows of Stem Stitch, and French Knots surrounded with Stem Stitch in place of a woven wheel. Beads intermingled with the different fibres create a touch of sparkle to set the piece off.

The second leaf from the left is worked in Fly Stitch, which transitions through colour and fibre: The tip is worked in stranded cotton, which is then blended through to coton perlé, then into wool. This area is then accented with bugle beads. The middle leaf is worked in Long and Short Stitch using stranded cotton and coton perlé. The right-hand and left-hand leaves are both worked in laidwork in wool and Fly Stitch in stranded cotton, and bugle beads have been added.

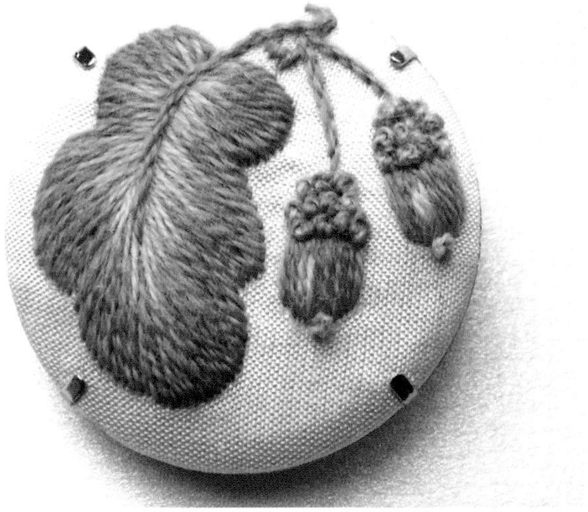

Brooch by Marg Dier. The oak leaf and acorns are worked with fine 2-ply wool in Long and Short Stitch, Satin Stitch, French Knots and Stem Stitch. Using finer wools allow the stitcher to work smaller scale motifs that can be mounted as jewellery.

Necklace by Marg Dier. The oak leaf and acorns are worked with fine two-ply wool in Long and Short Stitch, Satin Stitch and French Knots. This piece combines both crewelwork and goldwork with the addition of metal threads and small sequins.

This piece, designed and worked by Flo Collingwood, combines crewelwork and appliqué with accents of goldwork. The patterned fabrics are outlined in puffy couching and Buttonhole Stitch, which sit alongside areas of trellis and Satin Stitch.

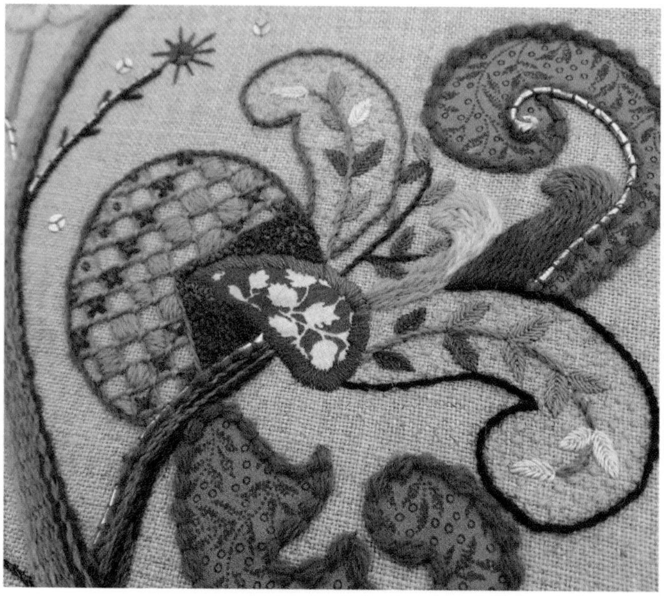

In this example elements of Japanese thread and spangles (goldwork threads) add a touch of sparkle and create a dramatic contrast to the crewelwork stitches and applied fabrics.

Worked by Helen Stevens, this piece combines traditional crewel and goldwork stitches, with emphasis on solid filling stitches, to create a fresh take on both techniques.

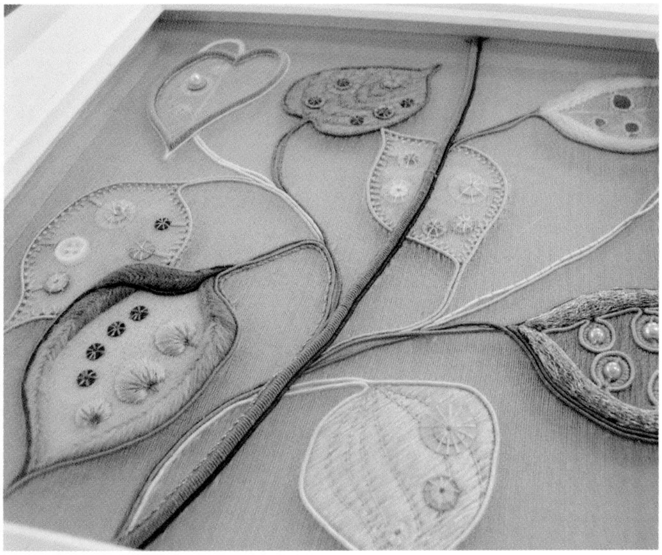

'Study of Honesty', designed and worked by Jenny Adin-Christie. This piece is worked on a delicate organza and combines crewelwork stitches with shadow work (a whitework technique) along with silk-wrapped pearl purl and silk-wrapped gimp. It also has the traditional elements of stitches and materials worked on the reverse of the fabric.

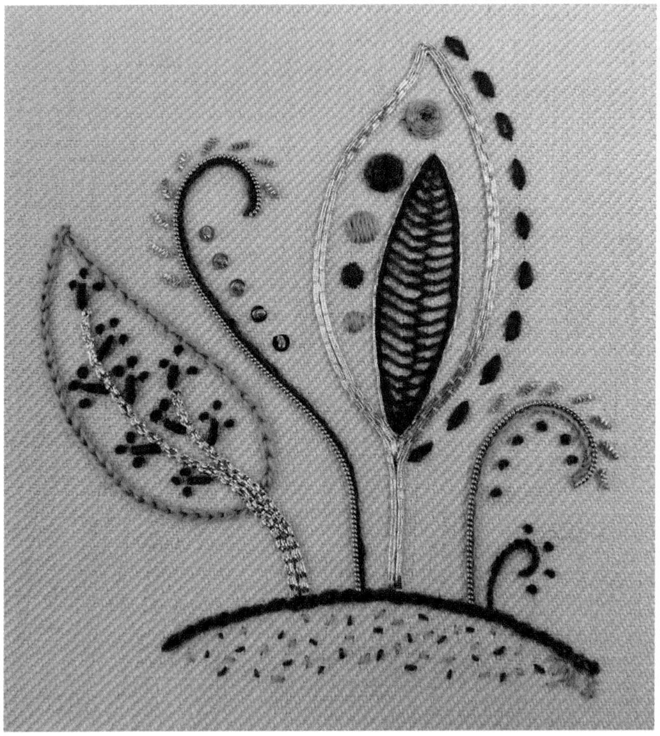

Worked by Helen Stevens, this piece combines traditional crewelwork textural stitches such as Cretan Stitch, Chain Stitch and seeding with couched pearl purl, rococo and passing threads.

'Study of Eringium', designed and worked by Jenny Adin-Christie. Worked on a delicate organza, this piece includes traditional shadow work stitches in wool with pearls, beads and small sequins. In addition, it has elements that are worked on the reverse of the fabric.

Motif Templates

Designed and worked by Shelley Cox, this section of a larger aquatic themed piece uses a variety of stitches, which creates a range of textures.

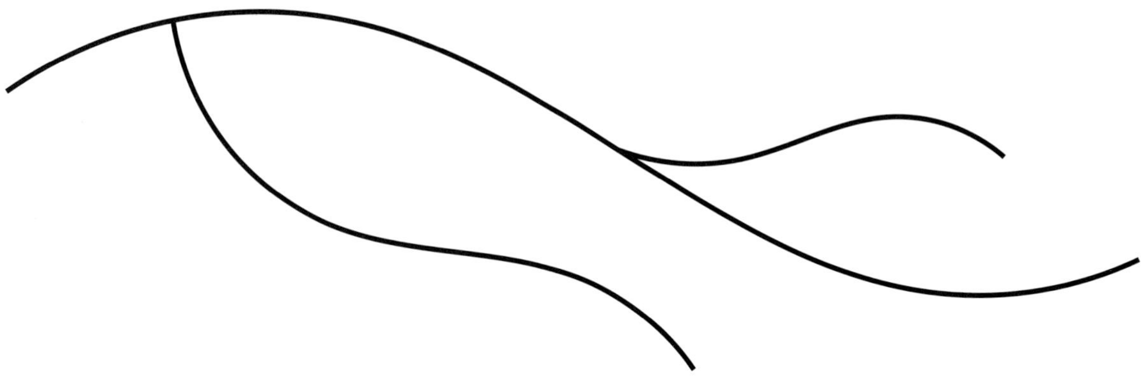

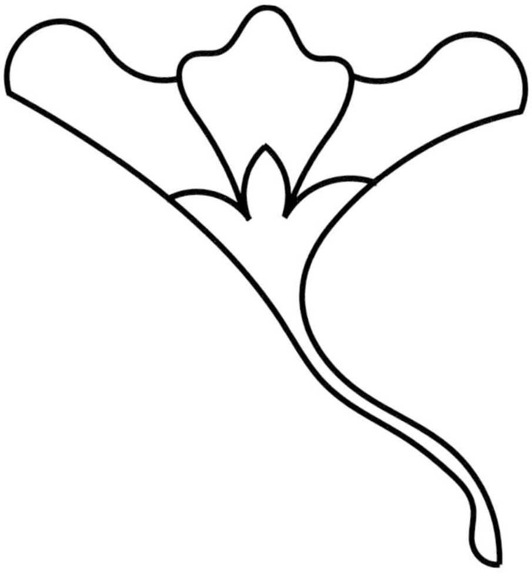

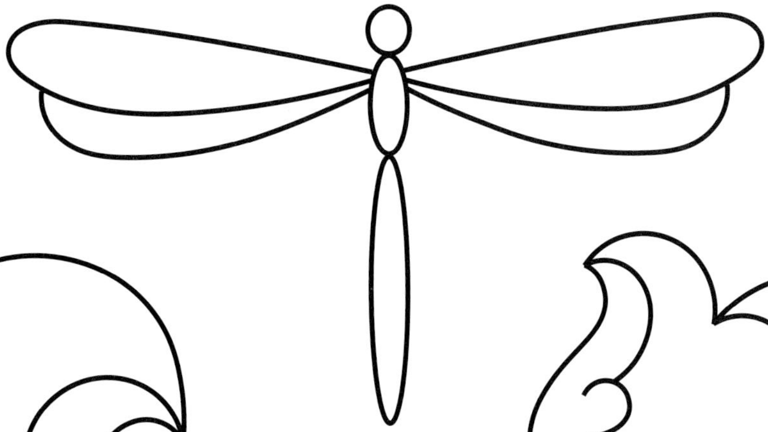

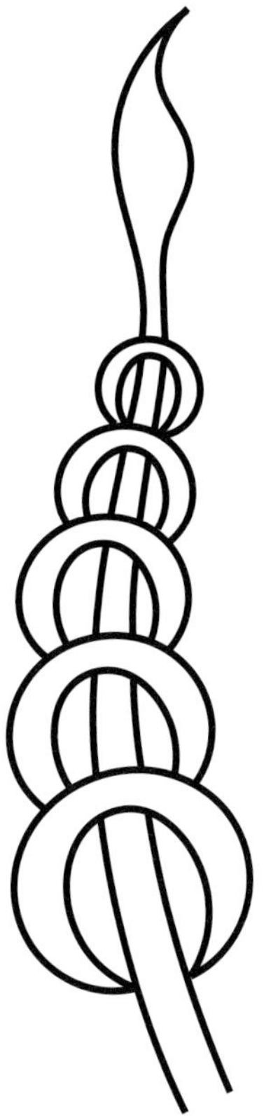

Suppliers

Appleton's
www.appletons.org.uk

The Bluebird Embroidery Co.
www.bluebirdembroidery.co.uk

DeVere Yarns
www.devereyarns.co.uk

Hand Embroidered
www.hand-embroidered.co.uk

John James Needles
www.jjneedles.com

Laurelin
www.laurelin.co.uk

Renaissance Dyeing
www.renaissancedyeing.com

Sarah Homfray
www.sarahhomfray.com

Designed and worked by the author, this piece use trellis as a focal point balanced with open and densely worked areas.

ABOUT THE AUTHOR

Becky Quine was taught embroidery from a very early age; from this, she developed a passion for working with a needle and thread that she pursued throughout her school years and early career. After spending many years in administration, the opportunity arose to change track and she joined the Royal School of Needlework.

In 2015 she graduated (with Distinction) from the RSN's Future Tutor Programme. During the course, Becky embraced the opportunity to learn new techniques and expand her knowledge of embroidery, especially crewelwork. She was also privileged to work on several high-profile RSN projects including an Oscar dress for Naomie Harris in 2013.

She continues to work on behalf of the RSN in their commercial studio, teaching her own portfolio of Day Classes and on the Certificate & Diploma, Future Tutor and Degree courses. She has taught across the UK, Ireland and in the United States.

Designed and worked by the author, this piece is a contemporary twist on the Jacobean style.

Index

Related Titles from Crowood

978 1 78500 539 8

978 1 78500 563 3

978 1 78500 252 6

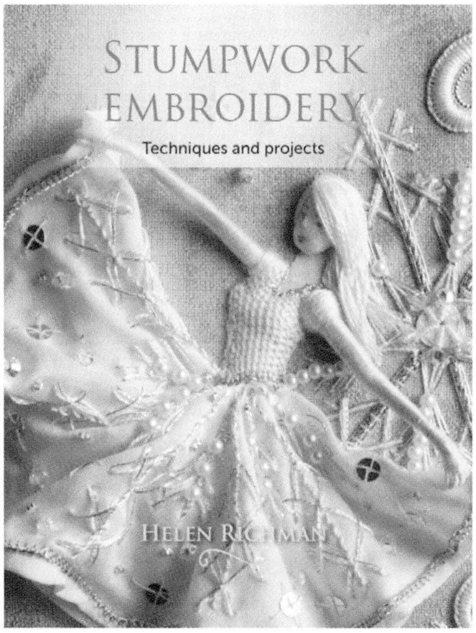

978 1 78500 294 6

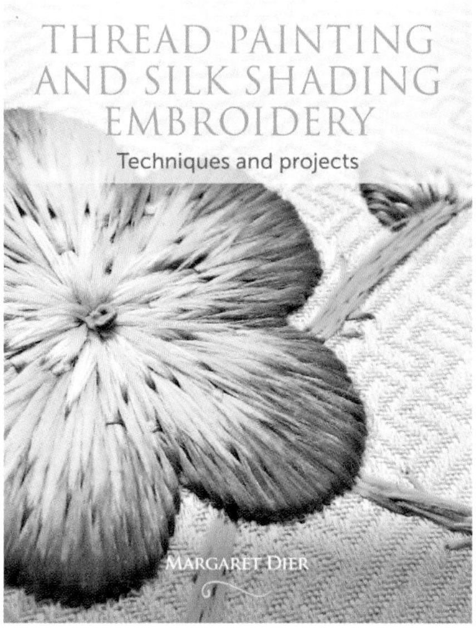

978 1 78500 477 3

978 1 78500 647 0